A Psychosocial Exploration of Love and Intimacy

A Psychosocial Exploration of Love and Intimacy

Joanne Brown

First published 2006 by
PALGRAVE MACMILLAN
Houndmills, Basingstoke, Hampshire RG21 6XS and
175 Fifth Avenue, New York, N.Y. 10010
Companies and representatives throughout the world.

PALGRAVE MACMILLAN is the global academic imprint of the Palgrave Macmillan division of St. Martin's Press, LLC and of Palgrave Macmillan Ltd. Macmillan® is a registered trademark in the United States, United Kingdom and other countries. Palgrave is a registered trademark in the European Union and other countries.

ISBN-13: 978–1–4039–9502–5
ISBN-10: 1–4039–9502–8

This book is printed on paper suitable for recycling and made from fully managed and sustained forest sources.

A catalogue record for this book is available from the British Library.

Library of Congress Cataloging-in-Publication Data

Brown, Joanne, 1965–
   A psychosocial exploration of love and intimacy / Joanne Brown.
      p. cm.
   Includes bibliographical references and index.
   ISBN 1–4039–9502–8 (cloth)
      1. Love—Psychological aspects. 2. Love—Social aspects. 3. Intimacy (Psychology) 4. Intimacy (Psychology)—Social aspects. 5. Psychoanalysis. I. Title.

BF575.L8B745 2006
152.4′1—dc22   2006040170

10 9 8 7 6 5 4 3 2 1
15 14 13 12 11 10 09 08 07 06

Printed and bound in Great Britain by
Antony Rowe Ltd, Chippenham and Eastbourne

Contents

Acknowledgements

I would like to thank my friends and colleagues at the University of East London and at the Tavistock Clinic in London for providing an intellectually stimulating and emotionally supportive environment in which to enjoy working. My thanks go to Prof. Barry Richards, Dr Carole Satyamurti, Prof. Michael Rustin and Margaret Rustin who supported the development of my work in Psychosocial Studies and in psychoanalytic observation methods. I also benefited from my encounter with the Free Associations project. I would like to thank my sister Lorraine Brown for including me in her reading and interests as we grew up and for her unassuming and generous support since. My thanks also go to Martin Klopstock for his support of this work in its earlier stages. I would also like to thank Marie-Jose Loncelle-Burris for her guidance in my more personal encounter with psychoanalysis. I am grateful to the people who talked to me, and told me about their experiences. This book would not have been possible without them. Finally, I am indebted to Barry Richards for his continued support of my work. I dedicate this book, with thanks, to him and to our daughter Maria.

Part I
Introduction

1
The Demise of Romantic Love?

1.1 Introduction

Is the ideal of romantic love an ideal out of reach? What happens to us, internally, when we fall into love, or lust, or into daydreams about the amorous other? When does the sensation of playful flirting transform itself into the seriousness of romantic longing? What do we really long for? Do we long for a heightened sense of ourselves and of our more vital desires? Or perhaps the narrative of romance promises to deliver us from the everyday, the mundane, from temporal reality, and ultimately from certain aspects of ourselves. Alternatively our romantic longings may be excited by the hope for a sensuous and penetrating sense of recognition. Is romance our secularised form of faith and passion, the Western world's ongoing soap opera and religion (see Kristeva, 1987)? And what happens to committing oneself to a cause other than oneself if the religion of erotic love rules the day, as Bertilsson (1991) asks. And why deconstruct a narrative, which, like any good novel, play or drama, reconnects us to a sense of life as vital and to a sense of ourselves as impassioned beings? Is the romantic narrative, as Pearce and Stacey (1995) imply, the best story we've got for anticipating the future with?

Romance, from a feminist viewpoint, is a disabling ideology for women, distorted by power and in a deeper sense, by narcissism. Sociologists argue that romantic love emerged as the necessary correlative of the conjugal family unit and is a debased myth derived from mystical religion. Is romance therefore a bourgeois invention aimed at routinising our passions? Did romantic love emerge as the necessary bedfellow of a specifically Western form of economic individualism? Why, in short, has romantic love been deconstructed and derided by feminists? Moreover, existentialism declares that romantic love is

3

unrealisable as an ideal and contemporary sociologists applaud its demise. Will psychoanalysis join the deconstructive critique of the romantic ideal? In fact, did psychoanalysis prepare the ground for a sceptical inquisition of our romantic aspirations?

This book will be clearly organised around a single question: is love possible? It will provide conceptualisations of love and of its possibility from sociological, philosophical and psychoanalytic viewpoints. The thematic continuity between these different schools of thought can be found in their critique and deconstruction of romantic love ideals. Alternative conceptualisations of love, from each of these schools, will be presented as contrasts to, and a critique of, a romantic conception of love. The theoretical deconstruction of romantic love outlined above will be contextualised in contemporary debates about late modern society as postmodern, therapeutic, narcissistic and as characterised by identity crises. However, each school of thought also gives us an insight into the compelling nature of romantic love and of the needs which it promises to fulfil. One of the questions that this book will pose is whether we are witnessing the emergence of a new discourse of intimacy in everyday life.

It is not the aim of this work to provide a full-scale study of changing attitudes to love and romance in contemporary Britain. It is not assumed that the existence of a debate in critical, social and psychoanalytic theory about whether romantic love is possible leads to a change in an individual's lived experience of romance or practice in the name of it. Indeed, it is in the disjunction between theory and practice or intellectual ideas and felt experience that we can perhaps understand Jackson's (1993) ironic claim that 'Even sociologists fall in love'.

Nevertheless, sociological literature has been reviewed (Giddens, 1992; Beck and Beck-Gernsheim, 1995) which draws upon empirical studies suggesting that romantic love is now a 'category in crisis' (Pearce and Stacey, 1995) in terms of everyday, lived experience. To explore the relationship between discourses of love and changing social formations, qualitative interviews have been carried out. A methodological approach that combines existing modes of biographical analysis (Plummer, 1983; Denzin, 1989a; Riessman, 1993; Wengraf, 2001) with new psychosocial modes of analysis (Hunt, 1989; Day Sclater, 1999; Andrews *et al.*, 2000; Hollway and Jefferson, 2000a) has been explored, because it is better able to address the social *and* psychic meanings of love.

Although it is not possible to establish the nature of the relationship between the social, psychoanalytic or philosophical deconstruction of romantic love and the status of romantic love in empirical reality, illustrative empirical material drawn from ten in-depth interviews will be presented in Chapters 10 and 11 in order to look at everyday discourses of love.

Material from biographical, narrative interviews will be presented in order to look at how people from two age groups (in their thirties and over and in their seventies and over) conceptualise love and view its realisation or possibility in their own lives. While romantic love is not deconstructed by the older age group, romance is not a love ideal that their material circumstances (war, poverty etc.) were altogether conducive to. Mrs Archer, for example, equated love with sex and the workhouse, and did not elaborate on her needs for psychic intimacy and emotional attunement when asked about her experiences of love and marriage:

A: Yeah, I knew him at school. We used to stand on street corners and have a little waffle.
I: Did you?
A: Kissing and cuddling.
I: Mm.
A: Where there was a lamppost. Our mothers used to say to us, 'If you get in trouble you'll go to the workhouse'. That was their saying.
I: Was it? Mm.

What can be seen, in the younger age group, is a tension between a post-modern ironic view of romantic love and a need for an exclusive, romantic, intimate relationship:

R: I, I was just about to say that maybe, you know, the person who's feeling in love has got, has got to be susceptible to that, maybe they've got a special need, you know, in their life to feel special. But I can't even agree with myself on that, because too many people feel it, and I think you can't sort of say that everybody has got this pathological need
I: Mm.
R: to feel in love. Surely, I mean that it's just pleasant as well.

The interview material will be used in order to ask in what way the conditions of late modernity are conducive to a questioning of the self, gender relationships and love, and in order to ask how we can interpret this phenomenon. Although the older interviewees have not taken part in a cultural transformation of intimacy, the material and structural conditions of their lives affected the discourse of love that they could position themselves in and these conditions were not conducive to a romantic idealisation of life. Thus, there is a complex interaction between one's psychic and social self, and it is by analysing this dynamic interplay that we can understand why romantic love is deconstructed, and speculate on what this deconstruction, disinterest or preoccupation with love means for an interviewee.

In order to understand the compelling nature of romantic forms of love (in songs, films, art as well as in everyday life and fantasy), this book will argue that a psychosocial explanation of its origins and functions needs to be provided. This book will address the inadequacy of the sociology of emotion which continues to afford the intellect and reason too much control over feeling and the irrational. It will also highlight the inadequacy of an exclusively defined psychoanalysis of affect in which the structural, historical forces in peoples' lives might be under-represented. Thus the importance of a psychosocial approach to narrative and to understanding subjectivity will be argued for.

Although emotion and culture form the content of the book, the disciplinary perspective (psychosocial studies) is innovative and the philosophy and method of this approach will be clearly detailed. This book will offer procedural guidelines on qualitative methods and demonstrate how biographical, narrative interviews can be used to investigate emotion in contemporary society. The method developed uses insights and practices from sociological methods, psychoanalytic, observational methods and psychosocial approaches to narrative. The importance of reflexivity in the research process (as, for example, a corroborative measure on interpretations made) will be demonstrated.

This book will take a captivating theme as its focus, but it will be distinctive because books on love tend to be exclusively sociological, historical, social psychological, cultural or psychoanalytic. A psychosocial study of emotion creates a discursive dialogue between these perspectives and does not reside exclusively in one discipline. The approach adopted here demonstrates how to work in an interdisciplinary way by specifically combining the sociology of emotion and psychoanalysis of affective life in order to understand the vicissitudes of love and its transformation in contemporary culture.

The book's educational features will be in its

- explanation of how to do interdisciplinary work;
- discussion of how to combine different discourses and professions – in this case, clinical work and academic research;
- clear exposition of major schools of sociological, psychoanalytic and philosophical thought;

- methodology section, offering an explanation of sociological, psychoanalytic and discursive approaches to biographical studies;
- demonstration of an innovative disciplinary approach in theory and method.

This text will take questions that are centrally important to peoples' lives (what is love, is it possible, what can we realistically expect from intimacy?), but it will embed these questions in theorisations of what love is, or ought to be, and in the cultural contexts in which we live. This book will ask a bold and arresting question (about our need for attachment) which is relevant to the social sciences, the humanities and to psychoanalytic studies.

Although this book is written for an academic audience and outlines various academic debates, it is relevant to debates in wider society. The question of the relationship between emotional attachment and sex was discussed by all of the interviewees and this discussion is relevant to contemporary discussions about sex education and how sex and sexuality are taught. Psychoanalysis, for example, alerts us to the fact that sex is psychosexual and sex education could benefit from exploring the fantasies, emotions, self-image and so on that define one's sexuality. As Mitchell (2003) points out: 'When Susan [Mitchell's client] experiences sexual yearning for her lover, the longing does not simply bubble up from bodily tissues, but emerges in the context of a subjective world she has constructed and maintained' (p. 80).

The younger interviewees in this study were more willing to talk about this subjective world than their older counterparts, and this raises the question of whether they have imbibed the tenets of a culture in which the importance of emotional literacy is argued for. The UK organisation 'Antidote', for example, campaigns for an emotionally literate culture at home, at school and at work, and 'Personal, Social and Health Education' (PSHE) is now a part of the UK's national curriculum.

This work can therefore contribute to discussions about what constitutes emotional literacy or emotional intelligence and reflexivity in relationships. A book on conceptualisations of love and de-traditionalisation processes is also relevant in the context of the plethora of media representations of men and women trying to understand what constitutes a fulfilling relationship or whether romance has to be the central axis around which one organises one's life (*Bridget Jones*, *Friends*, *Love Actually*, *High Fidelity*, *Sex and the City* and so on). The twenty-first century has also been referred to as the 'Singles Century' (Dennison, 2000) as the rise of the single person is, we are told, the greatest social phenomenon of our time. Thus, it is interesting to look at how the younger interviewees' experience being single and at how being single is perceived by their friends and family and by themselves.

However, the use of dating agencies is also increasing and Mills and Boon novels are, of course, still highly successful, thus indicating that we are still a romantic or 'object seeking' nation and this work will give us some insights into why romance is compelling for interviewees like Rachel:

> *R:* 'Well what does in love mean? What does it mean? you know, you want to be dead special to somebody and you want to feel that erm really lovely feeling that you feel when you first get together with somebody, and is it just being egotistical or something? Erm I still would find it difficult to say erm that just having a companion and being content with somebody cos you get on well and, you know, more ... was more of a friendship is as nice. I mean I can rationally say it is, but erm I don't think it's as strong a feeling. Maybe that's the emphasis on feeling rather than thinking.

This work will also contribute to discussions about whether contemporary society can usefully be referred to as therapeutic or more critically as narcissistic (e.g., its fascination with the emotional and psychic lives of the participants who people reality TV shows like *Big Brother* and *Wife Swap*). One of the central questions that this work asks is whether contemporary socio-cultural conditions have 'encouraged individuals to open up psychic space in an attempt to explore oneself and one's relationships' (Craib, 1994, p. 173) and it also asks how to evaluate this contemporary trend.

1.2   Structure of the book

Chapter 2 discusses the question of whether psychosocial and sociological accounts of intersubjective relations are commensurable, noting that they are differentiated by the use of psychoanalytic theory in psychosocial studies. What is distinctive about psychosocial studies is highlighted by briefly comparing it to the sociological imagination. The sociological imagination shares a similar concern with psychosocial studies in understanding the 'interplay of man and society, of biography and history, of self and world' (Mills, 1959, p. 4). However, in order to understand the forces that have most strongly affected an individual's life, the sociological imagination focuses on the social structures that have framed it. It is explained in Chapter 2 that the significant difference between the psychosocial imagination deployed in this study and the sociological imagination is that, for the former, 'man', 'biography' and 'the self' are understood via the terms of psychoanalysis (a theory of human nature and the development of mind). In psychosocial studies, psychoanalytic theories about different states of mind are also used for analysing an epoch's culture and the unconscious or latent meanings of social discourses and social phenomena. Examples of this are given.

Chapter 3 does not provide a detailed history of the emergence of romantic love or of the actual socio-economic and cultural conditions that accompanied its emergence. Instead it presents an overview of sociological, cultural and feminist theories of the emergence and function of romantic love. It looks at the philosophical, political and literary influences or lineage discernible in the romantic narrative and argues that it is a contradictory 'story' to position one's self in (partaking of religious ideals, enlightenment thinking, romanticism and socio-political changes in the eighteenth century).

The state of mind expressed in courtly love (via De Rougemont's 1983 work) is explored, because the romantic narrative partakes of it. Sociological views that are discussed link romantic love to the emergence of a sense of self (humanism), an upsurge in radical feeling in the eighteenth century (romanticism, enlightenment, French revolution), urbanisation (modernisation) and industrialisation, patriarchy and the unequal access to economic resources for men and women.

It is argued that sociological, cultural and feminist theories of the emergence and function of romantic love deconstruct it as an unrealisable state of mind (mystical and romanticist), and as undesirable as a social practice (for women and isolated nuclear families). This represents a view of love as impossible (it is unrealisable and undesirable). However, sociological views that link romantic love to processes of individualisation and enlightenment thinking are by contrast introduced as theoretical positions in which love is seen as realisable and desirable (because romantic love is seen as a progressive democratisation of intimate relations).

This question of whether romantic love is impossible or possible is situated in the context of psychosocial debates about the conditions of modernity/late modernity which, it is argued, are conducive to theorisations and experiences of identity crises. It is explained that the conditions of modernity/late modernity create a cultural climate in which 'all that is solid melts into air'[1]. Thus, the self, intimate life and the possibility of love are critically questioned in both theory and in everyday life.

Two contemporary examples of the sociology of emotion (and its way of seeing love) are discussed. The first is a social-constructionist, discourse-analytic approach and the second emphasises the importance of studying processes of de-traditionalisation, changes in gender relations and the evidence for the democratisation of love and intimacy in practice and discourse. In both cases romantic love, both as a 'natural' emotion and an ideal type of intimacy, is subjected to critical scrutiny. The first example is introduced as representing a view of love as impossible (from an essentialist or humanist viewpoint), while the second example, is a possible, but reworked, ideal typology of love.

This chapter ends by explaining that sociologists have traditionally been interested in sex, sexuality and the family, but not in love. The way in which this neglect of emotion is redressed by the emergence of the sociology of emotion and sociology's questioning of its own disciplinary boundaries is discussed.

Chapter 4 explains that what are otherwise incommensurable discourses and disciplinary perspectives have been united by their deconstruction of romantic love. Whereas Chapter 3 focused on theories of when and why romantic love emerged and on the religious, philosophical and political influences on and in it, this chapter focuses on why romantic love is undesirable and self-deluding as a state of mind.

A brief overview of existentialist, Lacanian and cultural views of the self-deluding nature of the romantic lover is provided. It is explained that it is useful to discuss an existentialist view of love relations in order to understand the debt which the new discourse of love and intimacy owes to existentialist ideas. It is argued that the concept of authentic love in existentialism shares some interesting similarities with the Freudian view of 'mature' love introduced in the following chapter. The existentialist view of the impossible nature of love also provides a thematic link to a view of love as impossible from within psychoanalysis (Lacan). Barthes is introduced as offering a more celebratory elaboration of Lacan's notion of the ever-desiring but insatiable romantic lover. Romantic love is marked by impossibility in all three accounts, because of ontological insecurity, insatiable desire and the thesaurus of meaning that it represents.

Chapter 5 discusses 'love in the age of psychoanalysis'[2] in order to assess whether psychoanalysis paved the way for a view of love as impossible or possible. Romantic love is deconstructed (as it is in the other theories) but also love is reconceptualised, as this chapter details.

Freud's view of love is also tied to an understanding of our existential condition and human natures, but he does not tie an understanding of love to socio-economic or cultural conditions. Romantic love is deconstructed by Freudian theory, because it describes a state of mind that is not reality based (it deposes the 'reality ego'), and from Freud's work, the defining features of 'mature' love are outlined. It is explained that psychoanalysis offers us the 'romance of disillusionment' (Phillips, 1994, p. 40), but without declaring love to be impossible. In this chapter a view of love emerges that is dependent upon the strength of a reality ego and the ability to mourn. It implies that love is defined by an ethical sensibility which attenuates narcissism. This chapter explains that in the Freudian view of love there are two principles of mental functioning (pleasure-narcissism and reality-mourning) and that romantic and mature love can only be understood by reference to infancy and childhood and the extent to which we inhabit infantile or childlike states of mind. This reconceptualised view of love is developed in Chapter 6.

Chapter 6 introduces a distinction between an associative (pleasure principle) view of the mind and moral (reality principle) view of the mind. The view of love as possible offered by Freud and Klein adopts both and it is argued that an understanding of love has to be informed by the dialectical understanding of the relation between these two views of the mind. In this chapter the importance of a relational view of the self (foregrounded by Klein) is highlighted and the centrality of the concepts of loss and mourning to Klein's understanding of love are discussed. The depressive position is referred to as a metaphor that can provide a container for an integrated view of love (neither derided nor rendered easy). This chapter details the way in which Klein deepens a Freudian understanding of the concept of the reality ego and introduces us to a view of love which ties it to mind, body and object relations. The idea of a reconceptualised, observant ego (neither wholly narcissistic and associative nor realist and moral) is introduced as the basis of a psychoanalytic view of love which is possible, but not romanticised.

Klein's concept of depressive love and the idea of the observant ego are then brought into dialogue with a one-sided view of the ego as narcissistic or as securely moral and self-present. In this, a Kleinian view of the mind, ego and object relations is brought into dialogue with postmodern views of the self and mind which critique realist views of the ego (and the possibility of love). It is argued that the psychoanalytic view of selfhood and love is indebted to humanist and modernist philosophies but that it is sensitive to postmodern critiques of their presuppositions.

A psychoanalytic reconceptualised view of love is brought into discursive dialogue with the views expressed in Chapter 3 (that it is a social script and is democratised) and Chapter 4 (that it is only narcissistic, there is no reality ego and we should enjoy this bittersweet 'dialectical bliss'). Psychoanalysis, it is argued, offers us a position on love which is not naively possible, nor despairingly or ironically impossible. Thus, we start to see a psychosocial debate on love emerging by creating a discursive dialogue between all the positions reviewed up to this point.

What we see building up from Freud through to Klein is an extremely complex view of love, which is less one-dimensional than views of romantic love as a false ideology, an exchange mechanism, a fear of freedom, an end to our wandering desires and so on. A detailed exposition of a psychoanalytic view of love allows us to look at the state of mind expressed in romantic love and the view of the mind assumed in existentialist, Lacanian and sociological discussions of love. Chapters 5 and 6 therefore offer examples of the way in which psychoanalysis can be used as a form of application, critique and discursive dialogue.

Chapter 7 compares and contrasts two views of love as possible, using conceptions of love and intimacy from the sociology of emotion and object relations psychoanalysis, and so develops the discursive dialogue between a contemporary sociological account of love and intimacy and the psychoanalytic object relations perspective. Psychoanalytic views of love are now brought into dialogue with a contemporary sociological view which is used to critically question the ahistorical view of love found in psychoanalysis. Freudian and Kleinian psychoanalysis can be used to uncover and critique the states of mind that impossible and possible views of love assume, but it does not posit a dialectical relation between social and psychic or emotional change in the way that the new sociological discourse of intimacy does.

This chapter does not provide a detailed account of the sociological explanation for this new discourse of intimacy (female emancipation and autonomy, for example), because the aim is to compare it as an ideal type of love with an object relations account of love. The artist, Mills (1959) said, is interested in an intellectual age and style of reflection, rather than with historical social structures and the large historical scene. What is described in the new discourse of intimacy is a new style of emotion, a way of feeling and vocabulary of motive which, according to Mills, is the artist's concern. The new discourse of intimacy (as documented in contemporary sociology) is studied as a new style of reflection, and we do not seek here to provide an explanation of the emergence of this new discourse in terms of the large historical scene (however, the empirical material in Chapters 10 and 11 does raise the question of how structural, historical forces affect the discourses of intimacy that people position themselves in).

Chapter 8 explains that everyday accounts of ideas and experiences of love, romance and marriage will be used in order to relate the theoretical ideas presented so far to a body of empirical material which has been gathered via a qualitative method. This interview material is interpreted from a psychosocial perspective and the specific focus is on how love is thought about and whether it is believed to be possible.

This chapter also briefly discusses the place of biographical studies in sociology and introduces the difference between objective and interpretive approaches to biographical methods. It points to the variety of methods that can qualify as interpretive. The increasing interest in the social sciences in narrative studies is highlighted and their relevance to the psychosocial studies project is explained. Discursive or social-constructionist approaches to narrative studies are discussed and they are compared to psychoanalytic and sociological approaches to narrative. Denzin's (1989a) idea of a new life history approach (which partakes of both objective and interpretive methods) is introduced and the version of psychosocial studies (and of a narrative approach) presented in this book is situated within this tradition. This chapter ends by detailing the similar methodological concerns which narrative studies and psychoanalytic observation methods share and emphasises the way in which the chapter has served to highlight the working assumptions which will inform the analysis of the interview material presented in Chapters 10 and 11.

Chapter 9 provides an overview of the broad aims related to the interview material and Chapters 10 and 11 present a detailed discussion of the findings. This involves identifying and illustrating the major themes to have emerged and examining the substantial differences that can be seen between the accounts given by the two different age groups studied. These chapters will emphasise the importance of psychoanalysis in understanding contemporary culture, but more specifically they will combine psychoanalysis with socio-cultural theory in order to illuminate the vicissitudes of romantic love. They will demonstrate the need for a socio-psychoanalytic analysis of love ideals and love talk via case material from two clearly demarcated age groups (people in their seventies and over and people in their thirties and over).

Chapter 12 concludes by arguing that this work has contributed towards contemporary debates on the nature of modernity, by specifically focusing on conceptualisations of love and new cultural discourses of intimacy. At the same time it provides a critical understanding of a psychosocial approach in both theory and method, through the example of studying love and intimacy.

This work also contributes to discussions about how to produce grounded psychosocial theory, by specifically developing a psychosocial approach to narrative studies. It will, therefore, be contributing to debates in the philosophy and method of biographical studies.

2
A Psychosocial Approach to Emotional Life

2.1 Introduction

A psychosocial analysis is characterised by its attempt to avoid studying the individual in isolation from his or her social context, and those working in this field generally embrace critical psychology/psycho-analysis and critical social theory, but beyond this common endeavour, significant differences of approach can exist among psychosocial theorists. This is partly because, as an overriding framework, psychosocial studies can contain many versions of both sociology and psychology. For example, when doing psychosocial analyses, we could be using a post-structuralist sociology and psychology (Squire, 2000a) and employing discourse analysis as our method of investigation. Or we could be combining critical theory with object relations psychoanalysis and employing film theory (Yates, 2000) or life histories as our methodological tools (Hollway and Jefferson, 2000a). Alternatively, we could be analysing the psychological effects of certain discourses (in divorce law, for example), using narrative analysis (Day Sclater, 1999).

The strength and simultaneous weakness of psychosocial studies is that it often draws on history, politics, feminism, literary studies, psychoanalysis and so on in order to complete its intellectual journey. What we are therefore faced with when trying to use psychosocial studies as an interdisciplinary approach is the problem of holding our analyses across seemingly incommensurable disciplinary boundaries.

Until recently (in the United Kingdom), the University of East London's Psychosocial Studies degree (launched in 1983) was the only psychosocial studies degree available. The psychosocial studies area which emerged at the University of East London (UEL) grew out of the undergraduate discipline of sociology, but was to a large part influenced by its close academic

15

links with the Tavistock Clinic, which is predominantly informed by Kleinian and post-Kleinian psychoanalysis. The Tavistock Clinic in London (the United Kingdom) is a National Health Service (NHS) psychoanalytic psychotherapy training and educational institute with a community mental health purpose. I taught for many years in the Psychosocial Studies subject area at UEL and at postgraduate level in Psychoanalytic Studies at the Tavistock Clinic, where I was also trained in psychoanalytic observation methods. The psychosocial approach developed in this book emerged in the context of my work at UEL and at the Tavistock Clinic.

At UEL, the psychosocial area emerged, because many sociology students were interested in working in the welfare professions, and as such psychosocial studies emerged from the demand for teaching which combined sociological and psychological insights: 'They needed a knowledge base to enable them to locate welfare interventions in broad social and historical forces, and also tools with which to think about interpersonal relationships, and how individuals come to experience the world in different ways' (Richards, 2000a).

Richards explains that the term 'psychosocial' has gained a wide currency in social scientific research across the last three decades, as part of the overall trend to interdisciplinarity. He states that in spite of the fact that references to it were unusual before the mid-1970s, they have increased markedly since: 'The PsychINFO database shows a trebling of references to 'psychosocial factors' and 'psychosocial development' from the 1970s to the 1980s, and almost a further doubling to the 1990s, when there were over 13,000' (ibid.).

It is therefore not surprising to learn that a degree in Psychosocial Studies is now available, for example, at the University of East Anglia and there are Psychosocial Centres at Birkbeck College, London, the Open University and the University of the West of England, Bristol and so on. A psychosocial approach to psychoanalysis is also a major part of many UK Masters programmes in Psychoanalytic Studies (e.g., at Leeds Metropolitan, Brunel and the Tavistock Clinic).

2.2   Interdisciplinarity and the sociology of emotion

In Brown (2000) three sociological trends are identified that could be seen to have catalysed the beginnings of a sociology of emotion, but they are also relevant to the understanding of the historical emergence of psychosocial studies.

The year 1975 is cited as the watershed year in which a distinct body of work began to take shape in the sociology of emotions (Bendelow and

Williams, 1998), and the sociological trends identified below can be said to have informed its emergence. Moreover, these trends have challenged the disciplinary split between psychology (the individual) and sociology (society), the strict demarcation of the personal and the political and the terms of modernity in which reason is split from emotion, mind from body and the subject from the object.

First, for example, we can see that sociology would have been obliged to rethink its neglect of emotion, due to the very psychologisation of everyday life documented by Rose (1990), Foucault (1976), Sennett (1977) and so on. Indeed, Rieff's (1966) 'triumph of the therapeutic' refers to the growth of psychological discourses which we can see as sociological facts in need of theorisation. More generally, psychosocial theorists (Marcuse 1969; Fromm 1976; Lasch 1984) were looking at the psychological effects of consumer capitalism and at individual sympto-matology in the conditions of late modernity. It is therefore no surprise to see that Hochschild's book *The Managed Heart: The Commercialisation of Human Feeling* (1983) is referred to as a 'landmark text' in the sociology of emotions (Bendelow and Williams, 1998), because it looks at the way in which people are increasingly used for their *emotional* labour in a promotional, consumer-based economy.

Second, what we also see in this period is the popularisation of the idea that the personal is political (second wave feminism) and the femi-nist challenge to the 'categorical split between reason and nature which establishes the terms of modernity' (Seidler, 1998, p. 194). Indeed, according to Benjamin (1988) the principles of Western rationality are based on masculine traits (separation, control, autonomy), which represent what she refers to as a psychic repudiation of femininity (inter-dependence, inter-subjectivity). Moreover, feminist calls for emancipation meant that the question of equal rights 'no longer came to a halt around our private lives' (Beck and Beck-Gernsheim, 1995, p. 2). This, in turn, is one of the factors which has catalysed a process of de-traditionalisation which is transforming intimacy in gender relations, family structures, sexuality and emotional expression. And this is another instance of a sociological fact which has obliged sociologists to extend their analyses of inequality to the private realm of relationships (Giddens, 1992).

Finally, the postmodern challenge to Cartesian rationalism and Enlightenment 'truths' (Derrida, 1967–72; Lyotard, 1984) has led to what Denzin (1989a) calls a reconfiguration in the social sciences more generally. Hence, the 'crises of the self' (Richards, 1989a; Frosh, 1991; Woodward, 1997 etc.) of late modernity have been matched by 'disciplinary crises' (see Denzin, 1989b) in which postmodern critiques of 'the modernist epistemological project' (see Usher *et al.*, 1997) have obliged disciplines like sociology and psychology to review their own disciplinary boundaries. In both sociology and psychology, for example, the individual/society dualism has led to a neglect of either history (psychology) or of embodied feeling (sociology).

Bendelow and Williams (1998), for example, explain that emotions had traditionally been banished to the margins of sociological thought, because the discipline had not attempted to rethink the relationship between knowledge and emotion. Emotions, she says, were generally treated as asocial and as somehow inhering in the individual. This meant that the social world was known through a 'disembodied Cartesian conception of reason', which Seidler (1998, p. 194) explains led to a disdain for that which was personal/emotional. It is for this reason that Bertilsson in 1991 concluded that 'love's labours had been lost in social theory', arguing that the emotions had been treated in an instrumental and functional way. It is perhaps unsurprising, therefore, to find that the contemporary work on the sociology of emotion promises an 'ontological commitment to different ways of knowing' (p. viii) and a challenge to Cartesian rationalism, and that the 'emotions have come of age' (p. xxvi) in sociology.

Brown (2000) does not argue that the sociology of emotion and the psychosocial study of emotion are the same. Nevertheless, the sociological trends outlined above can be seen to have influenced the emergence of both psychosocial studies and the sociology of emotion. This book will, however, clearly distinguish a sociological way of seeing love from a psychosocial approach to love that is informed by social theory *and* psychoanalysis.

2.3   The philosophy and methods of psychosocial studies

In 1959, Mills wrote *The Sociological Imagination*, the conceptualisation of which is very similar to what might be described as a psychosocial imagination, as we will shortly see. It is not the aim of this chapter to enter into a detailed discussion of Mills' work, but his description of the sociological imagination (in Chapter 1 of his book) does provide us with an interesting platform from which to think about how it distinguishes itself from a 'psychosocial imagination'.

Mills' stated aim was to realise the promise of the social sciences, which, in his view (in 1959), had become pretentious and mediocre.[1] He describes the sociological imagination as a quality of mind that 'seems most dramatically to promise an understanding of the internal realities of ourselves in connection with larger social realities' (p. 15), without which people will not Mills argues:

- 'define the troubles that they endure in terms of historical change and institutional contradiction' (p. 3);
- 'possess the quality of mind essential to grasp the interplay of man and society, of biography and history, of self and world' (p. 4);
- 'cope with their personal troubles in such ways as to control the structural transformations that usually lie behind them' (ibid.);
- be able to 'understand the meaning of their epoch for their own lives' (p. 5).

'The first fruit of this imagination', Mills argues,

> is the idea that the individual can understand his own experience and gauge his own fate only by locating himself within his period, that he can know his own chances in life only by becoming aware of those of all individuals in his circumstances. (p. 5)

Mills is arguing for a humanistic, interventionist sociology, which does not only deal in metatheory, but also attempts to conjoin the biographical and historical.

Mills argues that in the 'absence of an adequate social science, critics and novelists, dramatists and poets have been the major, and often the only, formulators of private troubles and even of public issues' (p. 18). This was especially so, he argues, in the nineteenth century when the social sciences were attempting to conform to a positivist science.[2] However, Mills maintains, that by the late 1950s, the sociological imagination was becoming the intellectual common denominator of the times. That is, 'popular categories of criticism were becoming as much sociological as aesthetic' (ibid.).

A psychosocial analysis therefore needs to be placed in a particular tradition of sociological thinking, because it shares a commitment to studying life as a biographical and historical project. However, there are significant differences between a sociological imagination (manifest in the sociology of emotions, for example) and a psychosocial study, because the latter explicitly tries to combine psychology/psychoanalysis and, broadly speaking, sociology.

The object of sociology as a field of knowledge has been, as Rustin (2000, p. 43) states, 'to develop valid generalisations about societies, their component structures and processes and developments'.[3]

Although this book is sensitive to the macro worlds in which people live and the way in which they are filters by means of which they might experience the world, it does not aim (in theory or empirical method) to 'develop valid generalisations about societies, their component structures and processes and developments'.

In the introduction to their edited collection on biographical methods, Chamberlayne *et al.* (2000, p. 20) draw a distinction between King's use of biography in order to emphasise 'class welfare systems and family relationships' and Hollway and Jefferson's 'decision to explore certain theoretical questions relating to anxiety and fear of crime'. That is, although Hollway and Jefferson do refer to historical social structures (changes in the forces of production and employment), their aim is not to develop 'generalisations about societies, their component structures and processes and their development' (Rustin, 2000). Instead their aim is to provide a psychosocial analysis of subjectivity, but with a particular emphasis on exploring how psychoanalytic concepts can be used to understand the discursive positions that their interviewees occupy. That is, they explore the links between their 'defended subject' (of Kleinian theory) and the 'discursive subject' (of social or social-constructionist theory), thus offering a psychosocial explanation of the relationship between their interviewee's 'lived life' and 'told story'.[4]

This book can be understood in a similar context to that of Hollway and Jefferson's (2000a) and Day Sclater's (1999) in which (broadly speaking) sociological explanations of emotion or individual lives are combined with psychoanalytic reflections on them. However, these sociological explanations are not necessarily intended to provide generalisations about national forces of production, systems of political domination or international anarchy (the facts of history, or our chief enemies, as Mills, p. 13 describes them[5]).

The sociologist is, Mills claims, primarily concerned with these historical social structures and with the large historical scene. This means that their primary concern is, he says, with the changing structure of continent-wide society, industrialisation, rates of investment, war, world history, imperialism, totalitarianism and so on. Mills explains that the sociologist looks at literary moods, families, persons, creeds, jobs, neighbourhoods, at structures of societies and their components, at different social orders and at change and continuity through this world historical lens. Mills makes a distinction between the sociologist and the artist. The latter, by contrast, is primarily concerned with an intellectual age and style of reflection (styles of emotion, ways of feeling and vocabularies of motive) and not necessarily with 'the large historical scene'.

According to Mills' definitions, the psychosocial approach to the study of emotion (and narrative studies) in this book does not systematically qualify as 'classic social analysis' (1959, p. 21).[6]

Therefore, despite some similar objectives between a sociological and psychosocial imagination, significant differences exist in the use of the term sociological. Also, the sociological imagination could be seen to be in danger from a sociological reductionism. That is, (like the sociology of emotion) it rests on the idea that if we can place the individual in their socio-historical context, we will have the most significant facts about their life to hand.

However, psychoanalysis adds to this equation theories on human nature and on the development of mind. From a psychosocial perspective, we need to define 'our troubles' in terms which go beyond, yet still retain, an emphasis on 'historical change and institutional contradiction'.

The model of psychosocial studies presented in this book argues for the importance of bringing an essentialist psychoanalytic account of affective life into dialogue and debate with historicised sociological and cultural accounts of emotion and social phenomena. It involves using object relations psychoanalysis as an analytical tool with which to analyse a social phenomenon or discourse, rather than the social phenomena or discourse being explicitly used to interrogate or deconstruct the discourse of object relations psychoanalysis.

However, object relations psychoanalysis is critically engaged with by the importation of psychoanalytic concepts into a sociological context which emphasises, for example, that it is our societal 'feeling rules'[7] which legislate for what can be expressed and that it is our discourses of emotion which name certain sensations/feeling states as constitutive of a discrete emotion and therefore socially construct that which we take to be love, envy, jealousy and so on.[8] That is, the essentialised account of emotion in object relations psychoanalysis is implicitly questioned by a psychosocial 'way of seeing'[9] which critiques any ahistorical study of affective life. A psychosocial study of emotion therefore both demonstrates the strength of psychoanalytic concepts in a non-clinical field, while also challenging a study of conceptions of the mind in isolation from theories of society.[10] A discussion of the humanist/anti-humanist (essentialist) debate will emerge from this juxtaposition of approaches.

2.3.1   The psychosocial study of emotion

The philosophy and method of a psychosocial study of emotion have not yet been exhaustively discussed, but attempts to define the possibilities and limitations of this field are emerging (see Brown, 2000), and the demonstration of the psychoanalytic sociology of emotion as a 'way of seeing' can be seen in the recent work of Richards on envy (2000b), Yates on jealousy (2000), Price on happiness (2000), Hollway and Jefferson on fear (2000a) and Clarke (2003) on hatred.

In the above examples, a psychosocial study of emotion is operationalised in three main ways. First, it can be identified as a form of applied psychoanalysis, in which a psychoanalytic conceptualisation of a specific emotion is used as a tool for understanding contemporary social formations or a specific social phenomenon (Richards, 2000a, applied the concept of envy to questions of political leadership and electoral success).

The second form assumed by a psychosocial study of emotion is closer to psychoanalytic critique: a psychoanalytic understanding of affective life is used to examine educational discourses of learning (Price, 2000) or legal accounts of mediation (Brown and Day Sclater, 1999).

Third, a psychosocial debate can be constructed in a more dynamic way, such that a 'conversation' is constructed, for example, between a psychoanalytic understanding of jealousy, contemporary discourses of masculinity and the conditions of late modernity (Yates, 2000). Or, similarly, a psychoanalytic understanding of the unconscious is simultaneously combined with a sociological understanding of gender in order to provide a more complex account of learning in the classroom (Price, 2000).

In this third category, psychoanalytic accounts of affective life are brought into dialogue with, broadly speaking, sociological discourses of masculinity, learning and intimacy in the manner of both applied psychoanalysis (to demonstrate the relevance of a psychoanalytic concept to a discourse or phenomenon) and psychoanalytic critique (to expose the inadequacy of a contemporary discourse of affective life) but also to hypothesise about the dialectical relation between social and psychic change.

The above are, to some extent, artificial distinctions and one research project may contain instances of all three modes of analysis (application, critique and discursive dialogue), but as already stated, psychosocial studies more generally and a psychosocial study of emotion more specifically have only recently begun to be defined.

We have so far only referred to the way in which a psychosocial study of emotion can be understood conceptually, but what about its empirical grounding? How is a psychosocial study of emotion brought down from the level of application, critique and discursive dialogue to the level of lived experience? Or, from a more 'grounded theory'[11] perspective, how is psychosocial theory generated out of the empirical material gathered? Richards' (2000a) applied version of a psychosocial study of emotion used political advertising as empirical material, Price's (2000) psycho-analysis as critique takes educational discourses and classroom observation as empirical material, whereas Yates (2000) uses film as an empirical grounding for her psychosocial research. Each project needs to clarify what the empirical material is being used for: to generate psychosocial theory, to test a hypothesis, to critique an existing discourse or to demonstrate the strength of a psychoanalytic concept.

This book will contribute towards the definition of the possibilities and limitations of a psychosocial study of emotion conceptually, but it will also explore the question of how empirical material (life history interviews) can be used to refine or test it.[12]

2.4   Tensions in psychosocial research

Clinical psychoanalysis and academic learning represent two different methods of learning and knowledge generation, and their incommen-surability is inevitably encountered when 'practising' psychosocial studies. Following Bion, Waddell (1988) makes a distinction between learning about things and being able to learn from the experience of the self in the world; likewise psychosocial studies can be seen to ask us to learn about things (from the book) *and* from the experience of the self in the world.

However, giving space to 'learning from the experience of the self in the world' is not always easy in an academic context, as Proctor (2001, p. 28) points out:

> In the renaissance of classical learning, Montaigne wrote against the increasingly academic nature of education. He believed it should teach us *how to live* – be useful in helping us to 'understand our-selves … confront death, quell our wilder ambitions, appease our melancholy or our physical discomforts'.

Proctor cites De Botton (2000), who ironically points out that education instead 'impressed on us the derivation and etymology' of ideas like wisdom or ethics (ibid.). This is overstating the case (and the limitations of education), but it is an important point, as it highlights the possible tensions in psychosocial research, which attempts to traverse the academic/clinical (or experiential) divide. It is perhaps for this reason that Craib (1998, p. 139), a self-confessed lover of ideas, wrote a paper called the 'Psychodynamics of theory'. In it, he described his ambivalent relationship to intellectual life. He said:

> My movement away from theory began when I entered psychotherapy as a patient, and continued when I later started training as a group psychotherapist. It was indirect: theory was rarely, if ever, the material of a therapy session, yet as I grew closer to my own life, theory became less important. Looking back on my life as a student and then as a lecturer, it now seemed that theory provided me with a way of living that I did not have to own and an arena for some fairly basic desires and feelings to be acted out.

Main (1967) lists the many uses to which ideas or 'mental food' can be put. He says that ideas can create idle mental fat or great energy, can whet the appetite, be treated with contempt, become a useful servant or dominating master, and be a friend or enemy. There is a whole gamut of feelings, he says, from curiosity to loathing, from evangelism to competitiveness, which greet and become attached to ideas and as learners/researchers we are implicitly being asked by the terms of psychoanalysis to know something of this whole gamut of feelings that we bring to education. As Barfood (2002, p. 40) explains: 'There is no notion in Freud's psychology of a learner with a disinterested curiosity about reality for its own sake.'

Psychoanalytic methods encourage a 'meditative review of analytic work',[13] but interestingly, as Gough (2003, p. 26) points out, 'discussions of reflexivity rarely make reference to psychoanalytic theory, despite a long and rich tradition of writing on intersubjective dynamics'. This gap in the literature on reflexivity is, however increasingly, addressed by psychosocial research (e.g. Hunt, 1989; Day Sclater, 1999; Hollway and Jefferson, 2000a) that incorporates the concepts and methods of psychoanalysis into its methods of data collection and analysis. This book will highlight what psychoanalysis can add to discussions of reflexivity, by specifically referring to how reflexivity is conceptualised and fostered in the courses on psychoanalytic observation methods at the Tavistock Clinic, London.

Most psychoanalytic clinical training requires students to study psychoanalytic observation methods as part of their preparation for clinical work. Observational methods are simply referred to as 'a training in self-awareness' (M.J. Rustin, 1989, p. 68)[14] and some of the insights from this method are referred to in Chapter 8. We will see how psychosocial research tries to incorporate and combine psychoanalytic modes of learning and knowledge generation and more traditionally conceived academic modes of learning and knowledge generation.

For example, academic writing tends to conform to a 'scientific' model in which one's hypotheses are carefully crafted and tested. What this model of presentation does, of course, is to establish 'rules of theorising'[15] which go some way towards protecting a discipline from charges of artistic licence or wild analysis.

However, infant observation writing tries to achieve the right balance between poetic or artistic capabilities (imaginative writing) as well as scientific or intellectual capabilities which commit this writing to a 'high standard of literal accuracy and correspondence with observed fact' (ibid., p. 73). Papers about infant observations attempt to integrate theory and experience and the task is therefore to stay 'experience near' (J. and A-M. Sandler, 1994, p. 1001) and be vigilant about using literature or making interpretations which are 'experience far'.

Researchers using the terms of psychoanalysis, may therefore need to try to achieve an academic style that has affinities with creative writing in order to prevent the 'metapsychology of analytic theory' (see Waddell, 1988, p. 313) from erasing 'the language of insides'.

Hunt (2002, p. 176), for example, argues that creative writers need to 'delve into the inner world, in order to create writing which, whilst not necessarily autobiographical in the strict sense, is deeply personal'. She refers to Heaney's (1980) definition of the writer's voice: 'finding a voice means that you can get your own feeling into words and that your words have the feeling about you in them' (ibid.). This is similar to the kind of writing that clinical work demands, because it is expressive of learning from the experience of the self in the world. Learning from experience and learning by the book are not necessarily mutually exclusive exercises, of course, but the rhetoric of science which is implicit in academic writing and research (hypothesis, method and results) and the modes of creative expression encouraged in object relations psychoanalysis can be difficult to reconcile.

What we can see from this brief discussion is that psychosocial research that incorporates the tenets of object relations psychoanalysis stimulates a reflexive relation to empirical *and* conceptual work. Hence Craib's paper on the psychodynamics of theory[16] encourages academics to add a psychology of knowledge (or psychodynamics of theory) to the sociology of knowledge.

However, it is not the aim of this work to demonstrate a psychosociology of knowledge.[17] What is being emphasised is that psychosocial research can catalyse the development of a self-reflexive approach to one's object of study (in a personal, individualistic sense and socio-cultural way). Hence this study has involved a struggle between writing about love academically and living through the vicissitudes of it in everyday life. One of the main questions that concerned me was how I could write about ideal-typical love (from existentialism, psychoanalysis and sociology) without falsely positioning myself as someone who lived up to these models of authentic, mature and 'pure'[18] relating.

By writing about love 'authoritatively', for example, did I position myself as someone who knew how to love with integrity, passion and self-composure? Did I implicitly position or present myself as someone who would know in rich detail what the secrets of a good relationship are? Did I, in any way, believe that by writing about loneliness, jealousy, vanity, the capacity to be alone, to be modest and generous that I would traverse the all-important developmental threshold from narcissism to a more honourable concern for others? Or did my very choice of this subject of study reveal my own struggle with how to mitigate jealousy, envy and hate with something less convoluted, messy and shameful?

I often struggled with the problem of how to create a kind of umbilical cord linking knowing about theories of love or psychoanalysis to, or with, my experience of relationships and of psychoanalytic psychotherapy. For example, I asked how I could pay heed to the psychoanalytic injunction to 'know thyself' and not use psychoanalysis as a 'mere intellectual puzzle' (see Bettelheim, 1983). How could I keep the different elements of my experience integrated and grounded or should I have quite self-consciously attempted to keep them distinct and separate? And if so, how? Lear (1990, p. 6), for example, reminds us that 'in trying to understand human subjectivity, the mind is trying to grasp its own activity'. That is, in our research projects, we are partly trying to understand ourselves.

I found the sometimes irreconcilable aims of learning and writing from experience and learning and writing by the book particularly difficult to combine and thus what is presented here is a form of writing that is mostly consistent with (but critical of) the 'scientific' textual tradition to which a social science/humanities text, broadly speaking, belongs.

However, whereas Part 2 can be referred to as traditionally conceived academic theory, Part 3 gives voice to everyday narratives and experiences of love. In Part 2 we will see what sociological, existentialist and psychoanalytic approaches offer in answer to the question 'what is this thing called love?' and in Part 3, after a discussion of methods, we will see how interviewees in their eighties and thirties answer this question.

Part II
Love Ideals

3
Modern Love
Sociological Approaches

3.1 Introduction

In this chapter what we will see is that a socio-cultural perspective on the emergence of romantic love as a story opens up a 'thesaurus of meanings'.[1] That is, it is possible to identify ways in which this love story[2] partakes of religious ideals, enlightenment thinking, romanticism and socio-political changes, which the story dialectically juxtaposes.[3] Hence Barthes'(1978, p. 148): 'I love you has no usages. Like a child's word, it enters into no social constraint; it can be a sublime, solemn, trivial word, it can be an erotic, pornographic word. It is a socially irresponsible word.'

Moreover, romantic love's historical emergence and ideological function is contested, and it is difficult to clarify whether or not social theorists are referring to romantic love as a state of mind,[4] social practice,[5] narrative[6] or discourse.[7]

As a story (in films, novels, songs etc.), romantic love has many plots, characters and endings, which resist any final definition or closure. This chapter will not, therefore, begin with a classic definition of romantic love, because its aim is to offer a socio-cultural 'way of seeing'[8] romantic love that will, in later chapters, be combined with a (psycho) 'analytic attitude' (see M.E. Rustin,[9] 1989, p. 20) thus offering a psychosocial study of emotion. Stories of love can then be seen as socially determined and as expressive of a primary human (originally infantile) need to be object related.

Broadly speaking, it will be argued that a sociological and socio-cultural way of seeing love presents an impossible view of romantic love, because the origins of love ideals are seen as largely socially determined.

However, although sociologists are interested in the social construction of reality, they also recognise the dangers of generalisation and of only focusing on the 'great universes of meaning that history offers up for our inspection' (Berger and Kellner, 1964, p. 24). Nevertheless, very often their focus on 'little workshops of meaning' (ibid.) subjugates this micro world to larger social realities, thus losing the uniqueness of the ways in which different people make sense of the same social reality.

However, Mills' description of the sociological imagination points to the theoretical inadequacy of a sociology which only deals in metatheory, because it will not be able to conjoin the biographical and historical. It is this abstract, 'masculinist' sociological style which explains Bertilsson's (1991) claim that 'love's labours have been lost in social theory'.[10] Jackson (1993) similarly bemoans the fact that sociologists have traditionally been interested in sex, sexuality and the family, but not in love. However, as we saw in Chapter 2, Bendelow and Williams (1998) claims that 'the emotions have now come of age in sociology' and Giddens (1992) is a part of this tradition in which sociology challenges its own nature/disciplinary boundaries, for example, stating that he deliberately attempts to base his own writing style on the more 'feminised' self-help genre.

Since the expressed aim of the sociology of emotion is to reclaim emotion as a source of knowledge about social life, we might assume that a psychosocial and sociological account of intersubjective relations would now be more commensurable. However, as Hochschild (1998, p. 5) tells us, the 'sociology of emotion does not focus upon a person's childhood development per se, or on injury and repair, but instead on the socio-cultural determinants of feeling, and the socio-cultural bases for defining, appraising and managing human emotion and feeling'.

It is the 'socio-cultural determinants of feeling' and the 'socio-cultural bases for defining emotion' which this chapter will highlight. That is, in Berger and Kellner's terms, this chapter will look at 'the great universes of meaning that history offers up for our inspection'. However, it is not the aim of this chapter to study twelfth-century Europe or indeed eighteenth-century Europe[11] and it will only, therefore, provide a brief overview of the sociological account of the emergence of romantic love (Watt, 1957; Collins, 1972; Stone, 1977; Sarsby, 1983; Hendrick and Hendrick, 1992 etc.) and of the philosophical/religious influences discernible in it (Gusdorf, 1980; De Rougemont, 1983; Day, 1996; Davies, 1997 etc.). Sociological perspectives (Berger and Kellner, 1964; Giddens, 1992; Beck and Beck-Gernsheim, 1995; Hatfield and Rapson, 1996) on the function of romantic love will be briefly reviewed. Feminist theory (De Beauvoir, 1949; Firestone, 1972; Sarsby, 1983; Radway, 1984 etc.) will be used in order to criticise the traditional sociological assumption that romantic love represented a new kind of freedom (specifically for women).

3.2 Courtly love: amour passion

As already stated, it is possible to identify ways in which the romantic love story partakes of religious ideals, enlightenment thinking, romanticism and socio-political changes. A socio-cultural way of seeing love involves looking at these influences in order to understand our 'private troubles in terms of historical change' (Mills) and in terms of the discourses which the romantic narrative may partake of and present us with.

What sociology tells us is that the historical emergence of the romantic narrative cannot be separated from the historical emergence of a sense of self, because theoretically, at least, romantic love is predicated on choice, self-definition and marrying for love. It is for this reason that many sociologists argue that the ideals of romantic love 'inserted themselves directly into the emergent ties between freedom and self-realisation' (Giddens, 1992, p. 40) in the seventeenth and eighteenth century.[12]

However, romantic love also depicts the loss of self, suffering, disruption, transcendence and passion, which tales of courtly love depict. Indeed, according to De Rougemont (1983) courtly love needs to be understood as expressive of a love for God and the divine. In order to understand the ways in which romance incorporates the ideals of courtly love, De Rougemont's analysis[13] of it will be used. The historical accuracy of his thesis[14] will not be the point of discussion, but his polarisation of marriage (aligned with romantic love) and passionate but chaste love[15] (courtly love) which he argues have different origins and are irreconciliable will.[16]

A popular understanding of courtly love refers to a Knight's love for a noble and inaccessible Lady. The Knight devotes himself to the Lady whose inaccessibility keeps his passion and torment aflame. This is a love that cannot be consummated and it facilitates an unrealistic idealisation of the beloved and fuels the propensity for passion and strong emotion. It is a transcendent, chaste love that is not earthly and never leads to union with the beloved. This is a type of love that leads to a loss of self, because one's whole being is consumed by thoughts and desires for that which is strongly idealised and forever unattainable.

Courtly love is not therefore referred to as a love rooted in the dictates of reality and reason. To the extent that romantic love incorporates the ideals of 'amour passion', it can be celebrated as a beguiling narrative, but cautioned against, because of its promise of the impossible: a life lived in a more ardent, passionate and sublime state of mind.[17]

Romance can therefore be associated with the ascendency of reason while incorporating resonances of cosmic fate, transcendence, religious ecstasy or conversion. For the sake of clarity, we can think of romantic love as both an heir of the Enlightenment and of, broadly speaking, religious passion, insight and obfuscation. In a similar vein, romance can also be thought of as partaking of rationalism and romanticism.[18] In Freudian terms this means that romantic love can either serve the reality ego or be used in order to fulfil the needs of a pleasure ego; pleasure here signifying illusion, denial and the fantasised transcendence of our earthly limits (see Freud's *Formulations on the Two Principles of Mental Functioning*, 1911a).

Giddens (1992), for example, makes a distinction between amour passion and romantic love and Sarsby (1983) argues that romantic love is predicated on a notion of the 'thunderbolt'[19] – Cupid's arrow, against which we are powerless. Indeed, according to Sarsby there is a contradiction in offering passionate love as the prescribed condition for marriage, wherein this unbidden, uncontrollable emotion is regulated.

Amour passion can be likened to Nietzsche's celebration of Dionysian rebellion in the face of rationality (see Bertilsson's 1991 discussion). That is, amour passion is marked by urgency, passion and sickness and while the ego is overwhelmed, it enjoys its own despair.[20] Hence Jackson (1993) argues that there is a narrative closure in romantic love (the heroine who becomes a bride – mother – completes and leaves the story), because passionate love and long-term affection are incompatible. Passionate love, for example, is supposedly the precursor of long-term affection, but it is disintegrative, fuelled by obstacles and insecure. The paradox is that romantic love tries to incorporate amour passion and still be a generic social force tied to existing institutions like monogamy and marriage. What is being emphasised by social theorists is a reason/passion dichotomy or, in psychoanalytic terms, a polarisation between affect (sensation, emotion) and thought in the narrative of romantic love. De Rougemont offers us an analysis of the roots of this dialectic by reference to romantic love's incorporation of courtly ideals, which he maintains are essentially religious. It is interesting to briefly look at De Rougemont's account of courtly love, because we could hypothesise that theorists who emphasise the religious, romanticist and mystical subtext of romantic love (in the service of the pleasure ego) are more likely to subscribe to an impossibilist thesis on love.

De Rougemont, for example, is particularly interested in the myth of Tristan and Iseult which was formed in the twelfth century and which on the manifest level warns against that which is anti-social and disruptive of the social order.[21] Tristan and Iseult is about adultery and stages the conflict between feudal law and courtly chivalry in the twelfth century. There was, De Rougemont explains, a religious attempt to coerce, what he calls, human passion (aggressive/sexual impulses) and to 'contain the urges of the destructive instinct' (p. 22) and the break-down of marriage. It is passion which is therefore cast as disrupting our ability to think or reason and the myth, De Rougemont maintains, serves to warn us about the danger of seeking its rapture.

De Rougemont's main thesis is that the cult of passionate love in the poetry and songs of the twelfth century expressed the heretical beliefs of the Cathars. The material world and embodied self, according to this doctrine, was not created in God's image, but was created by a rebel Angel (the Devil). That is, our descent into matter is the work of Satan who wanted to escape the strictures of heaven. Hence, the material world is a perversion of God's spiritual creation of souls and consequently our souls are ensnared in bodies (a material life) foreign to them. We have therefore parted from our spirit which remains in heaven and with which we yearn to reunite. Courtly love speaks the same language as the Cathars in its renunciation of the earthly world (chaste love), devotion to God (the Lady as the materialisation of the divine urge[22]) and reunion with our spirit self (seeking transcendence beyond material love).[23]

There is a similarity here to Plato's (416–385 BC)[24] story of us forever seeking our lost half. In courtly love and Plato's fable, people are marked by lack, rupture and disintegration. In Lacanian terms, these stories dramatise the impossibility of ever fulfilling our desire to be self-pos-sessed and complete. Indeed, courtly love is a more ethical version of love according to Lacanians (see Salecl, 1994), because union is renounced and desire is sustained. It is in this context that we are led to understand the claim that 'I can't love you unless I give you up' (Salecl, p. 15). However, the Cathars did strive for union, but this was ultimately only possible by 'falling out of the material world'[25] – hence the link between passion and death.

De Rougemont thinks that the Troubadours probably used the sym-bolism of the Cathars, even if they were not members. Courtly love, as already stated, is therefore expressive of a desire for union (with God/the beloved), transportation (to God or divinity by the beloved) and transcendence (from our earthly state[26]). Courtly metaphors are there-fore resonant with Eastern mysticism and heretical religious beliefs, to which we are still in thrall via romance: The moderns, men and women of passion ... expect irresistible love to produce some revelation either regarding themselves or about life at large. This is the last vestige of primitive mysticism (De Rougemont, p. 282).

A myth is needed, De Rougemont (p. 21) alleges, to 'express the dark and unmentionable fact that passion is linked with death and involves the destruction of anyone yielding himself up to it with all his strength'. De Rougemont's is a complex thesis, but he believes that Tristan and Iseult and Romeo and Juliet exist to warn us against, in psychoanalytic terms, the inability to think through our feelings (passions). They raise up for De Rougemont the image of dying lovers, and declare that 'love like a force dominates you'.

> The terrible yearning wasting my heart;
> if I could name it, if thou couldst know it.
> Yearning now calls for death's repose
> What fate for me?
> Tis yearning and dying. (De Rougemont, quoting Tristan, p. 49)

Courtly love, according to De Rougemont, portrays the rapture and enjoyment of suffering, of the 'obstacles' which in Freud's (1912a, pp. 256–7) terms 'swell the tide of the libido'. Indeed, the single theme of the Troubadours' poetry, according to De Rougemont, was unsatisfied and unhappy love: the poet's plaint and the Lady's 'No' (p. 75).

Suffering has become in some instances, he says, a sign of redemption. That is, there is an assumption of another world and we become tempted by death to reach it. This can be seen in German Romanticism (De Rougemont, p. 222), which is contrasted with the 'disenchanted sadness' of the French. In Stendhal, it is claimed that we see a yearning for the sublime (which Rousseau laments too), when in his novel marriage replaces passion. Hence, passion is increasingly frowned upon by reason, in love's developmental history, and in 1822 there appears a scientific treatise on love (Stendhal' s 'De l'amour').

De Rougemont says that poets or theorists of love increasingly see the obstacles to love's transcendental power as internal and existential. Hence, of Chateaubriand, De Rougemont says: 'He has grasped that the drama takes place inside him, between intolerable laws of finite terrestrial existence and the desire for a transgression of our limits, fatal, but divinising' (p. 223).[27]

De Rougemont argues that Goethe's 'Werther', on the other hand, still believes that 'Charlotte' (his inaccessible beloved) is the route to transcendence (a prophetic being) and when he cannot unite with her, he commits suicide in her name. Stendhal, on the other hand, De Rougemont compares to a doctor studying his own malady. This examination of love continues, of course, when the 'psychoanalytic flag' is raised over the territory of normal love (see Bergmann, 1987, p. 157). Hence, a process of secularisation, rationalisation and individualisation means that love and its vicissitudes are eventually reduced to the human level.

However, De Rougemont maintains that romantic love is still influenced by the legacy of Christian sanctity (terrestrial vocation, humility, marriage with God rather than fusion, agape) and Catharist heresy (imperfect human love, the devil's world of terrestriality, the desire for luminous eros, fusion with the divine, transportation, passion).

De Rougemont concludes that passionate love is based on the illusion of living life to the full, of being free, transported and enriched. The myth offers the mind the 'mirage of infinite transcendence' and declares that 'love transports us beyond the misfortune of being a self' (p. 61). However, De Rougemont says that we are only free when we renounce the defeat and passivity of passion. There are links here to Freud's reality ego (1911a) offering greater satisfactions than the more passive and reactive pleasure ego. But while in thrall to this myth we cannot live life in the present and the mind recoils from an acceptance of limitation in ourselves and the other: 'Every possible love recalls us back to its bonds, reduces us to those limits of time and space – whereas the one goal of infinite love is compelled to be divine: God, our ideas of God, the deified self' (De Rougemont, p. 285).

Interestingly, De Rougemont implies that passionate love is ultimately a narcissistic phenomenon, when he states that Tristan's and Iseult's need for one another is driven by their own need to be aflame; they do not need one another to be as they are.

They love, he says, but not one other, thus echoing De Botton's (1993) point that our need to love is prior to the need to love anyone in particular (p. 12) or Lacan's claim (see Sarup, 1992) that we always fall in love in excess of the object. Passionate love can therefore be referred to as narcissistic, because according to the above accounts it is not object related or only object related as a means to a self-referential end (hence its theoretical deconstruction).

De Rougemont's work is helpful, because it gives us an entry point for looking at the different discourses that are discernible in romantic love and it sheds light on the contemporary social–scientific deconstruction of it. As already stated, we could hypothesise that theorists who emphasise the religious, romanticist and mystical subtext of romantic love (in the service of the pleasure ego) are the ones more likely to subscribe to an impossible view of love. Second wave feminism (De Beauvoir, 1949 etc.), for example, saw it (in Marxist fashion) as an opiate for women. Sociological accounts (Berger and Kellner, 1964) of romantic love see it as an ideology which restricts 'world building proclivities' and 'naturalises' marriage. An existentialist perspective (Sartre, 1943) and Lacanian view (Salecl, 1994) would argue that it promises to release us from our existential condition. Psychoanalytic perspectives (Clulow, 1993) would emphasise the manic flight from reality and post-structuralist accounts claim that the words 'Love' and 'God', do not refer to a metaphysical realm, but only to other signifiers (Shibles, 1974; Barthes, 1978). A view of love as possible, like Giddens (1992), however, draws on the rationalist heritage of romantic love and it then becomes the 'harbinger' of the pure, democratised, reality-based relationship (in the service of the reality ego).

De Rougemont provides a very Lacanian reading of desire, an existentialist reading of the human condition and a psychoanalytic analysis of a life and death instinct, without explicitly referring to them, but it is his attempt to describe human nature and the forces in the mind that makes his history of romance interesting.[28] The implication is, of course, that we should be careful of our passionate strivings[29] and the romanticism within us; his account is therefore a fruitful way into thinking about the views of love as impossible in social theory and psychoanalysis.

Hendrick and Hendrick (1992), Giddens (1992), Hatfield and Rapson (1996), De Rougemont (1983) and Sarsby (1983) all draw some kind of distinction between passionate and romantic love, and this is why this section began by describing romantic love as an heir of rationalism and religion, romanticism and the Enlightenment. De Rougemont has only been studied at length in order to evoke the state of mind dramatised in passionate love. Giddens, Hatfield and Rapson, and Hendrick and Hendrick all ask if passionate love is universal and they conclude that it is (felt at any age, in any ethnic group etc.). De Rougemont (p. 17) implies that its roots lie in our human natures ('it still remains to be seen what notion of love – what secret of our existence, of the human mind, perhaps of our history, this hankering must hint at'). Romantic love is also expressive of this passion and 'hankering' for self-transcendence, but it also depicts a more terrestrial, sober,[30] embodied love.

3.3   Romantic love

3.3.1   Introduction

As already stated, many social theorists refer to courtly love as prefiguring romantic love, but most sociologists cite the eighteenth century as the time when romantic love appeared as a new narrative form and model for conduct. That is, the historical emergence of the romantic narrative cannot be separated from the historical emergence of a sense of self, because theoretically, at least, romantic love is predicated on choice, self-definition and marrying for love. It is for this reason that many sociologists argue that the 'ideals of romantic love inserted themselves directly into the emergent ties between freedom and self-realisation' (Giddens, 1992) in the seventeenth and eighteenth century. Indeed, social historians describe an upsurge in radical feeling in the eighteenth century and Bertilsson, like Giddens, Beck and Beck-Gernsheim (1995), Stone (1977) and so on argue that in the course of its historical development, love becomes increasingly democratic and sexual-erotic (in contrast to the chaste and courtly love of the noble knight for 'his' lady).

Hatfield and Rapson (1996), for example, in their cross-cultural study of love and sex emphasise the difference between so-called collectivist and individualist cultures, in order to emphasise the specifically Western nature of romance. They point out that in the eighteenth century the Western world was being transformed in different spheres as follows:

1. the material sphere by urbanisation, industrialisation and technology. Love relations have to be understood in the context of the cultural changes that urbanisation led to;
2. the psychological sphere by individualism (hence romantic love is expressive of the self and self-definition);
3. the economic and political sphere by the rise of capitalism and a movement towards democracy (romantic love needs to be understood in terms of gender, which, it can be argued, 'set the terms for modernity' – see Seidler, 1998, p. 194);
4. the sphere of philosophy by the ideas of secularisation, science and the discovery or rediscovery (see Davies, 1997) of humanism.

1. Urbanisation, industrialisation and technology

Berman (1983), for example, divides the history of modernity into three phases. The first begins, he says, in the sixteenth to eighteenth century when people were beginning to experience modern life. He cites the work of Stone (1977)[31] who argued that in the late eighteenth century significant numbers of young people were forming intimate bonds that violated traditional family, class, religious and economic barriers. Socio-economic changes led to changes in interpersonal bonds that contributed to the demographic movements to cities, establishing the mobile type of nuclear family.

The second phase begins with the French revolution of 1789: an age of 'experimental upheavals in every dimension of personal, social and political life' (p. 33).[32] Here people have a memory of the premodern and an experience of the new and it is in this dichotomy, Berman argues, that the processes of modernisation (in social life) and modernism (in art and thought) unfold. He cites Rousseau as the first 'arch modern voice' (p. 35, in the second phase of modernity) and the first to introduce the use of the word 'moderniste'. He quotes from Rousseau's romantic novel, *The New Eloise*, in which the hero, Saint-Proux, writes to his love, Julie, about the experiences of modernity after his move from the country to the city: 'Everyone constantly places himself in contradiction with himself. The good, the bad, the beautiful, the ugly, morality, virtue have only a limited and local experience' (ibid., p. 18).

This means that his own love for Julie is questioned even as he reaffirms it: 'I don't know one day what I'm going to love the next' (ibid.). In Rousseau's hero we can therefore see the need for something solid to cling to in an atmosphere of 'turbulence and trouble', precisely undermining the stability of his beliefs. Berman echoes Rousseau's hero and argues that in the modern world, everything is 'pregnant with its contrary', adding that the modern voice 'resonates with self-discovery and self-mockery, with self-delight and self-doubt' (p. 32).[33]

The twentieth century marks the third and final phase of modernity, when the 'processes of modernisation expand to take in the whole world, and the developing culture of modernism achieves spectacular triumphs in art and thought' (ibid., p. 17). Here we find Berman describing a 'landscape of steam engines, automated factories, railroads, vast new industrial zones, teeming cities that have grown, telephones, newspapers, nation states, multinational aggregations of capital, expanding world markets' and so on. Berman claims that as the modern public expands in the twentieth century, it 'shatters into a multitude of fragments, speaking incommensurable private languages' (ibid.).

Hence, the very socio-economic conditions which romantic love partook of could be seen to have already sown the seeds of their own destruction. That is, as Berman says:

> Modernity ... can be said to unite all mankind. But it is a paradoxical unity, a unity of disunity: it pours us all into a maelstrom of perpetual disintegration and renewal, of struggle and contradiction, of ambiguity and anguish. To be modern is to be part of a universe in which, as Marx said 'all that is solid melts into air'. (p. 15)

According to Berger and Kellner (1964), in Berman's second phase of modernity, the industrial revolution created a situation in which individuals had to turn to the private sphere for self-realisation,[34] which they characterise as the last area of private choice in a vast, impersonal public sphere. The public/private split which industrial life instituted thus inaugurated a search for a sense of freedom and choice within the confines of a private world. The accent for Berger and Kellner is on the isolation of the private couple and they are therefore interested in how couples construct their social worlds and create a mutually narrated biography of their life together. As modernity develops, Berger and Kellner argue that the 'marriage partner becomes the significant other par excellence, the nearest and most decisive co-inhabitant of the world' (p. 11). Thus, these two people try to stabilise each other's sense of self and identity and construct a mutually shared reality, which is according to Berger and Kellner a precarious undertaking. They argue that this construction of reality (marriage) is in need of validation (by ideologies like romantic love), precisely because of an 'ever-present glimmer or suspicion as to its social manufacture and relativity'.[35]

They maintain that the world is most often experienced as an 'external datum, a ready-made world that simply is there for us to go ahead and live in' (p. 3). Objectifying the world and marriage:

> serves to establish the stability of this world and at the same time to assuage the existential anxiety that, probably, inevitably accompanies the perception that nothing but one's narrow shoulders support the universe in which one has chosen to live. If one may put it like this, it is slightly more comfortable to be Columbus than Prometheus. (p. 16)

Romantic love (and especially romantic fatalism/positivism) therefore saves us from what De Botton refers to as 'the full horror of contingency' (p. 10). Hence Berger and Kellner claim that: 'Without marriage people are threatened by anomie in the fullest sense of the word.' (p. 23)

The function of romantic love, in this context, can be likened to the function of an autobiography (as described by Gusdorf): 'a theodicy of individual being, doubting its own value ... making a reconciliation to self' (p. 39).

Berger and Kellner imply that pre-industrial life shielded people from a sense of this anomie, because it was a collectivist society, which they depict in a romantic light ('the same social life pulsated through the house, the street and the community', p. 8). By contrast, they depict the now isolated conjugal family unit as living in an impersonal global public sphere (see p. 19). Berger and Kellner thus question what kind of freedom romantic love and the conjugal family unit gained in Berman's third phase of modernity.[36]

2. Individualism

Romantic love, according to Stone (1977), represented a new kind of freedom, which was narrated in novels of the eighteenth century. Stone describes a companionate marriage based on affection and equality and a change in attitude from distance deference and patriarchy to affective individualism. Stone does not share Berger and Kellner's romantic view of pre-industrial life. He provides a gruesome list of common ailments not conducive to romantic longings. He argues that the individual was subsumed by kin, village or state with no privacy and therefore no freedom of choice or movement. Romantic love, however, was said to emerge in a society which emphasises individuality and self-identity.[37] Hendrick and Hendrick (1992) argue that the awareness of choice was a major correlate in the emergence of a sense of self, adding that this eventually involves the choice of partner. Hendrick cites Baumeister's (1987) study of the emerging process of self-definition in which 1830–1900 is mentioned as the flowering of the historical emergence of a sense of self.[38] It is then, they argue, that the problems of selfhood began to intensify, such as the nature of self-knowledge, how one defines the self, what it means to be fulfilled etc.[39] However, according to Gusdorf (1980), Christianity expressed this fascination with personal life, because self-examination (of sin) is central to it; the Renaissance testified to the freedom of the individual and the Romantic era, he says, exalted the genius. The virtue of sincerity, of telling all is, he maintains, crystallised in Montaigne's *Essays*, Rousseau's *Confessions* and Freud's psychoanalysis (see pp. 33–4). Giddens (1992) explains that romance emerges in the context of Berman's second phase of modernity[40] in order to insert self and other into a personal narrative which has no particular reference to wider social processes: it is an individualised love story.

Hence, we have become interesting to ourselves as a narrative object; a 'reflexive project' (Giddens, 1992) and the concepts of individuation and individualisation are some of those through which our experience of reality and ourselves come to be ordered. As Denzin (1989) explains our lives are constrained by the writing practices of our time and by the complex notion of the person that our society upholds.

For example, autobiography, according to Gusdorf (1980), does not exist outside of our own cultural context and it expresses a concern peculiar to Western 'man' in which the uniqueness of the self is prioritised. Gusdorf believes that the autobiography is not content to provide a CV, but is, as already stated, 'an apology, a theodicy of the individual being, doubting its own value and making in this literary genre, a final appeal or reconciliation to self'(p. 39). Interestingly, Giddens also uses literary or biographical metaphors to describe romantic love. It is, he says, a 'newly discovered narrative form providing a long-term trajectory oriented to an anticipated shared future' (p. 45). Moreover, romance, can be likened to the autobiography,[41] because it can also be seen as a means whereby we can rewrite and validate our identity.

Romance therefore expresses the concerns which Gusdorf refers to as peculiar to Western 'man' in which the uniqueness of the self is prioritised. He points out that in other cultures, the individual does not oppose himself to all others and lives an interdependent existence in which 'no one is the rightful possessor of his life or his death; lives are so thoroughly entangled that each of them has its centre everywhere and its circumference nowhere' (p. 30).

However, according to Hendrick:

> Because people do have choice, the possibility of linking choice of partner to romantic love can occur in ways not previously possible. Therefore, in the modern era, we have an increasing convergence of love or falling in love as a basis for marriage, and that convergence is based on the sense of self developing through the sense of choice as an aspect of one's personal being. (p. 24)[42]

3. The rise of capitalism and a movement towards democracy

The economic individualism of the eighteenth century is cited as the context in which the romantic novel first appeared in order to both express the social concerns of its day and to provide a new model for conduct. Watt (1957) explains that romantic love replaced courtly love as a new narrative tradition, because it tied love and courtship to freedom of choice. However, the fact that women could not realise the aims of economic individualism was, according to Watt, a reflection of the tension between patriarchy and individualism. The 1758 Marriage Act in England exemplifies this point:

> The husband and wife are one person in law; that is, the very being or legal existence of the woman is suspended during the marriage or at least is incorporated and consolidated into that of the husband; under whose wing, protection and cover, she performs everything. (Sarsby, 1983, p. 23)

Watt argues that the fact that men were deferring marriage until they were economically viable meant that spinsters and bachelors emerged as a new social concern and the romantic novel, he says, mainly concentrated on a courtship leading to marriage. The novel, he explains, was characterised by its attempt to draw a psychological portrait of its characters and thus contribute to a democratisation of intimacy, because ordinary, everyday detail became worthy of attention. For example, he points out that the novel wasn't written in Latin and one of the first novels (Richardson's *Pamela* first serialised in 1693) depicted a 'servant girl' marrying the 'squire' (Watt, 1957, p. 152). The novel therefore depicts romantic love as predicated on choice within the constraints imposed by gender expectations, class and ethnicity divides. However, women were as Watt points out de-carnalised and the ability to resist one's carnal desires is, therefore, shared by both courtly and romantic love, though the relationship is finally consummated in the romantic narrative. Watt explains this atmosphere of sexual repression by pointing to the fact that according to the Puritan view of marriage, sex outside of 'wedlock' was a sin. He claims that the middle classes saw the sexual excesses of the aristocracy as corrupt and romantic love therefore stressed the importance of friendship as much as carnal desire. Here is the basis for Stone's point that the romantic relationship is based on affection and equality rather than financial advantage or obedience.[43]

However, the main consumers of the novels that Giddens describes as 'flooding the bookshops' in the early 1700s were (middle class) women. Giddens quotes from a 1753 (p. 41) 'Lady's Magazine' which declared that 'there is scarce a young Lady in the kingdom who has not read with avidity a great number of romances and novels' (p. 173). However, Sarsby adds that it was not women's 'equality which made them avid readers about love, but their very dependency' (p. 68).

According to Hendrick and Hendrick and Sarsby an ideology was needed to justify women as unpaid labour and women in the middle ranks of society were not therefore supposed to be concerned with 'vulgar economic concerns' (Sarsby, p. 17). Hendrick refers to 1800–1900 as the century of male domination in which women were cast as weak, delicate of mind, the nurturing sex, maternal etc. According to Hochschild (1998), women learned to make a resource out of feeling and offer it to men (with sexual beauty) in return for material resources (or a validated, positive identity – see De Beauvoir 1949). Seidler (1998) tells us that men, on the other hand, 'do' emotional work to suppress feeling, because emotionality does not reflect well on their status as rational selves (p. 198).[44]

As already stated, according to Benjamin (1988), Western rationality represents a psychological rejection of the principles of femininity, hence Giddens refers to romantic love as feminised love, which was, for women, an assertion of autonomy in a context of deprivation. Moreover, Giddens cites women as the 'underlabourers of modernity' (p. 200)[45] having performed years of (in Hochschild's, 1983, terms) unpaid 'emotional labour'.[46] What we therefore need to add to Berman's analysis of the history of modernity is that the categorical split between reason (masculinity) and emotion (femininity) set the terms for it (see Seidler, 1998, p. 194).

While Giddens and Zeldin, for example, may applaud women as the intimacy revolutionaries, second wave feminists (De Beauvoir, 1949; Firestone 1972; Greer 1970) had a more critical view of the 'woman in love' (the title of De Beauvoir's chapter in *The Second Sex*). Their main point is that the sexual division of labour is non-conducive to the 'pure relationship' (see Giddens) or mutually constructed world (see Berger and Kellner). Romantic love is, they maintain, an ideological support for a short-term passionate involvement leading to a long-term unequal dependence. The nuclear family, according to second wave feminists, is claustrophobic, totally involving, sexually binding, and based on a philosophy of possessiveness, and yet it is held up as a woman's salvation. Indeed De Beauvoir argues that the woman in love desires her enslavement so ardently that she thinks it is her freedom.

According to R. Collins (1972) 'ideals are used as weapons' (p. 54) and the ideal of romantic love, 'including a strong element of sexual repression' (p. 67), is a woman's means for maximising her bargaining power in a situation where men control the economic world. His basic proposition is that men and women are unequals in physical strength and that in social structures where men can exercise this strength there is no need for an ideology like romantic love. He lists four types of social structure which have defining forms of sexual stratification and dominant ideologies: the low-technology tribal society, fortified households in stratified societies, private households in market economies and the advanced market economy.

It is the private household in a market economy where, he says, the centralised bureaucratic state exercises the legitimate use of power, and men, he claims, cannot therefore dominate women by brute force. He states that 'bilateral sexual property is a modern variant which arises with an independent bargaining position of women' (p. 59). However, a woman's main resource in the market economy is her sexuality and her status as a companion in the private household. The ideology of romantic love is, therefore he says, upheld by women, because it idealises her sexuality and renders her inaccessible. Sexuality can now only be referred to under its 'idealised aspect' (p. 68), that is, spiritual devotion, aesthetic beauty and interpersonal reliance. 'Sexual bargaining' he argues, 'now takes place by idealised gestures and symbolisation rather than the frank negotiations of traditional parents or marriage brokers' (ibid.).

The romantic love ideal is the (especially middle class[47]) woman's key weapon in acquiring power and status. However, the idealisation of women means, as Sarsby and second wave feminists maintain, that they are protected or barred from 'vulgar economic concerns' (Sarsby, p. 17). Women are kept, according to Collins in a 'fantasy world of aesthetic symbols' (p. 71).

So, although romance does afford a woman a form of power over men in which they can exercise their skills ('emotional literacy' etc.[48]), a fall into love for a woman also facilitates a falling out of herself. In short, romantic love is lambasted as the pivot of women's oppression,[49] by second wave feminists. They are consequently critical of romantic love as a social practice and as a state of mind and it is therefore possible to refer to this feminist sociological position as offering an impossible view of romantic love.

4. Secularisation, science and humanism

Humanist discourses in which a life beyond ideology is perceived are, in contemporary social theory, seen to be naive. Davies (1997), for example, explains that after the Second World War and after witnessing indiscriminate slaughter, contempt and a very modern and 'rational' (planned) extermination of a people, the very notion of the human was called into account. He maintains that it was then difficult to retrieve anything from the philosophy of humanism (enlightenment and romanticist ideals). Moreover, Davies points out that the concept of humanity could be hijacked and used to prioritise 'abstract man' over real people. The discourse of the essential human subject then legislates for the bounds of what it is possible to think or say and can ultimately become a threat to one's right to life. Humanism has also been accused of 'degenerating' into romanticism (p. 48) and into a pious 'religion of humanity' ruled by the few. Humanism, Davies says, has therefore become a term of 'sovereign condemnation', because it dissolves the particularities of class, race and sex in a singular universal essence, which tends to resemble the white, European male. Appeals to essentialism are seen to deny their own ethnocentric prejudices and it is in this context that we can understand the contemporary emphasis on 'identity and difference' (Woodward, 1997).

The essentialism that underpins the assumption that love and hate are emotions that are somehow innate or in our blood is thus problematised in postmodern and post-structuralist theory. Romantic love, for example, can be accused of fulfilling a similar ideological function to humanism naturalising socially constructed phenomena. Love according to Gay (1986, 87), for example, has been written about by 'popular poets, essayists, novelists' and so on as though it is a 'primordial energy', and 'universal solvent' (equally dissolving the particularities of class, race, ethnicity etc.). Writing about love in this humanist (universalist) vein, hides the historical character of its appeal, and it assumes the status of a natural emotion waiting to unproblematically occur. As an ideal-typical state of mind or associated social practice, it too then legislates for the bounds of what it might be possible to think or say. Hence, an impossible view of romantic love is sometimes informed by an anti-humanism.

Pearce and Stacey (1995) ask why the narrative of romantic love (and its consumption) has survived despite its deconstruction in feminist theory. Recalling the sociological equation of love with literature and narrative, they suggest that it survives because it is a classic script. It is not as Modleski (1982) says a monolithic, disabling ideology, but a script that we can enter and rewrite imaginatively. It is therefore the textuality of romance which we see being emphasised in the 1980s–1990s feminism, rather than the material powerlessness (or stupidity – see Greer, 1970) of women. Pearce and Stacey, for example, refer to romantic love's 'scripting possibilities' and argue that it offers room for self-exploration, and Radway and other writers emphasise the oppositional themes of justice and revenge in their theories of why women read romances. The romantic love story or song, they maintain, offers fantasy resolutions to present material circumstances and the consumption of romance is therefore expressive of the 'dreams of the oppressed'. In contrast to second wave feminism, the feminists of the 1980s–1990s state that we should take women's dreams and fantasies seriously and look at the imaginative triumph which romantic love stories enable women to experience. Indeed, according to Pearce, the forte of the romantic love story is that the characters are loosely drawn (empty) thus allowing us to fill them up with our identifications and needs.

3.4 The sociology of emotion: two contemporary examples

3.4.1 The narrative of romance

A socio-cultural way of seeing romantic love has involved deconstructing some of the different discourses or meanings that are discernible in the romantic narrative, and looking at the socio-economic and cultural changes which are conducive to the romantic sensibility or narrative. By looking at love in this way, we can begin to understand our own troubles as historically, economically and culturally constituted as Mills promised. In Chapters 9 and 10 the importance of a socio-cultural way of seeing love will be demonstrated, because interviewees' stories of love need to be understood by reference to, for example, their economic position, gender and age in order to understand how love is conceptualised and seen to be realisable. However, as already stated, a psychosocial perspective sees love as a play between our social, psychic and existential selves and an exclusive socio-cultural way of seeing love does not consider how these different facets of the self interact.

Indeed the socio-cultural way of seeing love has led to one contemporary position in which love is referred to exclusively as a discourse (interacting with other discourses with different lineages). From a social-constructionist and post-structuralist point of view, feelings are seen as social practices, rather than as 'natural' emotions, waiting unproblematically and universally to appear.

This is why 'love's labours' may still be lost in sociological theory, because although sociology is now keen to see emotions as corporeal, contextual and temporal and is keen to reinstate an embodied sociology, it is not so enthusiastic about seeing this body as a 'theatre for the mind' (Mc Dougall, 1986) that is *psycho*-somatic, rather than 'linguo-somatic' (Shibles 1974). That is, in contemporary sociology, language is in danger of constituting the limit of our world/research. The relatively new sociology of emotion is, for example, largely informed by discourse analysis (Pearce and Stacey) and philosophical linguistics (Shibles).

Crossley (1998), for example, discusses Coulter's (1979) work, which draws a distinction (following Wittgenstein) between sensations/feelings and emotions. Coulter says that emotions can't be localised (where do you love me?) and that they are different from sensations (like toothache). Emotions, unlike sensations, he argues are public and contestable. Sensation words, on the other hand don't refer, they shriek and exclaim (he gives as an example 'ouch' – see p. 18). Hence, Coulter argues that emotion words belong to our public dictionary and are subject to the language games of our culture, which Shibles (1974) argues we need to de-propagandise ourselves from. From a sociological point of view we can pay attention to the language game of romantic love, but methodologically we have no access to the private world of sensation: 'to think that words symbolise a metaphorical realm is to be shot through with Cupid's arrow: a cupidity for the unknown' (see Shibles, 1974, p. 356).

According to Shibles, the lover is captivated by a metaphor which becomes for him/her a fixation. Falling in love is like, he says, falling into a metaphor, but we speak of emotions as though we have a portfolio of them (p. 206). We should not look within to find our emotions, but at our language, which Shibles says captivates us. To speak of 'falling in love, finding love' and so on is a category mistake: the metaphor to myth fallacy. If we ask interviewees to tell us about their experiences of love, we are in this context, in danger of asking them to introspect on a 'vague abstraction'. The familiarity of the word love instead must be made strange, because metaphors, Shibles maintains, transform the world. Shibles, for example, says that we perform our words. Hence Barthes (see the following chapter) provides fragments and discourses of love and not truths.

In Pearce and Stacey's (1995) work, we can see one of the ways in which contemporary post-structuralist feminism looks at the psychological effects of the discourse of romance (see also Jackson 1993), rather than introspecting on love as though it is a 'pseudo-psychological entity' (Shibles, 1974). Similarly, contemporary work on the sociology of emotion calls for a philosophical problematisation of emotion, which critically re-examines our language games of emotion.

A discourse-analytic or social-constructionist position would not recognise love's status as a biological or psychological fact/need as object relations psychoanalysis implies (see Chapters 5 and 6). Thus, a psychosocial study of emotion is different from the sociology of emotion, because the former tries to combine the socio-cultural and object relations view of love. However, from the discussion so far, it is possible to see the ways in which a contemporary socio-cultural 'way of seeing' differs from the (psycho) 'analytic attitude' (see M.E. Rustin, 1989, p. 20) briefly referred to in Chapter 2. In Chapter 8, despite these differences of approach, a psychosocial method for interpreting life history data will be developed and in the cases in Chapters 9 and 10 the complex interaction between socio-cultural and psychological factors which influence people's ways of seeing or experiencing love will be discussed. As well as demonstrating a psychosocial way of studying love, the research question that is brought to these interviews will ask whether we are seeing an everyday deconstruction of love that resembles the theoretical deconstruction of love that we have begun to document. According to Giddens, for example, we are witnessing the emergence of a new discourse of intimacy, which he both charts and contributes to and I will briefly outline the main features of this discourse which forms one more example of a contemporary and significant socio-cultural way of seeing love.

3.4.2   The pure relationship and confluent love

The narrative of romantic love has traditionally been the dominant discourse of intimacy through which we have understood the psycho-sexual relationship of the adult couple. However, according to Giddens, the romantic narrative no longer describes a set of concepts and social practices which adequately captures, or prescribes, the practices for new social formations. According to Collins, it is in advanced market economies (when women are more economically independent) that the traditional system of sexual stratification is challenged, thus making the romantic love ideal less necessary. In this social structure he says that 'sexual bargains can be less concerned with marriage; dating can go on as a form of short-run bargaining, in which both men and women trade on their own attractiveness or capacity to entertain in return for sexual favours and/or being entertained' (p. 72).

The emphasis for Giddens is on the increasing number, especially of women, who are interested in relationships rather than the socio-legal arrangement of marriage. Giddens maintains that the term 'relation-ship', meaning a close and continuing tie to another, has only come into general usage relatively recently. According to Giddens (pp. 58–62) the more confluent love becomes consolidated as a real possibility, the more the finding of a 'special person' recedes and the more it is the 'special relationship' that counts.

It is women, Giddens argues, who developed romantic love and helped to dissolve it, but men, he says, are the 'laggards' in the transi-tions now occurring (p. 59). Men, he points out, have always fallen in love and have been influenced by romantic love, but in the current era, ideals of romantic love tend to fragment under the pressure of female emancipation and autonomy. Women are no longer complicit with the role of the phallus and with what Giddens refers to as men's 'lapsed emotional narratives' (p. 130). Whereas men have traditionally antici-pated their future in terms of an economic career, they have not seen romance as a way of engaging with future time, because it has been more closely aligned with amour passion for them (p. 57). The pure rela-tionship, however, seems to be less troubled by transcendent hopes and tragic experience than its predecessor, romance.

Intimacy is now being redefined as an emotional communication with others and the reflexive project of self refers to the way in which individuals are now continually obliged to negotiate who they are and what lifestyle choices they are making as traditions are swept away. Moreover, the future has to be worked for against a background of acknowledged risk (Giddens, p. 196). The reflexive project of self is an existentially inflected narrative in which I am always to some extent 'what I am not yet' (Sartre) and able to live with what Rylance refers to as Barthesian 'dialectical bliss'.[50] Addictions, Giddens claims, are the negative index of the degree to which the reflexive project of self moves to centre stage in late modernity (p. 76). Co-dependency, for example, is seen as an example of reverse reflexivity, because addictive relationships are not about choice.[51]

Giddens adopts what seems to be the language of neurolinguistic programming when he suggests that we need to overcome our 'negative programmes' in order to avoid fixated relationships. However, on the whole, Giddens prefers to use object relations psychoanalysis (rather than the post-structuralist emphasis on language) in order to think about how intimacy can be transformed further, but he uses at times a diluted form of object relations psychoanalysis. For example, he argues that the call to narcissism is the first stage of the development of confluent love, but this can be seen as the antithesis of object relating in classic psychoanalytic accounts. Giddens, is perhaps referring to 'healthy narcissism' or self-worth and assertiveness, that is, not a psychoanalytic idea of narcissism.

Also, his support for a transformation of intimacy in personal life is not confined to the world of adults, because children's rights should also be respected. However, an object relations approach to understanding 'the sexual activities of children' (see Klein, 1932) alerts us to the very real need for adults to set boundaries for children, because of what Freud would refer to as their weak egos and cruel impulses. It would not therefore be advisable, in this context, to grant children complete freedom of speech and action. These points of contrast highlight the way in which there are fundamental differences between a sociological and psychoanalytic approach to understanding intimacy, but there are nevertheless some interesting points of comparison too.

Giddens states that he wants to historicise object relations psychoanalysis, and largely does this by emphasising the way in which impulses towards subjection and mastery are a gendered phenomenon (in contrast to Sartre, Freud and Klein). Consequently, Giddens calls for an ethics of a day-to-day (socially conceived) personal life which corresponds to our wish for a democratic, participatory political life (in which we fight for freedom of speech and expression).

The model of the pure relationship is one which, like democratic politics more generally, encourages 'free and equal relations between people'. Giddens lists the principles of democratic politics (the constitutional limit of destructive power, accountability, pluralism etc.), arguing that these are the principles we see espoused in self-help manuals which he refers to as 'the texts of our times in the way that medieval manuals of manners were for theirs' (p. 64).

Moreover, the pure relationship is defined by its communicative potential in both sexual and emotional life. It is not necessarily monogamous or heterosexual, and it involves the cultivation of sexual skills and reciprocal pleasure. When reproduction was once a part of nature, Giddens explains that heterosexual activity was inevitably the focal point of reproduction. 'Once "sexuality" has become an integral component of social relations ... heterosexuality is just one taste among others, but such is the socialisation of reproduction' (ibid.).[52] Indeed, for Giddens, gay relationships are the pioneers of transformed intimacies.

Giddens ends his book by calling for a reconsideration of the way in which emotion has been counterposed to reason, ethics and morality. In contemporary society, he argues that passion has become a muted sexual experience, because there is no room for passion in an overly bureaucratised world. Yet, he asks, 'who can live without passion?' (p. 201) and he reminds us that confluent love is the fostering of non-destructive emotion and that it is also a resuscitation of the erotic. Eroticism, he says, is the cultivation of feeling, which is experienced in bodily sensations in a communicative context. In the pure relationship, Giddens hopes that eroticism will be sexually re-integrated within a wider range of emotional purposes, paramount among which is communication.

Interestingly, he concludes that a call for 'life politics' is akin to the renewal of spirituality. It is for this reason that Giddens states that what he supports is a radical pluralism and not a casual cosmopolitanism. Ours is a culture in which death has lost its place, he says, and instead the fascination with death has been taken over by an obsession with sex. Interestingly, in both existentialism and psychoanalysis, death and an awareness of our mortality and transience inform theories of 'authentic' or non-possessive intimacy.

Giddens' (1992) work, like Bendelow and Williams', is an example of the way in which sociology has reclaimed emotion as a source of knowledge about social life. Although Giddens' model of the pure relationship ultimately subordinates emotion to cognition, his work is nevertheless important, because (like Bendelow etc.) it is part of a tradition (see the Frankfurt School) in which individual symptomatology and character structure are tied to its socio-historical context. Thus, whereas psychoanalysis can be used to challenge the reason/emotion and subject/object split in Giddens' work, he addresses the individual/society dualism, which neither Freud nor Klein critically questioned.

Giddens says that his work represents an attempt to reinject modern social theory with a consideration of emotional ethics, passion and eroticism which perhaps explains why his own expressed aim is to stay as close to the self-help genre as possible, perhaps because in these texts he perceives an implicit critique of highly rationalised social theories (like a sociology informed by discourse analysis – see Craib, 1995; Seidler, 1998 etc.).

The existentialist maxim that existence precedes essence (see the following chapter) is the ontological basis of Giddens' argument, but what he is emphasising is that it is living in an increasingly de-traditionalised society which reveals this to us. Giddens argues that modernity is associated with the socialisation of the natural world, and he maintains that as 'nature becomes dominated by socially organised systems' (p. 34) we simultaneously see an intensification of processes of self-referentiality.

Giddens argues that as a new narrative form romantic love represented the harbinger of the 'pure relationship', because it involved an interrogation of one's own feelings as the precursor to entering a *relationship*, previously superfluous considerations for an economically convenient marriage (p. 58). Giddens, like Elam (1992) and Barthes (see the following chapter), tries to rescue romantic love from scornful trivialisation by arguing that it is and was a critical engagement with the maleness of society.

The 'pure relationship', however, is different from romantic love. It is 'entered into for its own sake, for what can be derived by each person from a sustained association with another and which is continued only in so far as it is thought by both parties to deliver enough satisfactions for each individual to stay within it' (Giddens, p. 58). 'Confluent love', which is a property of the pure relationship, is described as an 'opening out to the other'. It is 'active contingent love, and therefore jars with the 'for-ever, one and only' (p. 61) qualities of romantic love, which was both developed and then dissolved by women. Confluent love is, as Jamieson (1998) maintains, based on the ideal of 'intense disclosing intimacy', it develops 'only to the degree to which each partner is willing to *reveal* concerns and needs to the other and to be vulnerable to that other' (Giddens, p. 62). Confluent love is not about the future, or children, or power, it is fundamentally defined in terms of knowledge of self and other. Thus, the pure relationship is described as a facilitating environment for the reflexive project of self in which emotion is disclosed while autonomy is maintained. The relationship is capable of renegotiation as self and other change and is based on trust rather than vows of long-term commitment, which are contradictory promises in a context where contingency is acknowledged.

3.5   Love in the conditions of late modernity

Since the Second World War (in Berman's third phase of modernity) contemporary Western society has been variously depicted as postmodern (Lyotard, 1984), post-structuralist (Derrida, 1967–72), narcissistic (Lasch, 1984; Wetherill, 1997) and more recently as post-emotional (Mestrovic, 1997). Lasch (1984, p. 16) argues that 'ever since the Second World War, the end of the world has loomed as a hypothetical possibility and that this sense of danger has greatly increased in the last twenty years'. Lasch diagnoses our culture as one in which people are uncertain of their sense of place and of their own sense of self, 'which current concerns with identity registers' (p. 19). While many writers welcome these 'transformations of intimacy' (Giddens, 1992) and contestations of identity, contemporary Western society is also described as a 'culture of narcissism' (Lasch) characterised by troubled 'identity crises' (Frosh, 1991).

However, the 'indictment' of contemporary culture as destabilising and damaging can be contrasted with a more celebratory analysis of the conditions of late modernity. In contrast to the 'culture of narcissism' thesis, Richards (in Kennard and Small, 1997) has proposed that contemporary social relations are modelled on, or are similar to, a therapeutic sensibility.

Social theorists are perhaps increasingly interested in how people give narrative coherence to their lives, because 'standard biographies' have supposedly become 'choice biographies' (Beck and Beck-Gernsheim, 1995, p. 19), with all of the complications and 'shivers of freedom' that this brings. Love, according to Beck and Beck-Gernsheim, for example, is becoming a blank page that lovers must fill in, because a general process of individualisation, 'a Zeitgeist to "do one's own thing" ' (p. 3) removes us from 'traditional precepts and certainties'. They do not mean to imply that we are structurally, economically or politically free, but that we are being offered an oversupply of options (p. 7).[53]

Hence they begin their book, *The Normal Chaos of Love* with the following quote from Turrow's novel, *The Burden of Proof*:

> Listening to Sonny (his daughter), who was twisted about by impulse and emotion – beseeching, beleaguered, ironic, angry, it struck Stern that Clara (his wife) and he had had the benefit of certain good fortune. In his time, the definitions were clearer ... but for Sonny marrying late in life, in the New Era, everything was a matter of choice. She got up in the morning and started from scratch, wondering about

relationships, marriage, men, the erratic fellow she's chosen. (See Beck and Beck-Gernsheim, p. 1)

That is, as Berman said, as modernity develops, the public world 'shatters into a multitude of fragments, speaking incommensurable private languages' thus fracturing the discourse of romantic love too (see Pearce and Stacey). This perhaps explains why Beck and Beck-Gernsheim claim that, as a society, we are fascinated by 'great' love stories which in Gay's (1986, p. 97) terms 'surmount the obstacles, differences in status, religious or regional loyalties – that convention would throw in our path'. Hence, *Titanic* only weeks after its release in 1997 became (see Kramer, 1998) the highest grossing film of all time.[54]

The idea is that love and the world of intimacy have become more important to us,[55] but simultaneously subjected to critical irony, because the conditions of late modernity (metropolitan life)[56] are characterised by rapid change, by the de-traditionalisation of our 'feeling rules' and a consequent experience of status anxiety or existential unease. Moreover, processes of de-traditionalisation reveal to us the socially determined nature of our lives and, of course, loves.

This point is relevant to the way in which lovers might calculate the risks of a relationship at the start. That is, the knowledge of, and yet disavowal of, the impossibility of true romantic love can both be called upon with equal conviction (Pearce and Stacey, 1995, p. 37), because of the way in which we live at different levels of subjectivity: 'The new cultural permission for a rich, full satisfying emotional life has arisen just as new uncertainties subvert it ... the promise of expressive openness is undercut by fears of loss' (Hochschild, 1998, pp. 8–9).

Craib (1994, p. 169), for example, argues that 'the impetus of late modernity has been towards the isolation and fragmentation of the individual experience of the self'. He maintains that the risks and anonymity associated with living in huge systems, de-traditionalised societies and floating populations pushes us more and more into the world of intimacy, sexuality (see Foucault, 1976) and emotions. In 1994 Craib points out that it is significant that the last decade had seen the establishment of the 'sociology of the emotions' and he argues that ours is a culture obsessed with and terrified of emotion, that is, with that which cannot be controlled. He argues that our culture tends to increasingly deny 'the importance of disappointment' and this is evident, he says, in some forms of popular culture (the proliferation of self-help books) and in contemporary sociology (Giddens, 1992). There is, he maintains, the illusion of an all-powerful self, in which self-mastery and the management of messy emotions like hate, jealousy and envy is the new ideology for living.

It is important to situate the possible/impossible dialectic on love in debates about the conditions of modernity (see Richards, 1989b) and late modernity (see, for example, Lasch, 1984), because in theories of modernity/late modernity we can deduce one of two responses to our supposed identity crises. The first response is to declare that enduring feeling states/relationships are no longer possible and the second is to declare that freed from tradition, our relationships are opened up to creative possibilities previously unimagined.

3.6 Conclusion

The principal aim of this chapter has been to demonstrate a sociological and socio-cultural way of seeing love. This has involved looking at social structures and their effects on individuals and at discursive structures and ideologies and the way in which people are positioned in, and affected by, them. Collins, for example, looks at how a particular social structure 'caused' romantic love, while contemporary 'versions' of sociology deconstruct the various meanings embedded in the narrative, ideology or discourse of romantic love. Although these two areas of interest (social structures and discursive structures) are intertwined, they are also distinct, because deconstructing a story may not involve looking for the social structures that lie behind, or, indeed, engender it.

What we can see from the discussion so far is that love ideals do not have a consistent meaning throughout time and the way of deducing the meaning and function of the ideology of romantic love varies from author to author. However, what sociology explains about romantic love is that it is not an essential or natural emotion that is innate. Romantic love is an ideal or ideology that has to be understood in terms of philosophical and religious influences, changing conditions of modernity, a process of individualisation and the sexual stratification of society. In a 'classic social analysis' and in a socio-cultural analysis of romance, love is not studied as an emotion as such, but as an ideal that regulates the expression of feeling and impulse. A sociological viewpoint presents an impossible view of love to the extent that love is seen as a socially constructed ideal which is undesirable, because of its obfuscation of a reality-based relation between the sexes.

What sociology does not do (and cannot do) is study love as an emotion that 'inheres' in the individual. Although the emotions are 'now' relevant to sociology as Bendelow and Williams (1998) points out, they are not studied in the same way as psychoanalytic accounts of affective life. In arguing for the importance of a psychosocial study of emotion, the aim is to bring these two different types of explanatory frameworks into discursive dialogue and to operationalise a psychosocial interpretive strategy.

Conjoining sociology and psychoanalysis is necessary because what is not fully explained in sociological and social-constructionist terms is why, psychologically speaking, we might need to anticipate the future with the romantic narrative (of great or true love) in particular. This is an especially pertinent question if we are free to construct alternative narratives for ourselves.[57]

That is, although a discourse of confluent love might be discernible in people's narratives of love, our identification with romance is enduring and intense (see Chapter 10). Pearce and Stacey imply that this is because romance is always already a story (as can be seen in the story of *Beauty and the Beast* and films such as *Love Story* and the *Titanic*), even though it is no longer a single fundamental story.[58] Although Collins and Giddens suggest that the romantic love ideal will not be the dominant ideology governing sexual relations today, we continue to see romantic epics at the cinema (see Kramer, 1998) and romantic hopes and aspirations in everyday discourses of love (see Rachel and Zadie in Chapter 10).

In order to look at why the romantic narrative is psychologically compelling, Chapters 4, 5 and 6 will turn to existentialist and psychoanalytic theories which provide us with insights into the allure of romance by reference to a theory of being and a theory of mind. From object relations psychoanalysis we will also see an alternative conceptualisation of love that shares some similarity to the discourse of the pure relationship, at the same time as representing a significantly different approach to understanding love as an emotion only. From Chapters 4 and 5 we will see that not only structural and cultural forces lie behind our 'private troubles' (see Mills), since, as these chapters demonstrate, psychological and existential factors complicate our love lives too.

4
Love as Bad Faith
Philosophical Approaches

4.1 Introduction

This chapter will provide a brief overview of existentialist (Sartre, 1943), Lacanian (Sarup, 1992; Salecl, 1994/1998; Zizek, 1994) and post-structuralist (Barthes, 1978; Rylance, 1994) views of love. What we will see is that romantic love has been respectively deconstructed in the above theories as a metaphysical impossibility, a utilitarian demand (without reply) and as a thesaurus and endless festival of meaning. This chapter presents a theoretical critique of popular depictions of romantic love as either realisable or desirable. It does not aim to look at the work of each of these theorists in detail, because the aim is to provide a broad overview of their respective ways of seeing love as impossible or absurd.

Sartre's existentialist deconstruction of love is important for a psychosocial investigation into love and its vicissitudes for a number of reasons. First, Sartre's existentialism has influenced a Lacanian analysis of love (an investigation of the inauthentic). Lacan, for example, judged Sartre's conclusion that love is a 'metaphysical impossibility' to be 'absolutely irrefutable' (Sarup, 1992, p. 35) and Barthes' influential work on love draws upon both existentialism and Lacanian psychoanalysis (see Rylance, 1994, chapter 4).

Second, contemporary sociological views of love share similar features to existentialist ones (the emphasis on conscious choice). Existentialism, for example, is relevant for understanding the conditions of late modernity (in which love has become suspect and we are subject to identity crises as the existential parameters of life are laid bare). Also, Sartre's analysis of language as something that flees from us (1943, p. 373) finds contemporary relevance in social-constructionist positions on love as a discourse.

Third, there is existential resonance in object relations views of love (the fear of freedom or solitude), and separation anxiety is central to an understanding of the psychoanalytic view of reparative object relations.

Finally, existentialism informs De Beauvoir's analysis of *The Woman in Love*, and the feminist critique of Sartre's rationalist position (see Moi, 1990) also links up with the feminist critique of the psychoanalytic contention that separateness and a reality ego are the hallmarks of maturity (see Benjamin, 1988).

Despite fundamental differences between socio-cultural, existential and psychoanalytic ways of seeing love, common to all is the deconstruction of romantic love as an ideal form of love. This deconstruction of romantic love is broadly referred to as an impossibilist perspective, but from Giddens through to Sartre and Freud and Klein we can also see ways in which the romantic narrative is replaced by an alternative conceptualisation of 'authentic' love. After outlining socio-cultural, existentialist and psychoanalytic views of love, psychoanalytic and socio-cultural conceptualisation of 'ideal' love will be brought into discursive dialogue.

4.2   The 'being-for-itself' and the 'being-in-itself'[1]

Romantic love is deconstructed by Sartre, via an objection to the ontological possibility of oneness and merger between two people. According to Sartre the conscious *pour-soi*, or being-for-itself, is constantly evolving, (unlike the *en-soi*, or being-in-itself, which is the mute impassivity of the object world). We as subjects are what we are not yet. Consciousness is, therefore, equated with transcendence: to be conscious is to be constantly moving from one thought to another, both creating and nullifying and this permanent movement of thought or self-construction can only end in death. In the words of Quinidoz (1993, p. 193):

> All creative life, its movement constantly renewed and never accomplished once and for all, is a reflection of the ego as I see it: an entity in the process of becoming, constantly searching for its identity. Some may tire of this never ending search, but others may discover the whole excitement of life within it, because one never finishes becoming what one is.

We wish, however, to assume the status of an object which is what it is, which does not have to decide whether to live or die, to love or not to love. The chair I am sitting on is exactly that – a chair. Unlike me, it is not what it is not yet, and is not faced with existential choices.

In a sense then, there is no such 'thing' as the 'self', if what we mean by that is something definite and immovably fixed. Authenticity involves recognising this fact of existence and taking responsibility for what we make of ourselves, and our lives with others.

4.3   Contingency, the fear of freedom and bad faith

For Sartre, life has no inherent meaning apart from that which we choose to impose upon it, but he claims that we have a wish for magic healers and ready-made answers. Like children, a part of us continues to ask, 'but why?'. We are baffled by what Sartre refers to as life's absurdity and gratuity and we can suffer from an 'ontological insecurity' as discussed by Laing (1959, p. 39) or the 'fear of freedom' discussed by Fromm (1942). It is in love, then, that we can either invest the other with the answer to our need for meaning or use the love relation to escape our freedom:

> Surrounded by chaos we are understandably led to temper the full horror of contingency by suggesting that certain things happen to us because they have to, thereby giving the mess of life a sustaining purpose and direction. Though the dice may roll in a number of ways, we frantically draw up patterns of necessity, never more than when it is in the inevitability that one day we will fall in love. (De Botton, 1993, p. 10)

De Botton, in his *Essays on Love*, says that our longing for destiny is nowhere stronger than in our romantic life. This is because of the fear that the little sense there is in life is merely created by ourselves, that there is no God to tell our story or assure our loves (ibid.). There is a destiny to love, he says, but not a destiny to love a given person:

> Our choice of partner necessarily operates within the bounds of who we happen to meet and given different bounds, different flights, different historical periods or events, it might not have been Chloe I would have loved at all – something I could not contemplate now that I had actually begun to love her. (De Botton, 1993, p. 12)

According to Sartre the lover feels irritated and cheapened when he or she thinks that the beloved has chosen him or her from among others – Then if I had not come into a certain city, if I had not visited the home of so and so, you would never have known me, you wouldn't have loved me. This thought, Sartre says, grieves the lover (1943, p. 370).

This openness to further possibility and change means that ultimately I cannot say definitively that I will never leave you or that what I feel or say today will hold true in ten years' time. Love, like life, is contingent upon many things and it is this contingency from which as subjects we wish to flee, in what Sartre calls an act of bad faith. Bad faith is the denial of our status as subjects who live in a contingent world; it is a kind of repression:

> One puts one self in bad faith as one goes to sleep and one is in bad faith as one dreams. Once this mode of being has been realised it is as difficult to get out of it as it is to wake oneself up; bad faith is a type of being in the world, like waking or dreaming, which by itself tends to perpetuate itself. (Sartre, 1943, p. 68)

Sartre's world does not preclude commitment to another, but it does require that we recognise that this commitment will be subject to change and it is this existential freedom and choice that can be so vexatious to us.

4.4 'Being-for-others': Sartre's hell and the metaphysical impossibility of love

In 'First Attitude Towards Others: Love, Language, Masochism' (1943, p. 364), Sartre begins by saying that conflict is the original meaning of 'being-for-others'. This is because the other's look or gaze confers on me the status of a 'being-as-object' and this appropriation of myself by the other is for Sartre an unbearable contingency. As Sarup explains: What happens is this: to the other person, who looks at me from the outside, I seem an object, a thing; my subjectivity with its inner freedom escapes his gaze (Sarup, 1992, p. 35).

Others see us as we shall never see ourselves and we are trapped in an infinity of reflections in which what is inside is inevitably hidden, over-looked, misrecognised. For Lacan, the self we see in the mirror is an imaginary capture, an ego formed in fiction. Similarly, for Sartre, the mirror held up to us by others at once escapes us and, like the stare of the Medusa turns us to stone, fixes us in the other's perspective and (mis) perception of us. Sartre's notion of the gap of freedom and noth-ingness and Lacan's unconscious place an inevitable chasm between people which our declarations of love wish to dissolve:

> 'Proust's hero, for example, who installs his mistress in his home, who can see her and possess her at any hour of the day, who has been

able to make her completely dependent upon him economically, ought to be free from worry. Yet we know that he is, on the contrary, continually gnawed by anxiety. Through her consciousness Albertine escapes Marcel even when he is at her side, and that is why he only knows relief when he gazes on her as she sleeps. It is certain then that the lover wishes to capture a 'consciousness'. (Sartre, 1943, p. 366)

To Sartre, we can never know what the other is really thinking, their consciousness is their freedom and the thing which eludes us – the play of imagination, dreams, fantasies. No matter how much we may beseech the other to tell us what they are thinking, what's on their mind, their very freedom of thought can torment us and render us helpless. We are left only with an act of faith in which we decide, indeed choose, to believe that our partners do really mean it if they say that they love us, or that they do not think about leaving us for someone else.

These are the uncertainties that lovers at some point in their lives will face. Hence Phillips comments that lovers, second only to paranoiacs and psychoanalysts, are frantic epistemologists (1994, p. 41).

No two consciousnesses can be identical and no two people can be exactly the same. To achieve unity with another would, therefore, involve possessing the other's freedom of consciousness and transcending their very 'otherness' (for Sartre ultimately a metaphysical impossibility).

This imagined unity with another and the definitive casting out of our existential solitude is, however, what we desire. This is why in 'Being and Nothingness' (1943) the other is a tormenting alienation. Even the act of speech 'reveals to me the freedom (the transcendence) of the one who listens to me in silence' (p. 373), so that we are to some extent beings who fade under discourse:

> Thus the 'meaning' of my expression always escapes me ... for lack of knowing what I actually express for the Other, I constitute my language as an incomplete phenomenon of flight outside myself. As soon as I express myself, I can only guess at the meaning of what I express ... The Other is always there, present and experienced as the one who gives to language its meaning. (Sartre, 1943, p. 373)

In Sartre's discussion of 'being-for-others' we find the cry of Narcissus; only in this context he cannot bear the other limiting his freedom and grandiosity. This limitation on one's freedom is one that the lovers in Sartre's world freely choose as a form of bad faith in relationships which he characterises as sado-masochistic. To return to the myth of Narcissus, we can see that this kind of relationship is one that is portrayed between himself and Echo. She is only able to repeat everything he says; she has no voice of her own and, therefore, no contours of her own. Like many women who have silenced themselves for another, she is enslaved. For Hamilton (1982), both Echo and Narcissus, however, are trapped in a self-referential world much like the characters in *Being and Nothingness*: 'The more an adult is addicted to the mirroring relation, the less secure is his sense of both individuation and relationship. The mirror will never give him back what he wants. It will never show more than he can see' (Hamilton, 1982, p. 120).

Hamilton in *Narcissus and Oedipus: The Children of Psychoanalysis* (1982), claims that Narcissus's problem is over an unattainable proximity in which he does not know what an object (in Sartre's world a subject) is and in which there is a shutting out of the third term, the paternal or symbolic. The third term for Sartre is perhaps the awareness of the other's status as a being-for-itself which love relations, he argues, need to disavow. We then fall in love with an insubstantial hope: 'The lover demands a pledge, yet is irritated by a pledge. He wants to be loved by a freedom but demands that this freedom as freedom should no longer be free ... This captivity must be a resignation that is both free and yet chained in our hands' (Sartre, 1943, p. 367).

Sartre argues that in love we want to be the limit to the other's transcendence, to be their absolute, their 'one and only', 'forever and ever'. Yet the irony is that this enslavement of the beloved kills the love of the lover since if the other becomes an automaton or slave the lover finds themself alone. Thus, for Sartre, the lover does not desire to possess the beloved as one possesses a thing; he/she demands a special type of appropriation (ibid.). The lover wants to possess a freedom as freedom. To be somebody's absolute is to foreclose their future:

> The motive of my uneasiness and shame is the fact that I apprehend and experience myself in my being-for-others as that which can always be surpassed towards something else, that which is the pure object of a value judgement, a pure means, a pure tool ... But if the Other loves me then I become the unsurpassable, which means that I must be the absolute end. In this sense I am saved from instrumentality. (Sartre, 1943, pp. 368–9)

That is, we enter love relations as a narcissistic defence. In Sartre's novel, 'Nausea' (1965), Anny rejects Roquentin because she doesn't like the fact that he has changed since they last met. She eyes him with a curiosity which is almost hostile because she depended on his stagnation as her reference point by which to measure herself. Anny wants to use Roquentin as a mirror on which she can project any image that she likes. He needs to be transfixed in time and in her memory, so that she is not made doubly aware of life's contingency. According to Sartre one way in which we appropriate the other is by being loved or recognised as the other's 'supreme value'. As Sarup explains when two people do this simultaneously, they are almost locked in mortal combat:

> Each of the two beings endowed with such a Desire [for ultimate recognition] is ready to go all the way in pursuit of its satisfaction; that is, is ready to risk its life … in order to be 'recognised' by the other, to impose itself on the other as the supreme value; accordingly their meeting can only be a fight to the death. (Sarup, 1992, pp. 32–3)

The person we defeat or kill cannot, however, recognise us and so we overcome 'dialectically' (ibid.) and destroy their autonomy. Just as Narcissus can only see himself, we want the beloved to only see us, and yet both self-referential worlds end in death:

> At the start, each of the two consciousnesses can at any moment free itself from its chains and suddenly contemplate the Other as an object. Then the spell is broken; the Other becomes one means among means. The illusion, the game of mirrors, which makes concrete reality of love, suddenly ceases. (Sartre, 1943, p. 376)

For Sartre (1943, p. 377) this is the reason why lovers seek solitude because the appearance of a third person spells the potential end of their love. It is interesting to think that, psychoanalytically speaking, the appearance of the third term, of 'reality', is the guarantee of our love. Sartre is, therefore, describing a world in which the narcissistic dyad is the norm and in which there is a claustrophobic anxiety. Not surprisingly, he concludes by summarising the 'triple destructibility of love' (p. 377):

1. 'It is, in essence a deception and reference to infinity, since to love is to wish to be loved, hence to wish that the Other wish that I love him … hence the lover's perpetual dissatisfaction' (ibid.). The amorous intuition, Sartre says, is an ideal out of reach. ('I look for signs, but of what? What is the object of my reading? Is it: am I loved, am I loved no longer, am I still loved? I tirelessly seek in the other's face: What am I worth?' (Barthes, 1978, p. 214)).

2. 'The Other's awakening is always possible; at any moment he can make me appear as an object – hence the lover's perpetual insecurity' (ibid.). ('Love's value is ceaselessly threatened by depreciation' (Barthes, 1978, p. 24)).

3. 'Love is an absolute which is perpetually made relative by others. One would have to be alone in the world with the beloved in order for love to preserve its character as an absolute axis of reference – hence the lover's perpetual shame' (ibid.).

> We are two ships each of which has its goal and course; our paths may cross and we may celebrate a feast together, as we did – and then the good ships rested so quietly in one harbour and one sunshine that it may have looked as if they had reached their goal and had one goal. But then the mighty force of our tasks drove us apart again into different seas and sunny zones, and perhaps we shall never see each other again; perhaps we shall meet again but fail to recognise each other; our exposure to different seas and suns has changed us. (Barthes, 1978, p. 223)

4.5 Lacan's view of the lover's utilitarian demand[2]

Although Lacan judged Sartre's work on love to be irrefutable, Sartre's faith in self-consciousness is something Lacan was critical of. The Cartesian subject is identified with the ego, and consciousness, which Lacan reversed by saying 'I think where I am not, therefore I am where I do not think.[3] This is because when we consider the role of the unconscious and language the 'discourse of the master' (Sarup, p. 41) is undermined, or to use Freud's (1923) metaphor, the rider on the horse does not know where the horse is going. For Lacan the central function of the ego is to misrecognise:

> The child sees itself in the mirror, but the image is reversed. Identity is a mere outer skin that constantly distorts one's relations with others. When the fragmented body gives way to the armour of the subject – and to its identity, already alienating by definition – the 'ego' is formed. (Sarup, 1992, p. 65)

If there is no 'realist' ego, but only a narcissistic ego capable of misrecognition, how can we love? More specifically, how did Lacan answer the question – why is there love?

4.5.1   Lacan's love of the impossible[4]

Lacan's 'famous definition of love', Salecl (1994, p. 19) tells us, is that the 'subject gives to the other what he or she does not have'. Salecl says that the object of our love is the traumatic *objet-petit-a*. The *objet-petit-a* is, Sarup explains, Lacan's formula for the lost object which underpins symbolisation, the cause of and stand-in for desire (similar to Bion's notion that thought occurs as a result of the absence of the object). However, Sarup explains that our desire is insatiable and that this desire cannot be satisfied in the way that a need can: 'The child wants to be filled by the other, to be the other, which is why no determinate thing will do. It demands a love that paradoxically entails its own annihilation, for it demands a fullness of the other to stop up the lack that conditions its existence as subject' (p. 68).

'Need minus demand' is Lacan's formula for desire, and although the felt emotional need for love may be real, the kernel of this need cannot be demanded (i.e. articulated). We desire that which is beyond the lover and, from a Lacanian viewpoint, our love will only survive if it remains inaccessible (and we are thus shielded from the knowledge that there is no lost Aristopholeon half who will offer oneness and self-completion). Sexual relations represent a search for a completion to self-identity for which there is no satisfaction to be found. Only if love relations repeat this impossibility, will they keep our desire in motion.

Salecl interprets Wharton's *The Age Of Innocence* as an example of this realisation. It begins when the newly married Newland is in love with his cousin Ellen and yearns for a place where 'they would be freely able to enjoy their love' (p. 19), 'when the reality of his love will get a true form' (p. 20). Ellen assures him that no such place exists: 'Oh, my dear – where is that country? Have you ever been there? ... . I know of so many who have tried to find it; and, believe me, they all got out by mistake at wayside stations; at places like Boulogne, or Pisa, or Monte-Carlo' (p. 19).

Newland, Salecl explains, eventually renounces this 'utilitarian demand' and realises that he can only continue to love Ellen if he gives her up. Similarly, in 'From the Courtly Game to the Crying Game', Zizek (1994) argues that the above type of courtly love is the love matrix of today, portrayed in Jordan's film *The Crying Game*.[5] Zizek uses *The Crying Game* in order to dramatise Lacan's point that there is no relationship between what the loved one possesses and what the loving one lacks.

> Love is a demand (although it remains without the answer) that addresses being ... Some being that is inaccessible as long as it does not answer. Love addresses that point in speech where the word fails.

Confronted with this experience, the subject has two solutions at hand: the point at which he no longer has words, he can either try to encircle or to stuff it with a stopper. (Lacan in Salecl, 1994, p. 23)

The preservation of the other's enigma is, Salecl implies, dramatised in Campion's film, *The Piano* in which the characters played by Harvey Keitel and Holly Hunter are separated not only by different cultures and her marriage to his employer, but by the fact that she is mute. This is not, therefore, romantic love which 'strives to enjoy the whole of the other' (Salecl, p. 22). It is a true sublime love which 'renounces, since it is well aware that we can only enjoy a part of the body of the Other ... That is why we are limited to a little contact, to touch only the forearm or whatever else – ouch' (Salecl quoting Lacan p. 23).

Philips (1994, p. 40) says that romantic lovers are like detectives trying to find out something that will make all the difference – 'Lovers begin as prolifically inventive, producing enthralling illusions about each other (recycled from the past), only to be disappointed into truth.'

Falling in love is not, therefore, a good way to get to know someone, and knowledge, Philips says, can kill our desire. At least in courtly love the lovers renounce the consummation of their love, there is no utilitarian demand and the other's enigmatic elusiveness is cherished. Familiarity can breed contempt if it involves a voyeuristic search for the secret of the other, perhaps even the search for the 'right' person can begin to seem like a search for the last word, the final signified.

According to Salecl the only answer to the avowal 'I love you' from a Lacanian perspective, is 'I can't love you unless I give you up' (Ellen's statement to Newland, see Salecl, p. 20). Indeed, Freud said that obstacles are needed to swell the tide of the libido and courtly love does this since it is a love of the impossible. This is, according to Lacan, more honest, since what we have here is a love for the obstacle which forever thwarts love, an obstacle which is somehow a priori.

Copjec (1994, p. 2) explains that an 'object relations notion of an original intersubjectivity, of a meeting between two presumably reasonable persons, each receiving his definition from the other, is here [in Lacanian psychoanalysis] disassembled'. Instead, she describes, a 'missed encounter between two unknowns' and argues that it is this misrecognition that constitutes sociality and the public world ('the sphere in which the subject's innermost being goes unrecognised' (ibid.)). She maintains that what we can see in Rousseau's *Confessions* is a 'cry or appeal to the other to pay closer attention, to listen a little longer for what one's words want to say' (p. 3). What she calls an 'inarticulable remainder persists' (ibid.), and she therefore agrees with Brooks' analysis of melodrama (the 'grandiose gesture', 'the music', the 'expressive *mise en scene'*) as representative of a compensation for the felt inadequacy of language.[6] In Lacanian psychoanalysis, then, this 'inarticulate remainder' after the word is spoken, this desire which is denied any utilitarian demand, is what our love is aimed at. Courtly love is more sublime and honest since it knows this, whereas romantic love, aiming as it does at the appropriation of the other is in the service of oneself. It is nothing but the cry of Narcissus, a less exalted, earthly love in which we cry like babies and with our demands sow the seeds of the destruction of our love.

According to Lacan, where there is absence we invent a presence, but it is the very impossibility of love that keeps our love in motion. What Sartre describes as the metaphysical impossibility of love becomes for Lacan love's metaphysical necessity.

4.6 Barthes' thesaurus of meaning[7]

It is interesting to critically assess Barthes' work on love (1978) because it represents current theoretical interests regarding postmodernism and the self. According to Rylance, Barthes' *A Lover's Discourse: Fragments* needs to be placed in the context of a period of transition in Barthes' work in which there is a revision of his earlier post-structuralist position and in which his later works reveal a 'classically humanist appeal' (1994, p. 128).[8]

Rylance (p. 129) claims that it is in his later work that Barthes enquires into what most essentially constitutes the self, and in which he starts to see language as a human instrument with intersubjective dimensions rather than as a malign overarching system or something liberatingly impersonal.

Rylance points out that whereas in Barthes' earlier work language was seen as something almost violent, a 'cancerous outpouring' (Rylance, p. 30), in *A Lover's Discourse* the tone changes. Barthes sees these love scenes, these 'matching pair of soliloquies' (ibid.) as psychologically necessary, as 'ritualised exchanges of language goods' (ibid.). His lovers are, therefore, in a tragic–comic theatre in which there is no reality behind the appearance and there are no exits. Indeed, Barthes does not see love as an illness from which we must recover, a view he attributes to psychoanalysis (see Rylance, p. 117). Instead he looks at the enriching aspects of this theatre of meaning.

4.6.1 The decentred self

In the preface to *A Lover's Discourse*, Barthes quotes a mathematician who apparently said that we must not underestimate the power of chance to engender monsters. For Barthes the monster in the context of this book would have been one which tried to emerge from a 'certain order of figures, a philosophy of love, when in actual fact we can look for no more than its affirmation' (p. 8). Similarly, Elam (1992) in *Romancing the Postmodern* states that she does not want to write a modernist account of romance: 'a formula for the generic identification of romance' (p. 8). Each text must in some way redefine what it means by romance according to Elam, who quotes Henry James' general definition of romance as experience liberated, disembroiled, disengaged, disencumbered, exempt from the conditions we usually know to attach to it (Elam, p. 6). Elam argues that 'romance seems to be the terrain upon which female desire can work, outside of the testamentary realism that enacts male desire as law'. Elam concludes, however, that we can only stay out of the law for so long and that the return to realism highlights the impossibility of romance. Nevertheless, her book, like Barthes', is a retrieval: 'Like Foucault or Laing in their work on madness, Barthes attempts to retrieve the lover's discourse for a culture deaf to the subject, and insists, traditionally enough – that the lover and the mad person are in some respects alike' (Rylance, 1994, p. 117).

Romance, Elam (p. 157) argues, is seen to depend upon anachronism and a disregard for a serious understanding of culture, for in these 'silly novels written by silly women culture is reduced to mental mediocrity and clothed in a masquerade of ancient names'. Romantic reading is therefore counterposed to real learning. Apparently in 'The Mill on the Floss' (cited by Elam), the extraordinary impulse (or romance) in the novel is carried by Maggie who tries to turn away from romance in order to read 'real' books. Phillip, however, convinces Maggie that she is 'shutting herself up in a narrow self-delusive fanaticism which is only a way of escaping pain by starving into dullness all the highest powers of her nature.' Romance, Elam says, is a counter-discourse on history and the real (p. 158). The task, she argues, of realism is to protect various consciousnesses from doubt and within the terms of this realism, affective disturbance is merely the effect of excessive feminine sentiment. As Elam says desire cannot be dealt with by realism and we can surmise that she, like Barthes, would see the lover as forsaken by Freud (with his insistence on a reality ego). So Elam, like Barthes, is trying to rescue romance 'for a culture deaf to the subject', but more specifically for the women identified with it, because it is a discourse accessed differently by men and women. Similarly, far from seeing love as an illness from which we must recover, Barthes saw love as a rich festival of meaning, and his book, therefore, creates an 'encyclopaedia of affective culture' (Rylance, p. 118).[9]

Rylance (p. 116) points out that psychoanalysis was useful to Barthes, because he needed a psychology that was 'sensitive to selfhood as a dramatic structure'. This is because Barthes, like Lacan, holds the notion that the self, 'The "I" which approaches the text is already itself a plurality of other texts, of codes which are infinite or, more precisely, lost (whose origin is lost)' (Barthes in Rylance, p. 104).

Life is, therefore, characterised by an ambiguous instability, which entails both tragedy and comedy. There is no central self around which our many parts coalesce and, consequently, Barthes prefers an intellectual style which is able to cope with this conflict. His writing can, Rylance (p. 108) tells us, be read as 'novelistic montage',[10] and it tries to avoid any final closure or essentialism which hankers after the 'real' or 'true' self.

This partly explains the form of *A Lover's Discourse*. It is a book of aphorisms with neither beginning nor end. What we have instead is the 'incessant sliding of the signifier under the signified', and it is this play of the signifier which, as Barthes implies, the lover cannot bear.

To recognise this intertextuality and decentredness is problematic for the lover, who cannot live in what Rylance calls this 'dialectical bliss' (p. 118). Instead s/he tries to coerce the other into an imaginary world, a melodramatic theatre of love complete with scripts, roles and stage directions. In *Essays on Love* (1993), De Botton moves from discussions of romantic fatalism through to idealisation and the subtext of seduction, and says that in love we attach ourselves to primitive belief systems akin to tea leaf reading or crystal ball gazing (p. 10). This is a notion echoed by Winterson (1994, p. 5): 'You were careful not to say those words (I love you) that became our private altar. I had said them many times before, dropping them like coins into a wishing well hoping that they would make me come true.'

De Botton states that through romantic fatalism we avoid the unthinkable thought that, as already stated, the need to love is always prior to our love for anyone in particular (p. 12). De Botton accuses his main character of trying to construct a grand narrative, oblivious to the chance nature of his encounter with Chloe, his beloved. Lacking a coherent narrative himself, a fixed direction, a thematic unity, he looks at how his character hallucinates these qualities in Chloe. It is when she does not assume them that anxiety and heartbreak begin: 'From the outside (prior to epidermal contact), she seemed wonderfully controlled, possessed of a distinct and continuous character, whereas postcoitally I saw her as vulnerable, prone to collapse, dispersed, needy' (From his seventh essay entitled 'False Notes', p. 67).

The irony and poignancy here is that Chloe unbeknown to her is being auditioned, indeed, cast in a different part. She, like the signifier, becomes in her lover's 'imaginary' shifting, suspect, prone to collapse. Consequently, 'What catches Barthes's sympathy ... is the lover's forlorn effort to realise his impossible ambition – to live up to the factitious standards set by his own Imaginary' (Rylance, 1994, p. 117).

4.6.2 The imaginary

For Barthes, the 'truth' of love cannot appear, and it is the attempted reification (and deification) of love which forms part of the lover's tragedy. Love is structured according to the Lacanian phallus; it is a demand for completion and plenitude – in short, salvation. For Barthes, love is a state of the imagination, hence his lovers exist in the Lacanian imaginary, hallucinating a mirage of love, a well in the desert.

In Lacan's hall of mirrors, two people who lack being demand wholeness, and popular culture tells us that it is love which can provide us with the answer to the quest for ourselves. We are still in the shadow of Aristophanes'[11] theory which sees man/woman as originally a four-legged, four-armed, two-headed creature, which becomes divided and set to search for his/her missing half. Hence, in romantic literature and film it is love that will return to us our lost half and repair our damaged souls, and it is variously depicted as the panacea for our ills, the fruit of life, an opiate to which we can become addicted. For Barthes it is an endless play of signifiers which lovers do not want to acknowledge as shifting, suspect: 'Werther is not perverse, he is in love: he creates meaning always and everywhere, out of nothing and it is meaning which thrills him: he is in the crucible of meaning ... a kind of festival of meaning' (Barthes, 1978, p. 67).

For Barthes it is as though love is everywhere to be seen, and yet nowhere to be found and therein lies the lover's tragedy and Rylance emphasises Barthes' sympathy for the lover who is 'ignored, disparaged or derided' (p. 117).

4.6.3 The cry of Narcissus

The thought that love is inevitably narcissistic seems to preoccupy Barthes who declares that 'Werther is the pure discourse of the amorous subject – this bid is never anything but Narcissus' Cry, Me, Me, what about me' (1987, p. 67).

Freud (1914) describes narcissism (see Chapter 5)as the withdrawal of libido from the external world on to the subject's own self. 'The sick man', for example, 'withdraws his libidinal cathexes back upon his own ego, and sends them out again when he recovers' (p. 75). 'The charm of a child lies to a great extent in his narcissism, his self-contentment and inaccessibility, just as does the charm of certain animals' (p. 83). Thus, in narcissistic women, children and animals we see what we 'fancy for ourselves' (p. 85) – to be the core of creation, 'his majesty the baby'. The aim and satisfaction of a narcissistic object – choice is therefore to be loved and to increase one's own self-regard, but Freud maintains that 'a person in love is humble' (p. 93). That is, dependence upon a loved object lowers one's self-regard and narcissistic self-sufficiency, which only the satisfaction of being loved or of fulfilling one's ego ideal can once again enrich. A narcissistic object-choice confuses the boundaries between the 'me and the not-me', because the difficult work of recognising that we are dependent has been refused. According to Freud then, there are 'legitimate' means by which we can recover some of our lost narcissism, but where the ego refuses to develop out from a state of primary narcissism, illness – melancholia (1917) will follow. It is therefore no surprise to see that Freud likens narcissistic illness to sleep and warns us against this solipsistic world.

Barthes takes heed of Freud's warning and reminds us of the way in which we can try to possess ourselves and the other in a process of de-differentiation, thus explaining why for Barthes (1978, p. 11) 'the lover's world is one of adhesives and gummy coalescences'.[12]

In *A Lover's Discourse*, love is a play of meanings between our social and psychic selves, an auto-dialogue in which 'I love you' is not as generous or as loving as it might sound. Barthes maintains that to say 'I love you' is to proceed as if there is no theatre of speech, and as though this 'word-as-sentence' is always true. He says that it contains no information but its immediate saying or presence: 'no reservoir, no armoury of meaning' (p. 149). These are the words, however, that Barthes acknowledges we run after; for him there is only one response upon hearing them and this is: 'There is no answer' (p. 148). According to Winterson (1994, p. 153): ' "I love you", You did not say it first and neither did I, but when you say it and when I do, we speak like savages who have found three words and worship them.'

This 'savagery' and need partly explain why in love there is a temptation to coerce the lover into our own imaginary world. According to Barthes,

'I love you' are the words of the maternal, amorous dyad which we are reluctant to lose. When we 'fall' out of love it is this 'maternal' amorous language from which we are exiled. Barthes says that when there is no more resonance, when everything is calm, it is worse. We are most alive to our desires and nostalgias when uttering this 'love cry':

> Jealousies, anxieties, possessions, discourses, appetites, signs, once again amorous desire was burning everywhere. It was as if I was trying to embrace one last time, hysterically, someone about to die – someone for whom I was about to die: I was performing a denial of separation. (Barthes, 1978, p. 109)

For Barthes 'the "signs" of love feed an enormous reactive literature' (p. 154) in which 'those who seek the proffering of the word, I-love-you, are at the extreme limit of language, where language itself recognises that it is without backing or guarantee' (ibid.). Barthes paints a picture of Hollywood, literature, music and the lover therein, pining after this thing called love, and 'driven by unconscious forces behind him and enslaved by imaginary forces before him' (Rylance, 1994, p. 118). This imagined wholeness, however, is an illusion, an unattainable ego-ideal in which the lover demands the 'genitality of maturity and the maternalism of infancy' (Barthes, 1978, p. 104). Barthes ironises this tragic quest and leaves his lovers, after the utterance of their love cries with an 'inarticulable remainder' and a desire which cannot make any utilitarian demands (see Copjec, 1994). Hence for Barthes, the only answer to the avowal 'I love you' is: 'There is no answer'. The lover hopes for that which love might only be able to deliver in fairy tales:

> The Beast – held enchanted in his ugliness – loves Beauty; Beauty obviously, does not love the Beast, but at the end, vanquished, she, too, says the magic word: 'Je vous aime, la Bete'; and immediately, through the sumptuous arpeggio of a harp, a new subject appears. Is this story an archaic one? (Barthes, 1978, p. 153)

4.7 Conclusion

Sartre provides us with a very convincing portrayal of the insecurities, jealousies and self-delusions that the lover suffers from, which he understood as symptomatic of their 'fear of freedom'. The notion that romantic love contains an existential lie (love can save us from freedom – aloneness) that we psychologically need, but somewhere know to be false (we are responsible for ourselves and we are ultimately alone), renders our world one of self-deceit and fear. Implicit in Sartre's condemnation of bad faith in love is a radical rewriting of our partnership vows (with oaths of ever lasting love) and this 'free' love demands considerable emotional courage (because there can be no limits imposed on our freedom with promises of 'until death do us part'). Sartre's notion of authentic love or authenticity is based on the idea that we should live as subjects who do not deny our own or the other's freedom/aloneness in life. Love should not be used as a shield against mortality, transience and contingency or as a refuge from taking responsibility for the decisions that we have taken in life. Sartre's idea of authenticity lends itself to a view of love that is based on our capacities for rationality and thinking, because otherwise our love will be dominated by fear and ontological insecurity. Although Sartre understands the insecurities we face in confronting the maxim that 'existence precedes essence', what he calls for is responsible decision making. To take flight into emotion (love as the thunderbolt) is a way of abnegating responsibility for the meaning we confer on life and for the decisions that we take (when we might, for example, convince ourselves that we have involuntarily fallen into love).

It is the idea that romantic love is used to answer some problem about the troubling nature of existence that leads Lacan to endorse Sartre's critical analysis. For Lacan, we are incomplete, and existence is defined by its alienating quality. Subjectivity is marked by alienation and misrecognition, and love cannot deliver us from the vexatious nature of the human condition. Romantic love, according to the theorists presented in this chapter, offers us a palliative ideology for living. As an ideal, romantic love proves to be impossible to realise and undesirable, because it is a dishonest, and at times, dishonourable way to live. Barthes provides us with examples from the 'enormous reactive literature' that this search for love brings, highlighting the double binds, pains and raptures that the lover is beset by as he or she tries to realise love.

In the next chapter we will turn to Freud in order to see if his psychoanalysis, like sociology, feminism, existentialism, Lacanian psychoanalysis and post-structuralism, deconstructs romantic love as unrealisable and undesirable. Will psychoanalysis meet the deconstructive critique of romantic love that we have so far seen? What is distinctive about a Freudian view of love in contrast to a socio-cultural view of love? Will psychoanalysis offer us a reworked conceptualisation of love that has affinities with Sartre's authentic love or Giddens' confluent love? Will we find sympathy with a discourse-analytic approach to love as outlined in Chapter 3 Will Lacan's view of a fractured subjectivity and an impossible love be addressed by a Freudian view of a reality-based love? Will psychoanalysis lend itself to a view of love as realisable, desirable and indeed necessary for our psychological well-being? Will a Freudian view of love provide a critical contrast to views which deconstruct stories of love as postmodern subversion or sentimentality? And what will these socio-cultural, existential and psychoanalytic views of love have in common and how will they differ?

5
Transference Love
A Freudian Approach

5.1 Introduction

What is the view of love that we find in Freud? Is it a type of neurosis? A play of glands? A mirror in which we do not see beyond our own reflection? A furious master? What has happened to 'love in the age of psychoanalysis'? Freud said that he was wary of raising the psychoanalytic flag over the category of 'normal' love and intruding upon the territory of poets (see Bergmann, 1987), but this is exactly what psychoanalysis has done in the field of so-called normal and pathological love relations. The subject of love is perhaps most commonly thought about as a subject of romance, but what psychoanalysis offers us, according to Phillips (1994), is the 'romance of disillusionment' (p. 40). This does not mean that psychoanalysis counsels us in cynicism; this would indeed be antithetical to its aims.

However, conflict and hysterical misery are foregrounded by both Freud and Klein in their developmental narratives of mental stability and good-enough or indeed 'life-giving' (Symington, 1993) object relationships.[1] We will see that theirs is not a romantic idealisation of life, but their work nevertheless suggests that it is by resolving our conflicts and taming our misery that some of life's romance is more securely open to us.

Both Freud's and Klein's work posit love as a developmental achievement and the ability to love as the guarantee of mental health.[2] Freud (1914) said: 'we must begin to love in order not to fall ill, and we are bound to become ill, if in consequence of frustration, we cannot love' (p. 78). However, before we can distil from Freud's or Klein's work the defining features of love, we need to outline what the obstacles are to achieving this position from which to relate to the world. Despite the

74

inevitable differences in the experiences which we will have enjoyed/endured, there are common anxieties which Freud and Klein maintain that we will have all experienced. What they present us with is a meta-narrative of mental/emotional development, although their ideas are, they imply, inductively arrived at, because they are based on observational, psychotherapeutic work with adults and children. This work is undertaken with adults and children who are suffering because of the states of mind and, therefore, relationship that they inhabit. This mental disorder or dis-ease comes in an obvious variety of forms. But it might be justifiable to ask why we should take seriously a conceptuali-sation of love which is derived from work with people who might be 'labelled' as maladjusted, personality disordered, neurotic, psychotic and so on.

The answer is that psychoanalysis states that the dividing lines between rationality and irrationality and between sanity and madness are fine ones, and that we all begin life inhabiting a state of mind to degrees either narcissistic, terrorised, vulnerable, psychotic or hallucina-tory. We only achieve mental well-being when we overcome the infantile neurosis[3] which these psychotic experiences give rise to, and the contention is that these experiences are liable to be recatalysed in later life. Moreover, by looking at the depiction of so-called 'neurotic' love, it is possible to discern what an emotionally 'mature' love looks like. There are differences between Freud's and Klein's understanding of hate, love, loss and mourning, but for both of them, we have all endured a primary experience of anxiety. It is the defining feature of our biological/psycho-logical entry into life, the affect with which we are born, and in relation to which discrete emotions like love and hate must be understood.

What thematically unites a developing theory of love in Freud's work is the increasing emphasis which is placed on the reality ego.[4] Freud's 1911 paper 'Formulations on the Two Principles of Mental Functioning' is a very short article (merely four pages), but it can be used as a key paper for holding together the different papers which add up to a Freudian view of 'mature' love.

There are, of course, other papers (1921, 1923, 1930 and so on) that are relevant to a psychoanalytic understanding of love, which will be referred to throughout, but it is an emphasis on the reality ego which constitutes a critique of romantic love and it is the emphasis on mourning (e.g. our lack of love, inability to love and carelessness with those that we love) which provides a thematic link between Freud and Klein (repa-ration) and introduces the idea of an 'ethical'[5] love, which is relevant to the 'democratisation of intimacy' (Giddens, 1992).

The role of the reality ego, introduced in 1911, is developed and enlarged from Freud through to Klein and its role in working towards mature or reparative love will become evident in this and the following chapter. Freud's conception of love was, however, constrained by his quantitative view of the mind, against which he himself struggled (see Meltzer, 1978; Sandler *et al.*, 1991) and this position as an enlightenment thinker (see Gay, 1986) partially explains why Freud initially wanted to reduce psychology to neurophysiology.[6] Contextualising Freud's work in this period explains why he saw the reality ego as developmentally progressive.

Indeed, both Freud and Klein are modernist, humanist thinkers and any derived theory of love will reflect this. However, their work is also implicitly critical of any exclusively rationalist project, because of their emphasis on that which cannot easily be subjected to language and logic, and they do not offer us a romantic positivism (De Botton, 1993) or imperial ego (Brunner, 1994). Although the view of love that we find in psychoanalysis is committed to an enlarged field of vision ('where id was, there shall ego be'; Freud, 1923), observation does not necessarily afford control. The unconscious cannot, as Phillips (1995, p. xvii) evocatively said, be given elocution lessons and the unconscious contents in our minds can erupt into our love lives in ways that can be stealthy and unanticipated.

Hence, Phillips claims that we can find both an enlightenment Freud and post-Freudian Freud in psychoanalysis, because it is the very study of the unconscious mind which questions the self as an object of 'scientific' knowledge. That is, a psychoanalytic understanding of love is sensitive to some of the tenets of postmodernism (the ironising of 'Truth', certainty, rationality etc.) despite its roots in the 'Age of Reason'.[7]

5.2   The reality ego

Bergmann (1987) devotes a whole chapter to Freud's indebtedness to Plato in which he says that historically speaking, some of Freud's theory can be seen as a revival of tenets in Greek philosophy. In Plato's *Phaedrus* Bergmann tells us that the soul is divided into three parts, the temperate horse, the insolent horse and the charioteer. The charioteer beholds the vision of his love and his soul is then torn between these two 'masters': 'Plato visualised the conflict as taking place between the rational part of the personality and the appetitive. Of the two it is the appetitive which is the older. It is the part that remains awake when we are asleep or dreaming' (p. 145).

Nature fights Nurture in Freud's theory of the mind and love, as he attempts to replace religion with the intellect (1927),[8] the pleasure principle with the reality principle (1911a) and intellectual insight for erotic satisfaction (1911–13b, 1912). That is, Freud's scientific starting point may be biology, but it is a spirited body, the unconscious depicted as having a life of its own. We do not find dead matter, but animal passion, even 'spirits from the underworld' (see 1911–13b, p. 164).

It is the body, however, which is often seen as the seat of elemental passion (id), which the mind (the ego) must harness. To be identified with one's body (emotionality, de-differentiation) implies a less evolved state than if one were identified with one's mind (rationality). Love, being closely tied to the sensual can, as a result, be seen as something akin to sickness, a force of irrationality, potentially anarchic, primitive[9] and insane – the proverbial madman's[10] disease.[11]

A Freudian view of 'mature' love differs in important respects from a romantic concept of love (which is largely seen as an 'amour passion'), because of the psychoanalytic emphasis on thought and rationality, that is, the reality ego. While a psychoanalytic concept of a mature 'object relation' differs from a romantic grand passion, it also differs from the contemporary sociological account of an ideal love (see Giddens, 1992) which is informed by a different concept of reason. A Freudian view of mature love is not exclusively rationalist or romantic, but is informed by a model of the mind which posits a dynamic relationship between these two 'principles of mental functioning'.

In Freud's 1911 paper the role that we see being allotted to the reality ego is that of the 'internal observer' (Trowell and Rustin, 1991), because it is a developed 'reality-ego' which enables us to observe the intense workings of our own mind and thus be less blinded and driven by them.[12]

Bettelheim points out that Goethe played a dominant role in Freud's intellectual development, particularly his poem on Faust. The story of Faust is, as Bettelheim points out, that 'of a battle for his soul between the forces of light and the forces of darkness' (p. 64). Bergmann, as we have already seen, draws a connection between Freud's and Plato's view of the soul; in Plato's Phaedrus the sickness of the psyche is due to the wild, primitive part of the mind making its claims too loudly.

Hence Freud's two models of the mind (1900 and 1923) posit a mind in conflict, torn between the demands of an impulsive, instinctual, emotional life and the dictates of reality and conscience. Furthermore, these impulses which are sexually anarchic (1905) and aggressive (1920) form the vast seabed on which everything else rests and from which everything else grows. The fully conscious, waking self is therefore the tip of the iceberg, because our roots are buried deep in an instinctual, emotional life with which we are born. We may not feel, therefore, as though we can always be in control of parts of our mind and may speak from a position of passivity or enslavement when emotions like rage, despair or panic overwhelm us.

Freud analysed the extent to which our own emotional, unconscious life can alarm us, especially when it reveals our own capacity for destruction. In 1920, Freud (having now witnessed the First World War) introduced the idea of a death instinct or destructive drive in human nature and the aim of psychotherapy became one of strengthening the ego (1923), rather than one of emotional catharsis (1900), just as the aim of civilisation, according to Freud, was to institutionalise limits to our desires or instinctual freedom (1930). On both a cultural and individual level, Freud (1930) implies that a battle will ensue between destructive forces and more harmonious, integrative tendencies. The last line of *Civilisation and Its Discontents* is compelling, because it was written, as the editor tells us, as 'the menace of Hitler was apparent': 'Eternal Eros will make an effort to assert himself in the struggle with his immortal adversary. But who can forsee with what success and with what result' (p. 340).

While Freud argues that what civilisation needs to do is to bind members of a community together, he also argues that our moral ethics (e.g. love thy neighbour etc.) forget that 'man is a wolf to man' (1930, p. 302) and that there is a primary mutual hostility between human beings that threatens civilisation. In 1930, Freud reiterates his belief in the battle between a life and death instinct, and he argues that we have an inborn tendency towards carelessness, irregularity and unreliability. This is why we value beauty, cleanliness, order and aesthetics, because they each represent a countervailing force against what L. Miller (1989) describe as the psyche's tendency to disintegrate.

The Freudian conceptualisation of love that we can see developing is one that has a strengthened role for the ego (in 1923) at its core, and love is therefore being reconceptualised as a thinking rather than exclusively feeling-based state of mind. Freud's short paper on the reality ego is, as a result, central to his developing theory of love and it foreshadows Bion's introduction of the link between love and knowledge.[13] Hence, the question of what a mature object relation looks like in psychoanalysis is intimately bound up with the question of what kind of self-knowledge is envisioned. We will see both thematic continuities and fundamental differences between a sociological concept of self-reflexivity and a psychoanalytic understanding of the ongoing, always partial, process of self-understanding.

5.2.1 Narcissism and the pleasure principle: the 'weak spots in our psychical system'

In 1911, Freud describes two principles of mental functioning: the pleasure principle and reality principle. A mind dominated by the pleasure principle is one which turns away from, or represses, that which gives it displeasure (e.g., a high degree of tension), because it would rather be in a state of psychical rest and self-sufficiency. That is, as infants we are assailed from internal and external stimuli, and our nervous system, Freud (1915) writes, has the task of mastering these stimuli. This becomes less easy, he maintains, in relation to internal pressures, because 'no actions of flight avail against them' (p. 116). Infants can, however, in a psychological sense, avert their gaze from that which arouses tension[14] and this, Freud says, is the beginning of repression (1911a, p. 30).

Freud maintains that the infant is minimally related to the world/others and is too vulnerable to acknowledge the reality of its own dependency (for food and nurture), fragility (motor incapacity etc.) and complete helplessness (he/she couldn't survive alone). Primary narcissism[15] is in Steiner's (1985) terms, an example of 'turning a blind eye' (to know and not know something simultaneously) and it is an omnipotent defence against a terrorising vulnerability.[16] Hence the infant needs what Richards (1989a) refers to as a 'gentle disillusionment' out of this defended state of mind.

In pre-Oedipal stages infants/children are described as largely incapable of love, because of their weak egos (1911a), ingrained narcissism (1914) and unmediated instinctual life (1905, 1920).[17] In the myth, Narcissus does not enter into social relationships and he is doomed to suffer the experience of those who once loved him. He is fated to fall in love with himself, and as a result he gazes into his own, insubstantial, reflection in a pool. He cannot gain any recognising response and he dies, as he moves closer to the ephemeral image which he sees, but cannot reach. The fate of Narcissus is one of the 'morals' of psychoanalysis: unbridled self-referentiality leads to psychic death. Narcissism is therefore described as a state of mind that we hopefully emerge from as we mature.

However, another person's narcissism has, Freud says, a 'great attraction for those who have renounced part of their own' (p. 83). That is, the self-contented child, the adult who is self-preening, the inaccessible animal 'seem not to concern themselves about us, they are "people who keep anything away from their ego that would diminish it" (ibid.). Freud says 'it is as if we envied them for maintaining a blissful state of mind – an unassailable libidinal position which we ourselves have since abandoned (ibid.). Hence, our attraction to or envy of the 'rich and famous'.

This position is not however unassailable, because our narcissism is hard pressed by reality; we need others to survive both psychically and materially and energy and attention are gradually directed to/invested in the world around us, thus involving a decentring of our place/importance in it.[18]

Nevertheless, according to Chasseguet-Smirgel (1985), our 'ego-ideal' is the heir of primary narcissism and it is a state of mind to which we aspire (oceanic oneness, self-contentment, invulnerability). Primary narcissism is defined by an ego/object fusion (I deny the existence of separate others), by omnipotence (I am uniquely special) and by the wish not to be alone. It is a state of mind under the sway of the pleasure principle[19] in which object relations are possible, but only so far as they are a means of satisfying the self (hence anaclitic and narcissistic object choices). What Freud and Chasseguet-Smirgel tell us is that love can be used to recreate the narcissistic fusion we enjoyed/fantasised that we had with our carers. If we use love in order to inhabit an invulnerable (because fused) state of mind with the other, it is likely to lead, according to Freud (1914), to a 'crippling dependency' and to 'prodigious expenditure of libido on objects' (p. 96). This is, of course, exactly what romantic idealisation can lead to: the loss of self.

If romantic love leads to 'addictive daydreaming' (see Sodre, 1999) and wish-fulfilling fantasies (the pleasure principle), it is a narrative lending itself to what Freud (1911a) refers to as the 'weak spot' (p. 40) in our psychical system (the temptation to follow the path of least resistance, to be passive, reactive). Freud instead emphasises the importance of self-definition (efficacy), rather than passive dependency (dedifferentiation) and it is the reality ego, Freud states, that will enable us to 'to choose the line of greatest advantage instead of yielding in the direction of least resistance' (p. 41).

If romantic love itself, however, has become our ideal, functions otherwise allotted to the ego-ideal (work, analysis etc.) cease to operate. Narcissistic love can therefore involve a depletion of the ego and/or its enrichment (in an illusory way): the object is lost (you are a reflection of me) or the self is lost (I am fused with you). The person who is 'lovesick', Freud (1921) says, behaves towards their beloved like the group does towards their leader. The leader/beloved becomes for the group/lover a representative of their ego and/or ideal ego. In both cases, this means that the group/lover has adopted an infantile, idolatrous relationship towards their leader/beloved.

Indeed Chasseguet-Smirgel explains that the person in love can be dazzled by the radiance of the object and experience an 'ephemeral plunge into primary narcissism' (p. 56) as the breach between ego and ideal disappears by hallucination and wish fulfilment. This can lead to experiences of lucidity, luminosity and so on but not necessarily, she says, to genital or psychosexual satisfaction. That is, the object itself recedes into the background, because this is a love beyond the vicissitudes of the flesh.[20]

Sex, Chasseguet-Smirgel argues, can be an impediment to bliss and idealisation. She quotes Grunberger who makes a distinction between instinctual maturity (anality, messiness, reality, ambivalence) and narcissism (the wish for purity, fear of pollution, instincts etc.). The return to primary narcissism is a refusal of the mortal body which the ego, in healthy development, has to integrate. Hence, Chasseguet-Smirgel concludes that in luminous love 'the radiance of the object joins battle with the shadows of the instincts' (p. 57).

The world is, Freud says, severely limited if one cannot tolerate its frustrations (see 1930), hence Freud sees art and education (and analysis) as practices in the service of the reality ego, substituting insight for immediate sensory gratification and relief. That is, the world/psyche/other cannot be explored if one is driven to live one's life principally to avoid displeasure, that is, tension.

Moreover, to live one's life with the aim of avoiding tension involves a repression of a knowledge of existential reality. In Freudian terms (1930) we are assailed by three sources of suffering in life: illness and ageing, natural disasters and our relations with others. In 1930, Freud states that it is the third of these which can cause unparalleled suffering, and it follows that we will be tempted to turn away from others or enter into narcissistic relationships.

In both Freud and Klein, hate as a relation to objects (life, people) is older than love, because the infantile mind is not well-formed enough to deal with that which is 'disagreeable' (fears of falling, dying and so on) cognitively. The early instinctual impulse is to scream at, or turn away from, the object which is identified as the precipitating cause of, (while at other times appearing as a source of relief for), this terror and discomfort. In both Freud and Klein, because of the anxiety accompanying our entry into the world, the experience of ontological insecurity (rather than secure attachment) is, experientially, a priori.

What is emphasised in 1914 is the importance of loving from a position of ego-strength, rather than one's love being determined by the impoverishment of one's own ego (helplessness, need, dependency). If love is 'ego-syntonic', Freud rather soberly comments, 'it is assessed like any other activity of the ego' (p. 94). Romantic love, however, is often aligned with daydreaming, fantasy and deficient reality testing, especially, according to De Rougemont and Giddens, when it closely resembles its predecessor, courtly love or amour passion. Indeed, it was De Rougemont who said that tales of courtly love held up the image of dying lovers, declaring 'love like a force dominates you', and Freud echoes this in 1917: 'In the two opposed situations of being most intensely in love and of suicide the ego is overwhelmed by the object, though in totally different ways' (p. 261).

Hence Freud introduces us to a disquieting view of subjectivity in which the ego is not in Brunner's terms an 'imperial master', but subject to collapse, blindness and self-abandon and in Freud's early papers we are therefore invited to look at the ego position from which we love.

5.3   Sexual states of mind[21]

Before Freud, the sexual impulse was seen to be largely absent in childhood, only really awakening in puberty. However, Freud claimed that the first 'riddle of the sphinx' (p. 113) for all children is the question of 'where babies come from' and how they are made. Answering these questions was problematic for 'civilised men' (Freud, 1912b, pp. 255–4) for whom sex was seen as degrading, something 'which defiles and pollutes not only the body' (p. 255). Hence Victorian society could only find excuses for sex, he said, in the merits of the object and via marriage (which romantic love is the prelude to). Sex is a reminder, Freud implies, of our animal natures and of an almost beastly amoral self: 'The genitals themselves have not taken part in the development of the human body in the direction of beauty: they have remained animal, and thus love too, has remained in essence just as animal as it ever was' (1912b, p. 259).[22]

There is an affinity between the way in which Freud depicts the contents of the unconscious mind and the way in which Coltart (1992) makes use of Yeats' poem *The Second Coming* to do so. Bettelheim (1983) tells us that psyche literally means butterfly or bird, something delicate that we need to approach with care. Coltart, however, refers to the psyche as harbouring a 'lumbering beast whose hour has come at last to be born'(p. 2) (in analysis). Similarly, Freud (1923) refers to the id as a horse with greater strength than its rider (p. 364) and Coltart and Freud both describe material animality to evoke the power and viscerality of the unmediated psyche.

What Freud introduces us to in 1905 is the aggressiveness of the sexual instinct (see Klein's (1932) 'The Sexual Activities of Children'), which is 'a contribution derived from the apparatus for obtaining mastery ... which is ... ontogenetically, the older of the great instinctual needs' (p. 72).[23] Hence, there is a close link between aggressive and sexual tendencies (as in sadism and masochism), and pain can therefore be eroticised, just as sex can be tinged with aggression or 'mastery'.

In 1923, Freud refers to the id (the pleasure driven part of our minds) as full of sexual and aggressive excitations. These sexual impulses (masturbation, voyeurism, curiosity, a sexual/sensual pleasure etc.) are observable, Freud says, at three to four years of age (p. 92)[24] and these sexual instincts are, moreover, under the dominance of the pleasure principle, from which, in many people, Freud says, they are never able to withdraw. This means that sex is essentially used for narcissistic (i.e. masturbatory) ends.

Here then, we can see quite clearly how important the concept of the ego is to Freud's developing theory of love, because without it we would be subject to an unmediated instinctual life, which might lead to a compulsive or driven sexuality/aggression. He is also, of course, drawing our attention to a rather unromantic view of human nature. When considering child sexual abuse and bestiality, for example, Freud concluded that: 'we cannot escape from the fact that people whose behaviour is in other respects normal can, under the domination of the most unruly instincts, put themselves in the category of sick persons in the single sphere of sexual life' (1905, p. 75).

It is inappropriate however, Freud claims, to use the word perversion as a term of reproach, because we all have, or have had, perverse tendencies.[25] In adult life, however, the sexual impulse has to struggle against certain mental forces which act as resistances (shame, disgust, guilt, p. 93). However, the infant or child does not have a strongly developed ego and the mental dams against what Freud calls 'sexual excesses' (p. 109) are in the course of construction during these early years. The capacity for pity (concern for the object) is a late development and children can, therefore, be easily manipulated and are easily cruel (p. 111). The child's sexual curiosity (the epistemophilic instinct, according to Klein) is closely tied to sadism, because until the instincts are socialised, they have the character of ungovernability and violence (see Chasseguet-Smirgel, 1985, p. 66). The child's curiosity, therefore, needs boundaries for their own sake and for the sake of the other.[26]

From a psychoanalytic viewpoint, what we can already see is that an understanding of love cannot be complete without an understanding of the mental functioning of the infantile psyche, an embodied sensual life and propensity for feelings of hate. Moreover, Freud is beginning to set out what he thinks neurotic or perverse love looks like. It is his conclusion that it is love that has been brought back to an infantile state, which is characterised by ingrained narcissism, weak ego functioning and ungovernable impulses under the sway of the pleasure principle.

Moreover, in these early essays, a very sceptical eye is inadvertently cast over the ideals of romantic love or, its predecessor, courtly love in which love is depicted as ennobling, poetic or ephemeral. The reality ego may enable us to observe and contain the 'sexual excesses' and instincts for 'mastery' when they begin to rumble, but it does not deny their existence. Indeed, the reality ego is observant of the powerful viscerality of love. As Lucy Goodison points out:

> More than wanting to cosset the beloved we may want to eat them alive ... Romantic feelings and fantasies may be the blossoms produced by being in love, but its roots lie deeper in the earth. The power it feeds on is not essentially romantic, but one that tears at the innards. (Quoted in Jackson, 1993, p. 209)

Narratives of romance which exclusively 'focus on hearts and flowers or union of souls' (ibid.) are, in classic Freudian terms, neurotic, because they represent a repression of a knowledge of reality.

Freud implies that love is inevitably coloured by one's instinctual, unconscious life as much as by mindful reflection. That is, the existence of dreams, psychosomatic phenomena, and stormy sensations remind us of the fact that we can never just align ourselves with a triumphant reality ego.[27] There is, as Bollas (1992, p. 221) said, a semi-independent 'it-ness' to our own minds, which Freud's discussion of instinct and the body, and a mind torn between conflicting thoughts, feelings and drives evokes.

5.4   Oedipal fixations and transference love

We have already looked at the self-referential narcissist, who lives in a solipsistic world and leads a life of 'psychic retreat' (Steiner, 1993). Oedipus, on the other hand, enters the maelstrom of human relationships, but he never leaves the parental 'home' or indeed the parental bed. Sophocles' play, *Oedipus Rex*, dramatises infanticide, parricide, incest and Oedipus' attempt to bear witness to these forces of perversity as they manifest themselves in his family of origin. Faust's struggle (see Goethe's (1808) story of Faust) between his better self and powerful instinctual pressures (embodied in Mephistopheles) lead to the destruction of what he loves most (embodied in Gretchen) and this is essentially what happens in the Oedipal tale too: Oedipus destroys what he also loves most.[28]

Freud (1930) says that we are never so defenceless against suffering as when we love and risk losing what we love, and that this is the predicament for the child. We risk losing our parents' love, for example, if they reject us (Oedipus has his feet maimed and is left to die) or if our aggression, in turn, threatens to destroy them (Oedipus kills his father in an argument) and if our incestuous wishes threaten to destroy our parents as a creative couple (Oedipus then becomes narcissistically unique to his mother).

In 1925, Freud explained why it is that our earliest relationships are conflicted, rather than simply harmonious. He pointed out that the human infant is born prematurely in relation to most other animals and is dependent on its carers for an incomparably long period of time:

> Its (the human infant's) intra-uterine existence is seen to be short in comparison with that of most animals, and it is sent into the world in a less finished state. As a result, the influence of the real external world upon it is intensified. Moreover the dangers of the external world have greater importance for it, so that the value of the object which can alone protect it against them and take the place of its former intra-uterine life is enormously enhanced. The biological factor, then, establishes the earliest situations of danger and creates the need to be loved which will accompany the child the rest of its life. (Quoted by Chasseguet-Smirgel and Grunberger, 1986, p. 39)

This protracted dependency on its carers, and the awakening of the sexual and aggressive impulses, all bind the child to the parent in an intense and complex way. Thus, our first and prototypical love is ambivalent.

In *On the Universal Tendency to Debasement in the Sphere of Love* (1912b) Freud reiterates his belief that the 'affectionate fixations' of the child towards their parent carry along with them contributions from the sexual instincts, that is, components of erotic interest (p. 248). However, he states that these will ideally run up against the incest barrier: 'Consequently it [erotism] will make efforts to pass on from these objects which are unsuitable in reality, and find a way as soon as possible to other, extraneous objects with which a real sexual life may be carried on' (1912b, p. 249).

In the above paper Freud argues that the erotic cathexis of the parent has to be relinquished so that passion and tenderness can combine and cathect a new love object.[29] However, this process is complicated by the fact that the child does not want to renounce his mother and is rivalrous with his/her siblings and father/mother's lover. That is, the child is not narcissistically unique to his/her parent in the same way that they are to him/her. Indeed, according to Phillips, while a child's love for its parents is monogamous[30] (there are no substitutes), the child in return experiences infidelity early on.

Chasseguet-Smirgel and Grunberger (1986) refer to the Oedipal period as a period of solitude. It represents the period when the child's narcissism more fully hits 'reality' as he/she realises that they are separate from their parents' relationship or lives (to some extent) and must begin to enter the external world (nursery, school etc.) alone. Chasseguet-Smirgel and Grunberger point out that there is an implicit link between the child's prematurity and feelings of painful inadequacy because he/she has wishes that he/she is incapable of satisfying (p. 40), and Freud argues that the early efflorescence of infantile sexual life is doomed to extinction in the form of a feeling of loss of love, failure and inferiority:

> The tie of affection which binds the child as a rule to the parent of the opposite sex succumbs to disappointment, to a vain expectation of satisfaction or to jealousy over the birth of a new baby – unmistakeable proof of the infidelity of the object of the child's affections. His own attempt to make a baby himself, carried out with tragic seriousness, fails shamefully. The lessening amount of affection he receives, the increasing demands of education, hard words and an occasional punishment – these show him at last the extent to which he has been scorned. (Freud quoted in Chasseguet-Smirgel and Grunberger, 1986, p. 41)

Feeling a loss of love or failure can lead to a permanent sense of inadequacy. Hence Freud says that the person who complains that 'I can't accomplish anything; I can't succeed in anything' (ibid.), is arrested in infantile states of mind. Nevertheless, Freud said that it is our fate to be cast out of a fool's paradise in which we cherish fantasies of being loved above all else, and of never seeing this love transferred elsewhere. What also characterises the reality ego, although this isn't clearly stated in 1911, is therefore its 'capacity to be alone' (see Winnicott, 1958 'The Capacity to be Alone') and ability to mourn an idealised, unsurpassable self.

It is Freud's insight into the child's premature and somewhat unrequited experience of love which explains Richards' (1989a) reference to him as 'Freud the tragedian'. In the chapter entitled 'The First Duty' Richards implies that a disappointment in love is inevitable, but the importance of a gentle disillusionment is stressed (p. 39). Freud's introduction of an Oedipus Complex into every child's life implies that we will all suffer some disappointment in love and a tendency towards melancholia (or Klein's paranoia) as a result. Even a 'successful' resolution of Oedipal conflict leaves us with a narcissistic wound which a present love can recall in times of separation and anxiety. Indeed, according to Chasseguet-Smirgel, the Oedipus Complex entails a permanent injury to self-regard and a 'sense of inferiority'; the Oedipus Complex is dissolved, she points out, because of its lack of success. Falling in love in adolescence/adulthood is a means of effacing the wound to our childhood narcissism.

In later life love thus represents a demonstration against the herd instinct and the idea that we are interchangeable. That is, love fragments the collectivity in making one person unique and entails a narcissistic re-cathexis of the self echoed in many narratives of love (see 'Rachel' in Chapter 10). Chasseguet-Smirgel says that although adult love is not just an Oedipal substitute, it nevertheless revives Oedipal conflict and she maintains that we will only be able to restructure ourselves by re-experiencing Oedipal conflicts.[31]

However, it is difficult to remember Oedipal conflicts, because as Freud said, for many people, childhood is like a prehistoric period (1905, p. 91), and he argued that we all suffer from an infantile amnesia. Nevertheless, he also claimed (1930) that every experience is preserved in our mind (even if at the level of what Klein refers to as 'memories in feeling' (1957, p. 180). For Freud (1930) 'in mental life nothing which has once been formed can perish' (p. 256) and he elaborates on this by saying that while looking at a contemporary city we can still see the remains of ancient cities and so on, which can be preserved, destroyed or, indeed, excavated. This means that our early childhood experiences are available for reflection if we want to look at the contemporary traces of them. This will necessarily be difficult, however, because as Wittenberg (1983) and later Kleinians explain, we do not want to re-experience the chaos and helplessness of infantile states or see the past being re-lived in the present.

Moreover, the feelings and conflicts that we felt in relation to our parents might have been repressed, because, for example, of the pain (jealousy, inadequacy), danger (rage, revenge) or guilt (erotic sensations) that they raised. Also, these feelings might not be available for easy recall, because they are based on pre-verbal experiences. Nevertheless, these memories in feeling, sight, sound and smell are preserved in the unconscious mind and, like a *déjà vu* experience, colour later life experiences.

Indeed, we could argue that it is adult or adolescent psychosexual love which will open up the door to our 'prehistoric epoch' more than any other experience in life, because it will recall, like a faint memory trace, earlier highly cathected experiences of the need to be loved, cherished and caressed, and the fear of abandonment:

> If sex is the way out of the family, falling in love is the route back, the one-way ticket that is always a return … . What makes these transforming experiences possible – is the knowledge and desire of childhood. When we fall in love we are remembering how to fall in love. (Phillips, 1994, p. 39)

The Freudian contention is that we are (to some extent) imprinted, that we have preconditions for loving that may be entirely unconscious to us. Indeed, the 'character of the ego' itself 'is a precipitate of abandoned object-cathexes and it contains the history of those object choices' (Freud, 1923, p. 368). Hence, in a letter to Fliess (1899) that he quotes in his 1923 paper Freud remarks 'bisexuality! I am sure you are right about it. And I am accustoming myself to regarding every sexual act as an event between four individuals' (p. 373). That is, 'ghosts from the past' (Gay) and 'spirits from the underworld' (Freud, 1911–13b) make up who we are and how we love.

Because of a childhood prototypic plate or imprint, it is Freud's (1912) premise that 'new objects will be chosen on the model (imago) of the infantile ones' (p. 249). The reality ego is therefore one which has to get to know something of its own unconscious shadows: to make that which is unconscious conscious, because the more repressed our first experiences of close, intense and needy relationships are, the more insistent they will be in their reappearance.

That is, it is emotionally charged relationships that constitute the primary content of our early reflection (see Fonagy and Target, 1997) and the Oedipal tale warns of the dangers of being unaware, due to repression, of how they are liable to affect our future lives. Freud said that what is repressed exercises an attraction 'upon everything with which it establishes a connection' (1915b, p. 148). That is, there will be a 'return of the repressed' (p. 154) while ever self-reflexivity limits itself to a refashioning of our conscious life.

In psychoanalytic terms, although the trace of the 'original' object is normal, the 'shadow of the object '(1917, p. 258) is not. What this means is that we need to ensure that our present love isn't a sad, imitative love which draws its life blood from infantile prototypes. While influenced by these infantile prototypes, a 'mature object relation' would draw its life blood from the love of the person 'in their own right' and from the quality of the 'psychic intimacy' (see Stern, 1985) shared with them.[32] What this means, however, is that the ego or 'I' has to know something of its own narcissistic wounds, its old wish for omnipotence and Oedipal traumas so that the 'present act of love' is less affected by them.

Bettelheim points out that the meaning of the term 'Oedipus Complex' is symbolic and he says that it is a metaphor operating on many levels. Freud used it, he says, for its 'suggestive and referential richness' (p. 21) and he warns against a simplified reading of the myth. He argues that Oedipus's guilt and discovery of the truth are central issues in Sophocles' play. That is, Oedipus 'in fleeing Corinth, paid no attention to the admonitory temple inscription "Know thyself" ' and Oedipus eventually, he says, acts out his metaphorical blindness[33] by depriving himself of his eyesight.[34] Teiresias, the blind seer, who reveals the truth, necessarily has his sight directed inward. Hence: 'The guiding principle of psychoanalysis is that knowing oneself requires knowing one's own unconscious and dealing with it, so that its unrecognised pressures will not lead one to act in a way detrimental to oneself and others' (p. 24).[35]

However, in his papers on transference, Freud describes the extreme resistance which his patients showed to looking at their own wishes to be omnipotent, their Oedipal fixations and transference love. Indeed, in his 1911–13 and 1912 works, love is the means, par excellence, of avoiding insight.

A transference love is one in which parental imagos are 'transferred' to an object who is then loved with the passion and force of the infantile psyche, which anticipates rejection (the narcissistic wound), but desperately tries to undo it. Bak (1973) suggests that idealised romantic love is always preceded by a separation or object loss and the subsequent damage to one's own ideal self. The person who 'suffers' from being in love then undoes the loss by finding a substitute object. Love can therefore represent a nostalgic attempt to 'revive dead souls or cure the sick by love' (p. 5). Hence, according to Freud (1911–13b), the woman in love[36] is a 'child of nature' who refuses the psychical in place of the material and she becomes, in Freud's paper, the femme fatale, the woman scorned, the 'agent provocateur' who needs to assure herself of her irresistibility and omnipotence (p. 163). The female analysand's 'fall'[37]into love is a resistance, Freud says, to analytic treatment and a re-enactment of the fact that she has been in love for a long time with the 'wrong' person.

Although Freud said that 'psychoanalysis is in essence a cure by love' he did not intend to offer his patients a romantic idealisation of themselves or of the therapeutic relationship. He was wary of the manipulative ways in which love can be used to avoid insight and to avoid taking responsibility for psychic work and psychic change.[38]

What Freud is implying is that unreal, idealised, romantic love verges on the pathological in the same way that transference love does. Romantic and courtly love, like transference love, are fuelled by obstacles, lack a regard for reality, are less sensible about consequences and are blind in their valuation of the loved person. Indeed, idealised love became by 1921 akin to magic, spells and hypnotism. Hence Freud studied the degradation of the ego in love and group psychology, arguing that 'from being in love to hypnosis is evidently only a short step' (p. 77). That is, romantic love, in Freudian terms, is predicated on weak ego functioning as we willingly become spellbound. Although Freud recognises that we can be totally overwhelmed by the love that the other inspires, the concepts of idolatrous, romantic or transference love have very little in common with the Freudian view of love that we can see developing. A 'mature' object relation or love is one in which the ego or 'I', while still in thrall to the beloved, can observe the dynamics of their relationship with them.

Hence, if psychoanalysis is a cure through love, it is a love that pays heed to the reality principle and stresses the importance of understanding, work and change. As already stated, love therefore becomes inextricably tied to thought and reality testing in Freud's psychoanalysis and it is the 'thinking self' (see Craib, 1994, p. 170) that conjoins the contemporary sociological account of transformed intimacies[39] and the psychoanalytic contribution to our understanding of love.[40] It is interesting to note that however historically contingent Freud's theories of 'mature' love are, there are traces of his ideas in the contemporary sociological concept of self-reflexivity. The difference, of course, was that Freud was less concerned with the refashioning of our conscious life, and was more interested in analysing the 'shadow of the object' (1917, p. 258) which either darkens or irradiates our inner unconscious life.

5.5 Insight, mourning and love

Freud's 1917 paper is crucial to our understanding of the development of the concept of love from Freud through to Klein, but also for understanding one of the most important tasks of the so-called reality ego. This task involves, as far as possible, psychically separating, first from our parents or carers and later, from current partners. This process of psychic separation, as a child, will mean that a process of individuation and self-definition is possible. It is in 1917 that Freud talks about the 'shadow of the object falling upon the ego', and he is essentially interested in depression as symptomatic of the inability to mourn an experience of not being loved as a child (whether real or imagined). The melancholic is subsequently unable to love herself or the other as an adult. The ability to mourn becomes, as we will see, a precondition or part of 'healthy love', because the concept of 'genital' or 'depressive' love gives central place to our capacity to feel loss and aloneness and to withstand separation anxiety (see Quinodoz, 1993).

Freud's 1917 paper raises the question of what happens to the many children/infants who suffer a 'disappointment in love' (p. 257) in pre-Oedipal stages of development when the child (due to its prematurity) has a precarious relationship to its carers. A common reaction to this disappointment, Freud said, was to deny it (the pleasure principle), but as we know repression 'exercises an attraction upon everything with which it meets', hence feelings of loss, anguish and aloneness live on in the unconscious mind. A loss of love, moreover, ushers in retaliatory responses (the self-preservative drive or aggressive impulses) and thus pain and anger dominate the child's mind. The world has offered the child an experience which is extremely disagreeable (in Freud's 1911 terms) when his/her ego is already weak and beset by 'sexual excesses' and impulses towards mastery (Freud, 1905). An early catastrophic experience of loss therefore impairs the development of a reality ego, precisely because the reality of rejection is unassimilable. What the child does to avoid losing their parent/carer is to become like them, to identify their own developing ego with theirs.

To be like somebody undoes our separation from them and identification is therefore a simple psychological mechanism which ensures ego/object fusion and repudiates ego-aloneness. However, Freud's 'critical agency' or super-ego then views the ego as the disappointing object and 'I' then receive all of the retaliatory attacks directed at those 'I' most needed, but felt abandoned by.

It is then that the symptoms of melancholia appear: low self-esteem, delusional expectation of punishment, cessation of interest in the outside world and inability to love (1917, p. 252). Nevertheless, by a strange act of love, Freud says that the masochism (self-laceration) keeps the object relation alive. An attempt to manically free oneself from one's objects (to triumph) will lead to self-attack, because the masochistic link to the object is threatened with extinction. Love or an intense object relation/cathexis can therefore escape destruction by perverse means. That is, the person is attacked, but cannot be released, they are loved and hated simultaneously and the melancholic essentially therefore suffers from an ambivalent relation to his/her significant others.

If we are unconsciously identified with a loved, but rejecting, and then hated parent/carer our future object choice and ways of loving will inevitably be adversely affected by these unconscious prototypes. For example, we may choose an ambivalent person to be with in the future (somebody who inspires contradictory feelings to the point of torment) and relate to them from the vantage point of infancy/childhood.

Freud's 1917 paper suggests that it is only psychological separation that allows us to move out of identificatory states of mind and into the realm of 'choice', rather than a 'refinding'. The role for the ego is crucial here: 'The topographic point of view with its emphasis on the unconscious and the past tends to make love only a replica. The ego, on the other hand, is conceptualised as less bound to the past and capable of finding new solutions to old problems' (Bergmann, 1987, p. 180).

A capacity for separateness is necessary in order to pave the way for a non-incestuous object choice[41] and in order to avoid over-identified, claustrophobic relationships. Indeed, projectively identified relationships become, post-Freud, the prototype of the aggressive ego/object relation. There is a difference between merger and closeness, as there is between an object choice and an object identification,[42] which Freud's developing theory of love and critique of romance tries to clarify.

Bak (1973) argues that love can be examined midway between mourning and melancholia, because love narrows the field of consciousness, involves an exclusive concentration on the object and involves an identification with the object. According to Bak, Goethe is the outstanding romantic prototype, displaying a convergence of love, death, suicide and melancholia – 'Ah your face. It follows me everywhere. It is poison. Opiate, Wine, Narcotic' (p. 1). What is striking about Goethe's Werther however is, as Barthes (1978) said, that 'the cry of Narcissus is all pervasive: Me, Me, What about Me' (p. 67).

In 1923, Freud recognised the passionate nature of this cry when he wrote that 'to the ego living means the same as being loved by the superego (i.e., the internalised parent)' (p. 400), adding that without this 'protecting and saving function' the 'ego lets itself die'. The 'infantile anxiety of longing' to be loved and fearing separation (loss) is therefore one which we are likely to remember (as a 'memory in feeling'), and it might be one of the factors which gives to our later love a quality of urgency and poignancy, its passion.

The reality ego is not therefore a cerebral 'I', without feeling, but a part of our minds/self which can in Bion's terms think through feeling. It is Freud's 1917 paper that introduces an ethical component to any idea of a mature object relation, because it foregrounds the importance of mourning our early losses. That is, we will all have suffered from a wounded narcissism and it is analysis, Freud (1911a, 1912a) says, that will be the cure for this, not love. That is, it is the attempt at self-understanding that may protect the object from a sexualised voyeuristic intrusion, bid for mastery and exclusively defined transference love, precisely because it becomes known, conscious and, in more developed states of mind, mourned (1917).

In 1923, the aim of psychoanalysis changed from being one of emotional catharsis to one of strengthening the role for the ego, because psychoanalytic insight inevitably involves us confronting loss (our narcissistic wounds), thus paving the way for a love in which the 'cry of Narcissus' (see Chapter 4) is not 'all-pervasive'. Moreover, it is the concept of mourning which provides a thematic link between Freud's concept of 'mature' love and Klein's concept of 'depressive' love and it gives to the reality ego the role of thinking through the many ways in which destructiveness may manifest itself.

The previous sections in this chapter (narcissism, the pleasure principle, aggressively tinged sexual states of mind) highlight the Freudian view of the soul torn between a 'higher nature' (protected by the developing ego) and 'lower nature' (unmediated pleasure, destructiveness etc.). We can clearly see a link between Plato's Phaedrus, Goethe's Faust and Freud's psychoanalysis in their depiction of the embattled human soul, but Freud is distinctive because he looks at this struggle as it manifests itself in our childhood relationships, on the familial interpersonal plane, in addition to the adult intrapsychic one in the psychoanalytic view of human nature. This battle defines the human condition and it logically follows on that it will also colour and threaten our capacity for love. Freud's preference is for a reality-based love or state of mind/ way of life and in Freud's early psychoanalysis (1911a) neurosis is described as an alienation from reality and an inclination towards the repression of a knowledge of reality. To the extent that romance is excessively used to deny 'reality', it is therefore to be resisted.

5.6   Conclusion

The main objective of this chapter has been to identify a concept of an agency in the mind that underpins Freud's developing theory of love. In Chapter 3, the attempt to provide an overview of the historical emergence of romantic love opened up a 'thesaurus of meanings'. The word 'love' was said to perform a function akin to that of condensation in Freud's account of dreamwork: a single signifier, image, smell or other factor conceals a variety of meanings. Similarly, in this chapter too, the attempt to distill a bounded concept of love from Freud's work is beset by difficulty, because it is a highly condensed concept in psychoanalysis.

What is clear, however, is that in Freudian psychoanalysis, the capacity to love is a developmental achievement and the character of love is determined by the extent to which our ego has gone through the transformation from a pleasure ego to a reality ego. Freud's 1911 paper has been useful to consider, because although love might be commonly thought of exclusively as an emotion, this paper suggests that love is only possible when the reality principle (a form of rationality) defines our dominant mode of thinking. It is on this point that we can see a convergence between a psychoanalytic ideal-typical love and contemporary sociological accounts of new forms of self-reflexive intimacy. That is, both psychoanalysis and sociology presuppose that emotion combined with reason is constitutive of love. It is here where, to some extent, we see the Enlightenment/Romanticism divide traversed by Freud (anticipating post-Kleinian psychoanalysis). Love is tied to sexuality (as it is in sociological accounts – see R. Collins, 1972), but love is also analysed in terms of infancy[43] and psychic reality (and this is what Freud adds to the sociological discourse of love).

However, there is a convergence between contemporary sociology and psychoanalysis in their presupposition that mature or confluent love is an 'ethical' way of being with others. Giddens notes the similarity between the principles of intimacy in contemporary self-help books and the principles of democracy in classic political texts, and his model of the 'pure' relationship is modelled on these ethical, democratic principles (1992).

Although Freud did not provide an ethics of love, a call for 'honesty' and responsibility ('where id was, there shall ego be') pervades his work. This is an honesty that relates to the Faustian battle within us (Eros versus Thanatos) and it is obvious on which side he would align love. He did not, however, intend to be moralistic about our narcissistic, perverse or careless tendencies.

For there to be a real convergence of interests in a sociological account of ideal-typical love (and current practices) and a psychoanalytic account of mature love, the former would need to include an acknowledgement of love's bedfellow – hate. That is, if 'confluent love' and 'romantic love' are concepts of love that are uninformed by the dictum that 'we are far more immoral than we believe' (Freud, 1923, p. 400), they are both concepts of love that are, in classic Freudian terms, neurotic, alienated from 'reality'.

Freud adds, however, that we are also 'far more moral than we know', thus anticipating Klein's concept of depressive pain. Depressive pain is felt when the insight into our capacities for destruction leads to remorse and regret. What we are insightful about, of course, is the ongoing battle between pleasure and reality, or narcissism versus object relations and about sexual and aggressive states of mind, Oedipal fixations and transference love.[44] This means that our love/beloved will always be endangered by the 'otherness' or 'semi-independent it-ness' of our own embodied minds.[45]

Kernberg (1995, p. x), for example, points out that it was impossible for him to study the vicissitudes of love without the vicissitudes of aggression:

> I found the aggressive component of the universal ambivalence of intimate object relations equally important. So, despite the best of intentions the incontrovertible evidence forces me to focus sharply on aggression in this treatise on love.

And in this context, Colman (1993) argues that 'popular notions of romantic love as happy-ever-after are, in fact, sentimentalised dilutions of the Romantic' (p. 85) which deny the torment that an emphasis on passion, excess and the free play of the imagination can bring.

From a psychoanalytic perspective, in the romantic search for the picturesque, heroic, imaginative and transcendent, earthy impulses like aggression, boredom and polymorphously perverse sexuality are split-off. Colman (p. 87), for example, argues that what we often see depicted in romantic films is a story in which the characters are caught up in a longing for ideal love: 'This is the torment. Something at the heart of love, and not only adulterous love but any grand passion, runs counter to the possibility of its fulfillment. Reality is always an obstacle.'

This psychoanalytic conceptualisation of reality can be seen in Meltzer's (1988) claim that there are forces in the mind towards philistinism and perversion. Hence, for Freud we are born into anxiety, and for Klein our destructive impulses are our most alarming ones. Unlike romantic love, a psychoanalytic concept of love does not offer us a perfect internal state, a state which Klein (1963) likens to the longed for, wordless understanding between a mother and her child. Colman argues that the archetypal longing for ideal love is the longing for divinity, divine omnipotence and perfection (narcissism). What we can see then is that, as a described state of mind, romance like Romanticism is in danger of a self-referentiality,[46] which obliterates the other. In this context we can understand why Colman argues that the romantic spirit needs uniting with a rationality which can respect social obligations.[47] Colman argues that the ideal world is there to enrich the 'real' world and that it is a mistake to think that it really exists. Ideals, are according to Colman (p. 90), beacons to guide the way, but they cannot necessarily be achieved: 'She (Emma Bovary) seeks to obliterate the real world in a frenzy of hatred and frustration that gives her love a manic quality, driving her on to ever more extreme behaviour the more reality threatens to invade.'

There is, as Colman (p. 93) points out, a loss involved in recognising that we might not be able to fulfill our ideals and this, he maintains, is at the heart of tragedy: 'But it is preferable to the futile and doomed attempt to deny the gap by omnipotent fantasy a la Madame Bovary.'

Colman is not, however, prioritising marriage as a socio-legal reality, rather he is asking what it is that makes two people psychologically married and capable of fidelity to the 'ordinary' (p. 79). Kernberg answers by arguing that romantic love is the beginning of sexual love, but it is the latter that integrates aggression and polymorphously perverse infantile sexuality into a stable love relation. Hence in psychoanalytic terms genital or depressive love represents an attenuation of romantic love, because romantic love, like the amour passion described by Giddens and De Rougemont, does not enlarge the field of the ego or one's capacity for concern.

However, although psychoanalysis puts forward a concept of love that is different from romance, psychoanalytic insights can be used to understand the passion and compelling force of romance as a narrative/experience. Romantic love can be interpreted as a search for a 'mutual identification in depth' (Kernberg, 1995, p. 6) which will 'open the deep pathways of the unspoken multiple relations between human beings (ibid.)'. That is, the 'capacity for a depth in relation to oneself as well as to others' (ibid.), which Kernberg writes about, is what romantic love can be seen to promise. In psychoanalytic terms, this capacity for depth emerges from our first object relationships and the romanticist appreciation of the sublime (experienced in luminous love) can be said to be inspired by or likened to our very first 'apprehension of beauty' (Meltzer, 1988).[48] Our popular discourses of romantic love can therefore be likened to an object-relational understanding of our infantile longing for affective, non-linguistic attunements (see Stern, 1985).

The following chapter will refine the psychoanalytic reconceptualisation of love and understanding of romance by focusing on the work of Klein. It perhaps seems anomalous to refer to 'love in the depressive position', but Klein's theory of depressive anxiety lends weight to Freud's (1923) claim that we 'we are far more moral than we know', because as already stated, depressive anxiety refers to the pain of regret which we suffer when we destroy that which is life-affirming.[49] Moreover, it is interesting to note that Klein's work moves love out of the exclusive province of psychosexual coupledom and includes in the concept of love the ways in which we live and work more generally.

This expanded concept of love has consequences for the way in which we interpret life history accounts. Eighty-four-year-old Eddie, for example, spent approximately six hours telling the story of his life. Although love was a part of it, he devoted much of this time to telling me about his voluntary work with the youth centre in East London: writing plays, forming bands, leading gymnastic teams and so on. When finally asked directly about love, he referred to love as evident in the case of the soldier who risks his life for another on the battlefield and not to any 'grand passion'. What Eddie offers us, in classic Freudian terms, is aim-inhibited love, but without a reconceptualised understanding of love, we could be in danger of concluding that Eddie's life history is uninteresting and irrelevant to this study. That is, psychoanalysis implicitly warns against looking for 'evidence' of love only in tales of elemental passion, and opens up a more varied range of object relationships as evidence of love.

Nevertheless, as Rylance points out, Barthes implies that the romantic lover is forsaken by Freud. What psychoanalysis brings to romantic love's developmental history is, if Barthes is correct, a view of love as impossible. In this context, it is psychoanalysis, prior to any postmodern theory, that has therefore deconstructed romantic love out of existence by its very attempt to understand it. Indeed, we could say that just as Freud (1927) asked us to live in a world without the comforting illusion of God, so too, he asks us to live in a world without love.

This would, however, be a wholly mistaken view of what psychoanalysis offers, since psychoanalysis is aligned with love. Psychoanalysis does, nevertheless, ask us to live with a love reconceptualised and we can derive a concept of love that is different from romantic and confluent love, while sharing affinities with both from Freud's work. The 'pure relationship' which is based on self-reflexivity and reason is consistent with the Freudian rationalist project, while romantic love with its focus on excess, idealisation, emotionality recalls the appetitive id: driven, blind, passionate.[50]

While the pure relationship is, in Freudian terms, underpinned by the reality principle, romantic love is closer to the dictates of the pleasure principle and intolerant of a more sober view of reality. Love from a Freudian perspective, as stated in the Introduction, draws on both of these principles of mental functioning. It is necessarily linked to the idea of psychic work, because psychoanalysis introduces limits to our hopes for a transcendent, exclusively romantic love or perfect internal state/partner.

Despite the attempt to identify and delineate a theory of 'mature' love with the emphasis on psychic work and the reality ego, we must be careful not to make the mistake that Phillips said that psychoanalysis could be in danger of making more generally. That is, Phillips (1995, p.19) states that rationalising the unconscious is an aim, but also a betrayal of psychoanalysis, and we might add, of love too. It is worth paying heed to Barthes' claim that it would be 'monstrous' to produce a theory of love, and that we should instead look for its affirmation, what people say and do in its name. However, in Freud's defence, we could say that while poets, playwrights and so on can provide us with phenomenological descriptions of love, psychoanalysis tries to more systematically understand its genesis, prehistory and 'logic', precisely because of its central place in ensuring mental health. Hence Freud said that the poets had discovered the unconscious and that he had added science to it, and this is true in the case of love too.

6
Reparative Love
A Kleinian Approach

6.1 Introduction

In this chapter a Kleinian way of seeing love will be outlined. This develops Freud's conceptualisation of love and allows us to look at the compelling nature of romance by reference to infancy and the object related character of human nature. Both Freud and Klein, as already stated, are modernist, humanist thinkers and their theories of love reflect this, but their work is also sensitive to, although it precedes, postmodern objections to the idea of a rationally integrated, unified self. Indeed the ethical nature of ideal-typical love, according to Freud and Klein, is a consequence of our accepting the fact that we are not always rational and can be split-off, fragmented and destructive. Thus, ideal-typical love has, according to Klein, a reparative urge or quality.

The Kleinian way of seeing love, like a Freudian mature love, conjoins emotion and thought and the two principles of mental functioning discussed by Freud. In Kleinian theory the Freudian idea that the mind develops in the context of 'live company' with other minds is developed further (see Alvarez, 1992), as is the idea of psychic reality. The self becomes much more relational in Kleinian, as oppose to Freudian theory, but the nature of this relating can be seen as part or whole object based. By detailing Kleinian theory, we can ask which form of relating romance is conducive to.

In this chapter we will see that the loving self moves from being the reality-based self of Freudian theory to the observant self of Kleinian theory. The nature of this observation is, however, emotional, because we are asked to think through our feelings while observing our thoughts and actions. Since psychotic anxieties and paranoid states of mind are said to be a part of our entry into the world, this observation requires considerable emotional energy, because we are asked to discern the origins of these persecutory states of mind, which the 'art of loving' requires us to move out of. In Kleinian theory, love becomes one of life's core ingredients against which hate and envy battle. This battle is a lifelong struggle and an understanding of what love is cannot be separated from a discussion of this Faustian-like temptation to indulge one's narcissism and rage.

In this chapter the psychoanalytic notion of self-analysis is contrasted with the sociological idea of self-reflexivity. It will also highlight the similar emphasis that is placed on understanding how we cope with solitude in existentialist, sociological and psychoanalytic views of love. Here, perhaps, we can begin to see one ingredient of ideal-typical love that all three ways of seeing love share and, in psychoanalytic terms, it relates to our capacity to 'be alone' (see Winnicott, 1958).

Sartre, Lacan and Barthes condemn romantic love, because it rests on a notion of oneness, plenitude and the closure of the vexatious nature of desire and existential unease. At the end of this chapter, a Kleinian way of seeing love will be brought into discursive dialogue with these views of selfhood and love as impossible. It will argue that these impossible views of romantic love assume an associative view of the mind and narcissistic ego. Kleinian psychoanalysis, it will be argued holds a dialectical view of the mind and ego, thus acknowledging the possibility and impossibility of love.

A Kleinian way of seeing love looks at love as a state of mind and feeling, rather than prioritising love as a social practice, script, or ideology. However, the socio-cultural way of seeing love (the sociology of emotion) will be brought into dialogue with the psychoanalytic view of love in order to explore how we can study love as a socio-historical phenomenon, a facet of the human condition and a unique experience of object relationships. Concentrating on all three factors prioritises a view of love as a play between our social, existential and psychic selves.

First, however, this chapter will detail the Kleinian theory of our first experiences of hate, loss and love.[1]

6.2   Kleinian states of mind and modes of relating

Whereas Freud's work is seen to be constrained by a physiologically based description of emotional life, Klein's work offers us a psychological elaboration of that which can be seen as our biological inheritance. Thus, whereas Eros and Thanatos can be understood as organic (even if unsubstantiated) concepts, Klein's paranoid/schizoid and depressive metaphors refer to what psychological processes these impulses give rise to. Hence Klein supplements Freud's three libidinal phases with a consideration of the ego's earliest relation to its internal and external objects. Hence, the feelings of the paranoiac and those of the depressive have distinguishing anxieties, defences and fantasies. They represent different positions which we can take up in relation to people/objects. Indeed for Kernberg (1995): 'Identity is built up from identifications made with a relationship to an object rather than with the object itself. This implies an identification with both the self and the other in their interaction as an internalisation of the reciprocal roles of the interaction' (p. 11).

In 1940, Klein (p. 362) explains what she means by an 'inner world of objects'. She maintains that our parents are experienced as concretely alive inside us and that we have 'doubles' of everything (p. 346), which are altered by our own fantasies and impulses. It is the constant interplay between projection and introjection which creates our internal world, and our inner world of objects is, Klein argues, made up of infinitely complex relations. If they are predominantly at peace then a sense of security is established and our inner world is largely experienced as a place of safety rather than danger. This is because the ego is predominantly identified with good objects, which strengthen its ability to overcome some of life's adversities.

That is, it is not just the shadow of the object that falls upon the ego, but the shadow of the object relation, and all object relations are, from a Kleinian perspective, beset by anxiety. Klein for example draws a phenomenological picture of the infant's world as dominated by intense anxiety. Klein argues that although the infant's craving for life (Eros) is evident in the baby feeding and taking in its first good object-experience, this object (experience) is threatened by the infant's anxiety (the death instinct) and by the tendency of the psyche towards fragmentation and loss. This is the paranoid–schizoid phase of development (dominant until seven months) when the good object is repeatedly lost, showing an inability to root a good object securely inside one's mind.

In the paranoid phase of development, the infant seeks out the object who will help with the anxiety and terror that he/she is prey to and he/she then idealises the fulfilling, protective object that is hopefully found. This instance of positive relating is, however, threatened by the infant's own inability to believe in the benevolence of this good object (when he/she is left by it and by the possibility of the object's own depressed non-responsiveness).

So, when love (or relief and gratitude) is tempered by disappointment, a feeling of neglect or suspicion arises. What do we do? What are our defence mechanisms? Our most primitive defence mechanism, according to Klein, is to rid ourselves of these feelings. We don't simply repress bad experiences, we deflect them and project them out, but in doing so we alter (in fantasy) the character of the object that, at a previous moment, we loved. We also split our own ego in the process, because part of what belongs to us is perceived as belonging to someone else. This leads to an ego/object fusion in which both psychic responsibility and psychic separateness are denied. This projective identification is a powerful form of communication in which the other can be nudged into feeling what, in fact, belongs to us. It is for this reason, seen as a form of possession, mastery and narcissism. It is, quite simply, aggressive and centred on the survival of one's own ego, rather than with a concern for the other.

In this paranoid phase of development (and paranoid adult state of mind), the object is split into the good and the bad, and contact with the bad object is seen to be dangerous. What the infant or the adult stuck in a paranoid state of mind cannot do is acknowledge that the person/object is both good and bad, but not the persecutor we fear them to be. The infant cannot acknowledge that, for example, his or her mother is a whole object, perhaps behaving in more or less consistent ways. When the infant perceives a changed and now persecutory object, he/she is convinced that it is the object that has changed, rather than his/her perception of it. Klein maintains that the object changes in fantasy, because with an ascendancy of intolerable frustration or anxiety, the object is identified as the cause of our problems. This state of mind can be also be inhabited by the adult, and it is Klein's belief that we are always prey to this paranoid state in which one's peace of mind is inevitably disturbed.

In the paranoid–schizoid position the infant/adult relates to people as part objects. That is, they are either good or bad, but they are not perceived 'realistically'(wholly), because anxieties about one's own survival are predominant. One's mode of relating is dominated by a paranoid concern for oneself, rather than an altruistic concern for the other (and in this respect we might begin to ask what type of relating romantic narratives and experiences give rise to). However, ideally, as the ego becomes more organised and the infant begins to make the transition from the introjection of a part to a whole object, it feels remorse for its previous attacks on (and misrecognition of) the object it can now see more realistically and indeed love.

This new way of relating to people and experiencing the world signals the move into Klein's idea of the depressive position. In the depressive state of mind projection lessens, because depressive anxieties are seen to centre on the survival of the good object with which the ego is now identified.

The idea that it is the lover's own mind that destroys the love found forms one of the most poignant and painful aspects of love stories (though an external factor is often assigned this role[2]). This echoes Klein's idea that depressive anxiety is one of the most painful aspects of emotional growth. The depressed patient/lover, for example, carries around a sense of failure, according to Klein (they can't sustain a loving relation), but they find it easier to berate the object (Freud's model of melancholia), rather than their own aggression and inability to secure a good internal relation to the object.

There are, of course, 'real' persecutory objects and experiences, which Klein maintains will most likely result in mental disorder. However, even in a situation of 'real' persecutory objects, Klein maintains that one's inner world can be repaired with the introjection of good objects/experiences in later life.

Hence there is in Klein's analysis of the mind a struggle between love and gratitude and hate and envy. Klein argues that the experience of early psychotic anxieties and the manic-depressive state which follows is a normal characteristic of the mourning process in childhood. It is overcome when we can master our own hate, become less suspicious of our objects and unify their split aspects and mitigate hate with love. This increases our trust in our own reparative powers and secures our internal world, which, when checked against reality, decreases manic omnipotence and obsessional control. A Kleinian conceptualisation of love therefore requires us to think about the psychic reality that we inhabit and about the states of mind we are prone to feeling. A paranoid–schizoid relation to objects (projection, splitting, idealisation and so on) is a defensive mode of relating that militates against feeling appreciative of life and mournful for one's own inability to draw sustenance from one's total environment. The depressive state of mind is constitutive of ideal-typical love, but also of emotional maturity more generally.

There are two sets of feeling which loss precipitates: persecution and pining. Both involve us being dependent upon the object, but persecutory feelings express our dependency on bad objects which we attempt to escape from or control. Klein describes this as a suffering which leads to destructiveness and sterility. However, being dependent upon a good object and pining for it is a suffering which gives rise to reparative and creative sublimations. Klein explains that the lost objects we mourn for may deepen our appreciation of life and make us wiser about our own inner reality, thus strengthening our sense of character which has now become identified with a good object.

It is, in Klein's (ibid., p. 369) view, in experiencing the emotions of sorrow, guilt, grief, love and trust, that the infantile depressive position can be 'overcome'. Indeed, for Klein, sanity is secured through the internalisation of a good object, which becomes the core of ego functioning. The sanity of the ego is not therefore only guaranteed by robust reality testing (Freud's model), but by its dependence on good objects. The ego of Kleinian theory is much less monadic and 'independent' than the ego of Freudian (and sociological) theory. Indeed, we could argue that in Freudian theory the ego attempts to ensure its own survival, but a much less self-centred view of the healthy ego characterises Klein's position, because it is an ego which is characterised by its concern for others. When we learn to love depressively, we therefore simultaneously enter an ethical world.

Indeed, we may be powerfully drawn to the narrative of romantic love precisely because it promises the good object/relationship of Kleinian theory. That is, it might be hope that draws us to romance, rather than perversity and illness. But from a Kleinian point of view, romantic love is inevitably prone to dissolution (if only periodically), since it is Klein's contention that our minds are fluctuating all of the time. Love therefore has to live side-by-side with its bedfellows hate, envy and jealousy. And indeed most love stories do, to some extent, depict these feelings en route to consummation.

6.3   The relational self

What we can see in Klein's work is that there is no mental state which is objectless or conflict free. A narcissistic withdrawal is, in this context, a withdrawal to internalised objects via processes of projective identification, for example. That is, other people are identified with aspects of one's own internal world/self. Sandler *et al.* (1991) explain that patients who make excessive use of projective identification are trapped in a world made up of projected parts of themselves. This weakens their ego and sense of reality and increases their anxiety. This often underlies claustrophobic anxiety when there is no space between self and other. However, 'From the subjective point of view, of course, the objects that become identified with the self are not experienced as part of the self. When Narcissus gazes at his reflection in the water, he does not know that what he sees is himself' (ibid., p. 162).

· These processes of ego/object fusion occur in couples, and we might ask how often love functions as a form of projective identification and denial of separateness:

> Narcissistic constellations constitute a universal opportunity for withdrawal from the otherness of the other, from the '3rd dimension' of the object with its setting of boundaries and its sensual reality, into an intoxicating dual union if the otherness is experienced as threatening. (Kernberg, 1995, p. 221)

The fear of losing oneself in love is therefore understandable, because processes of projection and introjection are, from a psychoanalytic point of view, an inevitable part of being in a couple. Kleinian psychoanalysis emphasises the way in which the intrapsychic processes of two people piece together in complex and 'unseen' ways (principally through the concepts of projection, introjection and projective identification). Although Freud recognises that the ego is a 'precipitate of abandoned object cathexes' (1923, p. 368) and is therefore relational, it is Klein who foregrounds 'the interpenetration of our identities' (see Craib, 1998, p. 174) from birth.

As Shuttleworth (1998) explains, the 'new psychology of infancy' and object-relations psychoanalysis are both a part of the interactionist or intersubjective view of the mind in which mental life is seen to arise precisely in contact with other minds. The work of Trevarthen (1977), Stern (1985) and Butterworth (1991) supports the idea that the infant has a natural capacity for intersubjectivity and a theory of mind. This means that the baby does interact with 'other persons by searching for and reaching out to their underlying mentalities' (Butterworth, 1991, p. 1). This work is relevant because it lends empirical weight to Klein's contention that we are object related from birth, thus challenging the asocial view of the infant found in traditional developmental psychology and Freudian psychoanalysis. The romantic narrative can be read as dramatising the ways in which we are inextricably object dependent and related. Romantic love might not therefore be an arbitrary social construction, but a story relevant to our human condition and its object-seeking nature.

6.4 The thinking self[3]

The loving mother is the thinking mother in Kleinian theory, just as the loving self is also the thinking self in psychoanalysis and contemporary sociology. That is, ideal-typical love has a containing quality and this is derived from the ability to think through what is felt. Ideal love is not therefore identified with an uncontained or cathartic release of emotion. However, love is not identified with cerebral thought either, because it is inextricably tied to feeling – the feelings of remorse, sorrow, yearning, pining, gratitude and so on discussed by Klein. Indeed, the mind and our thinking capacities are not seen as developing in isolation from emotion, because from a Kleinian viewpoint all thinking is emotional.

Thinking and feeling are like two sides of the same coin as is evident in the psychoanalytic view of how the mind develops. That is, cognitive life arises in conjunction with, and through, emotional life.

Fonagy and Target (1997, p. 690) explain that, from an object relations perspective, the understanding of mental states is embedded in the family and that it is emotionally charged relationships which constitute the primary content of early reflection: 'The child's development and perception of mental states in himself and others thus depends on his observation of the mental world of his caregiver.'

In Bion's terms it is the mother's capacity for reverie, which is crucial to the infant's developing thinking capacities. And reverie is described as 'the mother's sensitivity to emotions, feelings recognised by the receptive part of the mind: this requires a space in the mind where thoughts can begin to take shape and where confused experience can be held in an inchoate form until their meaning becomes clearer' (M.E. Rustin, 1989, p. 20). This kind of mental functioning therefore requires a capacity to tolerate anxiety, uncertainty, discomfort, helplessness, and a sense of bombardment, because the mother is in interaction with an infant dominated by paranoid–schizoid anxieties and part-object relating.

The mother's containing capacities are, however, affected by the infant's temperament, for example his resilience or vulnerabilities, as well as by the mother's own adult identity and 'internal thinking mother' (Boston, 1987, p. 22).

Our capacities for Giddens' 'self-reflexivity'and confluent love are, in this context, dependent (to some extent) upon the relationships into which we were born.

Main (1985), for example, explains that the secure child may have more 'epistemic space' in which to review her actions, situations, or thinking processes, because her thinking processes are not compartmentalised. An insecurity of attachment[4] leads, Main says, to defensive thinking, which distorts, disorganises and limits access to memories, intentions and the recognition of options. Fonagy and Target similarly state that individuals differ in the extent to which they want to go beyond observable phenomena to explain action in terms of desire, belief and action.

In Kleinian terms, for example, the infant/adult might split his/her own thinking processes in order to limit knowledge of both oneself and others (see Steiner's 1985 reference to 'turning a blind eye'), because of an inability to bear the depressive anxiety which metacognitive functioning or the reflective function might require. Thus, we begin to see the way in which Kleinian theory problematises the 'reflexive project of self'.

6.5   The observant self: a friend of ambiguity?

The self-reflexivity that is called for in a psychoanalytic view of love is one that reflects upon the conditions of life (in an existentialist vein), the intrapsychic and interpersonal nature of unconscious processes and the responsibility that one is taking for one's own future. Craib (1994, p. 176) explains that, according to Symington (1986), Klein's delineation of the paranoid–schizoid and depressive positions needs to be supplemented with a third, which he names the 'tragic position'. This position is one in which we learn to accept that our past was as it was and that it cannot be undone. This militates against us taking up a position of victimhood, as does psychoanalysis, existentialism and contemporary sociology more generally. The idea of the tragic position has an existentialist flavour about it, because it re-routes our attention to the present and future, while understanding the place of the past in both. Thus ideal-typical love requires us to develop a sense of responsibility for our lives and loves.

However, what agency in the mind can be observant, self-reflexive, mournful and responsible? It might seem artificial to carve out a particular agency or to render the mind knowable in this sense. As Bion (1970) notes: 'The realization of mental space is ... felt as an immensity so great that it cannot be represented even by astronomical space, because it is unrepresentable' (p. 12).

In Winnicott's (1971) terms we might say that we are in search of an ego/self capable of tolerating paradox and, therefore, capable of play (like the signifier). Freud's idea that the id, ego and super-ego are like colours melting into each other and Klein's insistence that we move in and out of paranoid–schizoid and depressive states of mind, give credence to Phillips' point that students of psychoanalysis must be friends of ambiguity. This is why the ego is referred to as, ideally, observant. Enlarging the field of the ego, is no longer an enlightenment, imperialist gesture and, becomes more a case of enlarging the ego's capacity for observation and self-realisation.

The self-realisation described is not one of closure, but it involves developing an 'internal observer'.[5] This observer can, as Meltzer (1990) points out, watch the play of the mind like we may watch the play of children, without forcing their attention. That is, it is at once both the children playing and it is not; it has responsibility, without a will-to-power.

Bollas describes this as a stage when the ego or the Oedipal child discovers the semi-independent it-ness of its own mind, which then problematises the narrative authority of its own voice. This is an important psychic development in which the child comes into the presence of its own mind, which is, he alleges, a very arresting moment and a disturbing journey.

The curse that Oedipus uncovers, Bollas tell us, is that we have minds which can make us suffer, get us into trouble, can be lost, abuse us and others and produce nightmares. The Oedipal child develops a conscience when he/she realises that like Oedipus he/she created the nightmare. Hence, Bollas thinks that the Oedipus play 'places the audience in the position of the gods who could see the full course of events and yet, by identification with Oedipus, be drawn into the inner texture of his specific dilemma' (p. 219). This, he points out, mirrors the oscillation we all endure in life between our reflective self states and the 'location of the simple experiencing self' (ibid.).

What Klein maintains is the idea that as the ego becomes more capable of accepting psychic reality, then it will be able to apprehend the external world with more accuracy. That is, the 'external' may always be imbued with the kaleidoscopic colours of our own imaginations, but we may be able to watch the changing shapes it assumes, nevertheless. Here then is the compromise between the enlightenment and post-enlightenment reading of psychoanalysis: a depressive metaphor which argues for a vision of the ego with its roots deeply sunken in the id, but not driven or blinded by it.

6.6   Social theory, philosophy, psychoanalysis: love – possible or impossible?

In Barthes' 'A Lover's Discourse' the self is seen, as stated in Chapter 4, as a dramatic sequence, rather than an authentic unity, and life is, therefore, characterised by an ambiguous instability, which is both tragic and farcical. Lovers, therefore, live in a tragic–comic theatre in which love becomes an interesting piece of fiction, merely played out by one of our many parts. This is our associative unconscious which by a process akin to dreamwork forever produces new patterns. This infinity of associations, signifiers, texts or codes means that for Barthes (influenced by Lacan and Sartre) the origin of the self is lost. Just as we can only know the instinct or unconscious fantasy through its psychical representative, so too, can we only know the self through associations and signifiers which are shifting.

The question therefore is: how can two people who lack being (their origin is lost) demand wholeness? Narcissistic misrecognition of oneself and others is inevitable if we can assume only the existence of a narcissistic as opposed to a realist or reconceptualised ego. For negative psychoanalysis, the lover's discourse becomes an anti-humanist paradise. Here we find endless examples of the inauthentic, of self-idealisations and of self-delusions.

Love has too many associations; the latent content can never reveal itself, and the narrative (like the dream) may change daily. In this associative view of the unconscious and, therefore, the self, we are cast as passive victims of our own and each other's otherness. Monogamy becomes, according to Phillips (1997) a way of keeping the versions of ourselves down to a minimum, trying to keep the true story of who we really are in circulation.

But Barthes' exclusive focus on the unconscious as promiscuous association leads him to conclude, as we have seen, that the lover was forsaken by Freud. The lover according to the negative appropriation of psychoanalysis can be represented only by blind Narcissus and murderous Oedipus, or in Bollas' terms, the 'simple experiencing self'. 'Where Id was, there shall Ego be' becomes the enlightenment fallacy. The ego can only be manic or melancholic (the heir of narcissism), but not mournful, because it cannot mourn what it cannot see (its own internal world of identifications and object cathexes dovetailing with the external world).

This view of love as impossible can be compared with what De Botton (1993) refers to as the work of 'romantic positivists'. Self-help books sometimes, de Botton maintains, argue that with enough thought and therapy, love can be less painful, and practical steps are offered which can remedy heartache and disappointment. De Botton describes the tone as one of triumph and brave optimism. Thus, we find in them the champions of the Enlightenment in which knowledge becomes redemptive:

> Hamlet's fate could have been avoided with the help of a good
> Jungian analyst, Othello could have gotten his aggression out on a

therapeutic cushion, Romeo might have met someone more suitable through a dating agency, Oedipus could have shared his problems in family therapy. (p. 241)

Within this irony is the point that romantic positivism, with its assortment of practitioners, preachers, gurus, therapists and writers, depicts a kind of defensive knowingness and a denial of the importance of disappointment. Whereas in Barthes the ego can only be fragmented and reparative love is impossible, in what Craib and De Botton describe, it becomes all too easy and effortless. Here we have the extreme of a positive appropriation of psychoanalysis, in fact a distortion of it, in which we can be given a step-by-step guide to virtually any area of our intimate lives, an emotional quick fix, and be led to believe that the semi-independent it-ness of our minds (Bollas) can be overcome. This id quality is what Craib accuses Giddens of neglecting in his picture of the 'pure relationship'. Indeed, for Chasseguet-Smirgel (1985), the genital position requires instinctual maturity, that is, an acceptance of anality, messiness, ambivalence, rather than a courtly love which is beyond the vicissitudes of the flesh, the mortal body or the shadows of the instincts.

So far then, the extreme point of a negative or a positive appropriation of psychoanalysis leads us to the end point of narcissism. In the former case, the lover is a thinly disguised version of Narcissus (the ego is not recognised), while in the latter we find a narcissistic denial of our instincts, emotions and disappointments (the id is not recognised).

Interestingly, Sartre's work on love is also in danger of promising a management of emotion, despite his rich evocation of disordered states in love. This is because Sartre only recognises a monolithic, rationalist ego which is denied an infantile self. His concept of authenticity or authentic love is one which does not even recognise an unconscious area of the mind. Instead, Sartre's analysis of love is predominantly concerned with our fear of freedom (separation anxiety) which, he argues, propels us to live a life of bad faith.

Sartre's world is in some ways a phenomenological description of Klein's paranoid–schizoid position, one which can be real enough, but which can be resolved, even if not once and for all. If in Sartre's world 'hell is others' then, like Narcissus, we are condemned to hate that which is essentially relational in us and thus that which is beyond our control. Our search for liberty is then within a position of enslavement and love does indeed become a metaphysical impossibility.

Sartre's phenomenology of being in love paints a paranoid–schizoid inner world in which separation anxiety is intolerable. This implies that solitude is experienced as a nightmare, which as Quinodoz (1993) points out renders life itself nightmarish. This 'fear of freedom' may lead to what Sartre depicts, an infantile dependence characterised by the paranoid–schizoid phenomenon of clinging to and fleeing from the object. Security will then be looked for in static relationships in which movement is impossible because the anxiety is too strong. Hence Hamilton says that – 'Echo and Narcissus fit together perfectly; neither is able to initiate or sustain dialogue' (V. Hamilton, 1982, p. 120).

In Echo we find a masochistic fidelity, unmitigated anxiety and melancholia, whereas in Narcissus we can see an indifference to anxiety and an autistic withdrawal into his own internal world. Mollon (1993) in 'The Fragile Self' points out that in the myth of Narcissus, his origins are preceded by the pronouncement that he should not know himself, that he should remain in ignorance of who he is and where he comes from. This can be likened to him being put into a permanent sleep of bad faith. He becomes trapped in an incapacity to recognise himself and others. Violence, envy, sadism and masochism pervade this story:

> Narcissus could be understood as gazing at, and trying to grasp, his own deeper self. His recognition that it is his self that he is trying to reach, and that it is unreachable – he can never be united with himself – leads to despair and the whole episode ends in death. (Mollon, 1993, p. 34)

In psychoanalytic terms, what Sartre partly describes is the way in which we use love and the beloved as (ego) ideals which we hope will deliver us to ourselves. Our primary aim here is not a love based on concern for the other and reparation, but ultimately love as a self-defence and the expression of a narcissistic need.

Indeed, we could argue that Sartre describes a situation in which we try to use love as an almost 'autistic mental object'. According to Tustin: 'The function of the autistic object is to obviate completely any awareness of the "not-me" because it is felt to be unbearably threatening. It is to close the gap' (quoted in V. Hamilton, 1982, p. 161).

In 'The Fate of the Transitional Object' Hamilton makes the point that when transitional objects become autistic and are used as patches, they lose their playful and transcontextual qualities. When the transitional object is merely a comforter it lacks qualities of play, experimentation and is a simple substitute for mother functions. If we have a defective sense of intactness we can, therefore, fixate on external objects or addictions and love can become one such addiction. If love is being used in this way, as a mental object to which we cling, then the only thing which is really real is the 'gap', the absence, the unthinkable anxiety caused by separation. Hence Barthes':

> The other is in a condition of perpetual departure, of journeying; the other is, by vocation, migrant, fugitive; I – I who love, by converse vocation, am sedentary, motionless, at hand, in expectation, nailed to the spot, *in suspense* – like a package in some forgotten corner of a railway station. Amorous absence functions in a single direction, expressed by the one who stays, never by the one who leaves: an always present *I* is constituted only by confrontation with an always absent you. (Barthes, 1978, p. 13)

However, as Hamilton points out, transitional phenomena exist in a third area of experience, a resting place between inner and outer, involving, therefore, the toleration of paradox (as in jokes, art and play). If we fear these transitional areas and need to fix things in their 'proper' place (like Anny in *Nausea*) then life is lived compulsively, joylessly, in order to fill the gap. Hamilton cites the example of her patient, Jean, who loved mathematics, hated anthropology and found dreaming too disruptive. She avoided non-purposive behaviour because she felt like there were no boundaries in space and to let go of 'adhesive facts' she could cling to thus threatened her with an infinite fall. She could not, therefore, enjoy nonsense, formless spaces, dreams or her own awakening sexuality. In Sartrean terms, we could say that she was trying to assume the status of an object and robbing herself of her own freedom, and in Barthesian terms, she was incapable of enjoying 'dialectical bliss' or desire (Lacan).

Connections can be made between Sartre's concept of authenticity and Klein's depressive position, to the extent that both involve a recognition of the other's subjectivity, however elusive it may be. What Sartre sees as an a priori impossibility in love can, therefore, be re-interpreted as a love characteristic of pre-depressive states (see Klein) which expresses itself in a lack at the heart of desire and the inability to recognise the other: 'Whereas dependency implies non-specificity, transience, immaturity and helplessness, object relations are enduring, extremely discriminating and bridge gaps in time and space' (V. Hamilton, 1982, p. 5).

Sartre's depiction of love as a 'fundamental mode of being-for-others' assumes that lovers are unthinking and incapable of coming together as two 'beings-for-themselves', who can, in object relations terms, enjoy some third area of transitional space. However, Sartre does describe how vexed and painful relationships can be and these reflections on his position are not meant to be a dismissal of what he describes.

Sartre provides us with a philosophical explanation of why we both need love, yet at the same time are incapable of it, but he does not explore the intrapsychic dynamics of his lover's needs. Indeed this would be a limitation on the freedom of consciousness which Sartre's philosophy does not want to acknowledge. This is where Sartre and Lacan differ, because in Sartre we find a monolithic ego, a fully conscious Cartesian subject who is denied a psychoanalytic infantile self. There are thematic continuities here between Sartre's position and Giddens'. The argument that Craib makes against what he sees as the 'implicit management of the emotions' in Giddens' *The Transformation of Intimacy* (1992) is also relevant to Sartre's work. Craib (1994) tempers Giddens' optimistic analysis of the 'pure' relationship with his observations that the omnipotent self-constructing subject, capable of rationalising all messy emotions, 'negotiating rolling contracts' and 'effort bargaining', employs an illusion of power. In Klein's terms it is worth remembering that the paranoid–schizoid position is exactly that, a position, and not a stage that we come through, never to return again. Furthermore, as Craib points out:

> Emotional satisfaction involves the satisfaction of rows, attacks, hurting and being hurt; this is part and parcel of intimacy. I want to be clear: I am not saying that emotional satisfaction is not an important part of any relationship that involves intimacy; I am saying that it is fragile, by its nature unstable and contradictory, and it can involve negative, destructive dimensions that also might be essential to the health of a relationship. (Craib, 1994, p. 124)

Giddens' work, therefore, starts to look like it is endorsing a management of the emotions in which the attempt is made to make emotions safe, thus denying the fact that they are often terrifying. In an age in which we are experiencing fragmentation, Craib sees the establishment of a 'sociology of the emotions' as significant (p. 87). With the endless chat shows, soap operas and agony aunts, we are, Craib points out, being encouraged to 'speak' our emotions, but social inferiority is still attached to deeply feeling the ambivalences and potential 'messiness' of them:

> The ideas and experiences described by Giddens are, I am sure familiar to many people; we feel as though we should be constantly

reconstructing our selves, examining and justifying our relationships in a search for intimacy and commitment. What I want to argue is that these are illusory goals set by late modernity, carrying on the myth of self control and of the all-powerful self that can control itself. (Craib, 1994, p. 117)

Moi (1990) explains the management of irrational passions in Sartre's work with reference to gender. She points out that Sartre phallocentrically equates consciousness with maleness, and analyses the influence of Sartre's account of holes and slime on De Beauvoir's work. Anything which cannot be controlled, she says, becomes negative and repulsive (remember Narcissus):

> For Sartre, the viscous represents precisely what holds back transcendental consciousness, that which makes our ideas sticky and unclear; it is, he argues, a force which sucks us back into the past out of which we were struggling to protect ourselves. Sartre's ontology thus explicitly 'sexualises' the world. For him the in-itself is feminine and the for-itself is masculine. (Moi, 1990, p. 94)

Benjamin in *The Bonds of Love* (1988) similarly argues, as already pointed out, that Western rationality is a masculine rationality which entails a psychic repudiation of femininity (see the chapter entitled 'Gender and Domination'), of that which is seen to be irrational, undifferentiated and regressive. This leads to an unconscious horror at the sight of dependency because of the premium that is placed on separation and autonomy.

Sartre's horror at the thought of one's individual autonomy being eroded, rendering love relations almost 'unethical', has, therefore, to be considered cautiously. What Sartre does provide is a phenomenologically dense description of disordered states in love, which in turn influenced both Lacan and Barthes, thus explaining to some extent why love becomes for these two subsequent theorists a metaphysical impossibility.

6.7   Social theory, philosophy, psychoanalysis: on the sense of loneliness

The existentialist flavour of psychoanalysis can be found in the psychoanalytic emphasis on the importance of us being able to withstand separateness and self-definition/awareness, but both existentialism and psychoanalysis describe the sometimes intractable difficulties that we encounter when trying to be alone. In both theories, it is the ability to withstand solitude that becomes one of the defining features of 'authentic' or 'depressive' love. In 'On a Sense of Loneliness' (1963), Klein says that loneliness, if it is actually experienced, becomes a stimulus towards object relations, a solitude that replenishes, rather than destroys:

> Solitude can become lifegiving when the distrust and anxiety aroused by the inescapable transience of our existence and that of those dear to us can be overcome in favour of bonds of trust, when love becomes stronger than hate. It is this particular awareness of knowledge of our limits that enables us to truly benefit from them. (Quinodoz, 1993, p. 192)

However, what we often long for when we are lonely is, Klein suggests 'the result of a ubiquitous yearning for an unattainable perfect internal state' (1963, p. 300). This perfect internal state is one which narratives of love often promise – a penetrating, sensuous and completing sense of recognition and fulfilment. 'However gratifying it is in later life to express thoughts and feelings to a congenial person, there remains an unsatisfied longing for an understanding without words – ultimately for the earliest relation with the mother' (Klein, p. 301).

What existentialist and psychoanalytic accounts of love stress is the need for some measure of freedom between the ego and its objects, allowing oneself and the object to 'come and go' (see Quinodoz, p. 77). This 'letting go' is not done dismissively, with implicit 'hate', but with an appreciation of transience and an attitude of trust. Of course, these are ideal ways of relating and it is not always possible to meet what, at times, might seem like exacting psychoanalytic standards. However, they are there for us to reflect on, even when our behaviour does not evidence this trust of ourselves, our objects or the benevolence of the world.

It is the fact that we are not always easily reconciled to the world that may become the focus of our mourning as we recognise that our mind might be in conflict or subject to a sense of deadness. Or, we might recognise that we have been complicit in an unfulfilling life, but the implication is that it is mourning these psychic realities that will revitalise what we see and feel. Psychoanalysis does not idealise life or the mind. Instead psychoanalysis points to life's inherent disappointments and difficulties, while still encouraging a hopeful relation to it: 'Whether to see life as it is, will give us much consolation, I know not; but the consolation which is drawn from truth, if thy there be, is solid and durable; that which may be derived from error must be, like its original fallacious and fugitive' (Bion, 1970, p. 7; quoting from Dr Johnson's letter to Bennet Langton).

It is what Craib (1994) refers to as 'the importance of disappointment' which will enable us to adjust our expectations in life so that our ego, in Freudian (1930) terms, is 'modest'. However, it may be the case that accepting the premise that a perfect internal state does not exist will lead to a 'sense of loneliness', especially if we thought that love would deliver some ultimate panacea:

> Being in love with another person can be a wonderful state; it opens up depths of feeling and sensitivity to ourselves, to the person we love and sometimes to others, that we rarely reach in our everyday lives. It is easy to see why some people become addicted to it; the tragic, sad – perhaps at times unbearably sad – aspect of being in love is that it changes. We can imagine that with this person we have found our heart's desire, the understanding and the ability to understand that we have always wanted. In this sense, perhaps, it is a period of madness. (Craib, 1994, p. 123)

Although existentialism, sociology and psychoanalysis radically differ in some important respects, this does not mean, as we can see, that they should necessarily be split. Both psychoanalysis and existentialism, for example, argue for the importance of disappointment (Craib, 1994),[6] which is not to be confused with a cynical defeatism such as Hoggett discusses in 'The Culture of Uncertainty' (1992). Sartre's concept of 'responsibility' can be understood in the context of Klein's concept of 'reparation' since the former is necessary for the latter. A further connection can be made between Sartre's phenomenology of being in love and psychoanalytic insights into object relations. Both to some extent maintain that we need to learn to be alone in the presence of someone (Winnicott), to tame our solitude (Quinodoz) and to draw strength from our sense of loneliness (Klein). These similarities do not, of course, compensate for, or deny, the very real differences between psychoanalysis and existentialism.

In *The Taming of Solitude: Separation Anxiety in Psychoanalysis*, Quinodoz (1993) argues that the working through of separation anxiety is at the heart of the psychoanalytic process and of the transition from narcissism to object relations. We can, therefore, conclude that the loneliness that Barthes, Lacan, Sartre and Klein speak of has to be borne and tamed. If we hope that love will relieve us of this struggle then perhaps this is not Freud's 'mature love', Klein's reparative love, Sartre's 'authentic' love nor indeed Lacan's 'sublime' love.

6.8 Conclusion

In Klein's work, love is not reified, it is not a 'property' of the beloved and it will not definitively cast out solitude, pain or ambiguity. An emotionally 'mature love' will not blind us, it is in a sense 'sober' rather than 'intoxicating'. For Barthes, Lacan, Sartre and Klein popular notions of love as oneness, salvation and 'deliverance from evil' (i.e. from hate) are flawed, though they argue this for different reasons. Nevertheless, here we find some common agreement between these different perspectives on love. In a psychoanalytic context the depiction of love that we find in, for example, Greene's *The End of The Affair* is not 'mature', but rather a rich evocation of a painful state of mind, much like that we find in Barthes, Sartre and De Beauvoir.

By using Kleinian psychoanalysis, we can conclude that our adult psychosexual love will always be threatened by the 'otherness' of our own and of our partner's mind. Sartre's nightmarish world does exist, as does Barthes' world of 'adhesives and gummy coalescences' (p. 11) and from Freud through to Klein we can see that 'mature' and reparative love is therefore linked to psychic work. The emphasis on psychic work does, however, sometimes seem like a very rationalist enterprise and one hardly conducive to romance. It is therefore important to remember some of the oceanic, non-verbal,[7] pleasures that romance brings and it might not always be wise to subject these pleasures to 'hard work'. In using psychoanalysis to understand the intrapsychic and interpersonal nature of love, it is worth reminding ourselves of Winnicott's (1969) plea to respect that some areas of experience and of the psyche are incommunicado. To try to rationalise all of experience, as discussed by Phillips (1995), can become a betrayal of psychoanalysis and ultimately of our love.

7

Reflexive Love
Sociological and Psychoanalytic Insights

7.1 Introduction

In the previous chapter a Kleinian way of seeing love was brought into discursive dialogue with views of romantic love as impossible (which assume an associative view of the mind and narcissistic ego only). Although Kleinian psychoanalysis offers us a view of love as possible, it does not offer us the science of loving lampooned by De Botton (see the previous chapter). Kleinian psychoanalysis, it has been argued, holds a dialectical view of the mind/ego and can acknowledge the possibility and impossibility of love. However, a Kleinian way of seeing love does not acknowledge the dialectical relationship between self and culture, agency and structure, and subjectivity and discursive positions.

This chapter will therefore bring Kleinian psychoanalysis into discursive dialogue with a view of love as possible (Giddens' confluent love and pure relationship), but which prioritises an analysis of love as a socio-cultural phenomenon. Object relations theory will be used to critically question the model of mind/ego assumed by this view of love, but the socio-cultural way of studying love will be used to critically question the ahistorical view of object relations assumed by Kleinian psychoanalysis. This chapter will explore how Kleinian psychoanalysis and a contemporary sociological discourse of intimacy can be brought into discursive dialogue in order to study love as a psychosocial phenomenon. The psychosocial questions that this chapter raises will be discussed further in Chapters 8, 9 and 10 when the explanatory strength of studying love as a psychosocial phenomenon will be demonstrated.

As already stated, this psychosocial project is to bring object relations psychoanalysis into debate and dialogue with social and cultural theory. The pure relationship is a significant and contemporary sociological discourse of intimacy and it is a good example of recent work in the sociology of emotion/intimacy against which we can clarify what distinguishes a specifically psychoanalytic sociology of emotion/intimacy. Moreover, the concept of the pure relationship is already consistent (to some extent) with the broad aims of a psychoanalytic sociology of emotion/intimacy. That is, unlike the concept of the depressive position, the discourse of the pure relationship is a psychosocial concept, which posits a dialectical relationship between social and psychic or emotional change.

The discourse of romantic love does not describe ideal-typical conditions for intimacy from either a sociological or psychoanalytic perspective. The discourses of the pure relationship and depressive love both deconstruct the 'ideology' of romantic love, though *without* presenting view of love/intimacy as impossible and, in fact, both of these discourses can be respectively used to provide us with insights into the socio-historical/psychic meanings of romantic love.

This chapter will discuss Giddens' ideas of the pure relationship, and confluent love will be discussed and their existentialist and psychoanalytic traces will be highlighted. It will then point to the important differences between a sociological approach to intimacy and a psychoanalytic one. It will be argued that, from an object relations point of view Giddens deconstructs romance, while still retaining an idealised view of the nature of love/relating. While still providing us with a view of love as possible, object relations psychoanalysis is better able to rethink the relationship between knowledge and emotion (the expressed aim of the sociology of emotion) and acknowledge the objections to humanist concepts of love.

7.2   The existentialist and psychoanalytic ancestry of the pure relationship

Interestingly, for a sociology text, what we find in Giddens' work on intimacy is a curious mixture of social theory, existentialism and psychoanalysis, seemingly substantiating Denzin's (1989a) claim that there has been a reconfiguration in the social sciences as one response to the conditions of late modernity.

The emergence of a discourse of the 'pure' relationship demonstrates the relevance of psychoanalytic and existentialist insights into the felt conditions of late modernity. That is, to some extent, the pure relationship resembles the discourse of depressive love via its emphasis on an ethics of relating 'confluent love' and self-reflexivity. The pure relationship is dependent upon one's capacities for 'emotional labour' and 'emotional intelligence' (Hochschild, 1983; Goleman, 1996), which are psychoanalytic concerns. The existentialist flavour of Giddens' argument can be seen in his insistence that processes of de-traditionalisation (which give rise to the pure relationship) expose people to the existential parameters of life (Beck and Beck-Gernsheim's, 1995, 'shivers of freedom') and to the responsibility of choice rather than habit, addiction, custom and so on. In Giddens' depiction of the pure relationship we can therefore see a turn towards feelings/narrative and a recognition of contingency. Giddens' argument that the pure relationship is emerging supports Richards' hypothesis that a process of emotionalisation is occurring that has a specifically 'therapeutic' quality to it. There are three key core elements to this therapeutic sensibility, expressivity, knowledge and compassion, and we can see all of these concerns reflected in Giddens' ideal typology of intimacy (see Richards and Brown, 2002, for a critical discussion of the 'Therapeutic Culture Hypothesis').

The concepts of the depressive position and the discourse of the pure relationship both shift the focus of attention on to the relationship, rather than reified emotion (romantic love) and both rest on an understanding of love in which the relationship between knowledge and emotion has been rethought. The concept of the depressive position and the discourse of the pure relationship both portray love as a particular form of intersubjectivity[1] or recognition (see C. Andard and S. Grosz, 2000). This implies a more active searching for and reaching out to underlying mentalities/affective states (one's own and the other person's) than the reference to love as a reified *emotion* could perhaps suggest. The reworked definitions of love that we find in sociology and psychoanalysis do not correspond to a cathartic release of emotion, precisely because of the self-knowledge/ethics of relating which both imply.

Giddens' work does represent the attempt to reclaim emotion as a source of knowledge about social life, which he also ties to processes of reasoning, thus challenging the emotion/reason split inherent in sociology. However, he does not deconstruct the monadic individual of Western philosophy or analyse the limits to self-reflexive reasoning, despite referencing psychoanalysis. Nevertheless, his work does provide us with the opportunity to critically question the ahistorical discussion of love that we find in object relations psychoanalysis.

7.3 Love in the depressive position: some socio-cultural questions

Is the quality of care and concern that the depressive position describes more likely to be found among women, as Giddens' thesis suggests?

Where is the erotic element of 'love in the depressive position', where is its passion? Is it asexual? Is it more cerebral and emotional than visceral and embodied? Should psychoanalysis pay more attention to the bureaucratic, institutionalised worlds that people live in? Can 'therapeutic' individuals animate their internal world without the help of a more collectively embraced life-politics? How does one's social setting (age, gendered place and class position etc.) close down psychic space and potentially deaden it? Can we colonise the future with hopes of personal transformation alone? Does 'love in the depressive position' suggest that our task is an exclusively defined intrapersonal one?

These questions will be considered further in Chapters 9 and 10 when everyday narratives of love are analysed psychosocially. For now, what it is important to state is that Kleinian psychoanalysis is not considered to be a neutral discourse unencumbered by time, place or historicised positionings (gender, class and ethnicity etc.). Giddens' thesis, for example, provides an interesting platform from which to ask whether 'love in the depressive position' is an ahistorical internal phenomenon or a mode of relating contingent upon certain socio-historical conditions. Whereas Klein provides an ahistorical ontological description of the human condition and our fraught relationships, Giddens describes the historical conditions which, we could argue, are most conducive to her account of reparative relating. Neither Freud nor Klein, for example, questioned the extent to which their psychoanalytic aims were constrained or facilitated by the macro cultures in which people lived.

We could, however, hypothesise that the delineation of depressive love may be a more fitting conceptualisation of love for a society which encourages a reflexive relation to the self. That is, 'depressive love' is predicated on self-awareness and on the ability to cope with ambivalence, that is, to feel affirmation and negation simultaneously. This ability to cope with changing feeling states may be particularly important in a society described as 'pregnant with its contrary' and in which the modern voice 'resonates with self-discovery, self-mockery, with self-delusion and self-doubt' (Berman, 1983, p. 23).

However, these could be thought of as the very conditions in which reparative relating is least likely to emerge and instead hypothesise that view of intimacy as impossible will be the one we are most likely to encounter. For example, many writers welcome these 'transformations of intimacy' and contestations of identity, but contemporary Western society is also described as one of 'identity crises' (Frosh, 1991) producing a 'culture of narcissism' (Lasch, 1984). However, even if we could do a large-scale study of changing attitudes about love and intimacy in contemporary Britain, how could we identify whether contemporary cultural conditions are conducive to pure, narcissistic or reparative relating? This is where the deployment of a clinical concept in a non-clinical setting becomes interesting, because socio-political changes and manifestly 'ethical' modes of relating cannot necessarily be equated with the concept of an internal depressive position. These methodological issues will be discussed further in the following chapter.

7.4   The pure relationship: psychoanalytic reflections

As an ideal-typical relationship the pure relationship fails to acknowledge the fundamentally antagonistic nature of our relations to others (Klein's death instinct) and to our own existential condition (Sartre's – 1943 – fear of freedom; Freud's – 1930 – sources of suffering). Giddens does, of course, recognise resistances to the reflexive project of self, but he, nevertheless, believes that these can be overcome. Hence, in Giddens' pure relationship, we do not see enough of jealousy, envy or hate and despite his expressed aim to reinject social theory with emotion, feelings are once again finally subordinated to reason.

Unusually, for a sociological text, Giddens does try to address the subjective experience of love to the extent that confluent love is described as an opening up to someone in which we disclose our emotions and expect the other to do the same. The subjective experience of love is here based on knowledge and recognition, but unfortunately Giddens does not focus on what this feels like or on what kinds of feelings this self-disclosure might provoke, beyond saying that we should risk being vulnerable. Craib (1994) suggests that only emotions which are well-managed are expressible and he argues that the pure relationship is a model for the false self of late modernity.

It is also important, of course, to draw attention to the fact that the disclosure of what we feel or think is potentially very risky and possibly hindered by unconscious fears about loss, rejection, madness and so on. Indeed, for some people, the interest in their psyche, relationship, feelings may be threatening and, for other reasons, simply unwelcome. Moreover, a 'culture of expression' may be one that erodes an inner reserve and capacity to sublimate (see Wetherill, 1997) which alerts us to the possibility that the erosion of boundaries can lead to increased levels of anxiety. That is, a culture which is more explicit, open, de-repressed could be one which stimulates perverse elements of sexual excitement. Wetherill is particularly interested in the excessive sexualisation of culture, but his invocation of Winnicott's (1963) plea (already referred to in

Chapter 6) to respect a part of the patient that is 'incommunicado' is equally relevant to discussions of emotionalisation and the therapeutic sensibility (see Richards and Brown, 2002). The therapeutic sensibility (the pure relationship, reparative impulses), we might hypothesise, would respect[2] the fine balance between interaffective attunement (Stern, 1985) and the need for privacy. However, although Giddens is passionate about a concern for the other, his work cannot address the problem of unconscious communication which is not easily open to negotiation. The individual in Giddens' account is communicative, but very bounded and monadic. This monadic view of the subject contrasts with the relational view of the self (intrapsychically and interpersonally) found in object relations psychoanalysis (outlined in Chapter 6).

For example, Giddens refers to what he sees of value in the psychoanalytic setting: 'it provides a setting, and a rich fund of theoretical and conceptual resources, for the creation of a reflexively ordered narrative of self' (p. 31). However, his emphasis on autonomous self-development ignores the fact that the mind is developed in the context of 'live company' (Alvarez, 1992) with another, as are relationships. He cannot therefore recognise the 'interpenetration of identities' (Craib, 1998, p. 174) and the transitional spaces which relationships offer (me and not-me experiences). For example, that Freud's 'psychoanalysis is in essence a cure through love', does not only refer to the ritualised setting for self-narration, but also to the dynamic transference relationship, which is in fact the real setting in which the reflexive project of self takes place.

Craib points out that in current sociological thinking intersubjectivity is seen as a 'matter of shared ideas or shared language' (p. 172), whereas object relations theory argues that what predates and underlines this cognitive world is an emotional one. What we find between people then, is an unconscious communication, which Craib describes as the 'background noise to our encounters, a barely noticed feeling of comfort or discomfort' (p. 173).

Often, it is these background noises that determine the quality of the intimacy that we share with a partner and it is this non-verbal communication that psychoanalytic therapists try to apprehend and become attuned to. Stern's work is important when thinking about the adult's non-verbal life, because his description of the non-verbal communication between infants and adults is very evocative and reminiscent of the non-verbal communications that adults share, despite their entry into language. Infants are in interaction with adults from birth in their experience of what Stern calls 'vitality' affects. Infants predominantly experience other minds via 'a multitude of parental acts ... how the mother picks up the baby, folds the diapers, grooms her hair, or the baby's hair, reaches for a bottle, unbuttons her blouse. The infant is immersed in these feelings of vitality' (p. 54).

And the infant is according to Stern a keen observer of these qualities of feeling in action and emotion: 'Like dance for the adult, the social world experienced by the infant is primarily one of vitality affects before it is a world of formal acts' (p. 57). Stern argues that experiences in the domain of emergent (0–2 months old), core (2–7 months old), intersubjective (7–9 months old) and affective attunement (9–15 months old) continue irrespective of our entry into language, even though they are only embraced partially.

Giddens' work cannot address the way in which love and intimacy is made up of these experiences, which although powerfully communicative, are difficult to negotiate or renegotiate. We may not even be able to articulate what it is that makes us uneasy and even doubt the reality of certain experiences, precisely because they are born from wordless communications. Many qualities of feeling, according to Stern, do not fit into our existing 'lexicon or taxonomy of affects' and he judges our language to be too impoverished for these non-verbal experiences' (p. 54). These elusive qualities are therefore best captured by 'dynamic, kinetic terms, such as surging, fading away, explosive, fleeting, crescendo ...'(ibid.). 'For example, a 'rush' of anger or of joy, a perceived flooding of light, an accelerating sequence of thoughts, an unmeasurable wave of feeling evoked by music, and a shot of narcotics can all feel like rushes' (p. 55).

Hence our *social* scripts of emotion often try to capture the very vitality affects which give form to discrete emotions: a *melting* love, an *explosive* jealousy, a *fading* happiness and so on. This is where language may constitute the limit of our world, leaving some interviewees declaring ' I don't know, there aren't any answers' (Zadie – Chapter 10), as they encircle their experience of 'love' with different words which might leave some basic problems or pleasures untouched. Thus certain songs, novels and films become indispensable ways in which people are helped by artists, dramatists and so on to formulate their own private troubles and experiences.[3] It is music, for example, that enables 'Rachel' to tell her lover how she feels about him via its form and content. And it is music, of course, that can capture 'dynamic, kinetic terms, such as surging, fading away, explosive, fleeting, crescendo ...'. What we can see is that a psychoanalytic understanding of intimacy decentres the primacy of words, which Giddens' work, by contrast, cannot do.[4]

What Stern refers to as affect attunement behaviours, for example, occur outside of awareness and do not necessarily lead towards a cognitive empathic knowledge or response: they are for *communion* rather than *communication*. Stern argues that the subjective experiences that infants and adults share must be of a kind that do not require translation into language. What we can add to this is that the subjective experiences that lovers share are often not amenable to language or consciousness. Affect attunement, according to Stern, represents one of the ways in which we 'can get inside of other people's subjective experience and let them know we have arrived there, without using words' (p. 138).

Craib's 'barely noticed feeling of comfort or discomfort' may arise precisely because someone has arrived in our internal space, 'without using words', and a democratic bill of rights may not be able to address this wordless affective language. The idea that affects, predates and underlines our oral, conscious communication therefore problematises a sociology of emotion, which can only concern itself with rational decision making (albeit impassioned by a consideration of equal rights) or with the social scripts of emotion which our society makes available to us. What sociology cannot do is to conceive of an internal space in dialectical relation with the public language or discourse of emotion.

Moreover sociological accounts of emotion only speak to the Oedipalised adult, to the neglect of the pre-linguistic infant in the child *and* in the adult. Thus, in combining insights from infancy research and psychoanalytic theories of infantile states with sociological approaches to emotion, our adult and our infantile selves can be reunited.

A psychoanalytic sociology of romantic love, for example, could focus on the way in which one's ideas about love and the self are socially constructed (Watt, 1957; Gusdorf, 1980; Jackson, 1993). It could simultaneously employ psychoanalytic paradigms in order to explore romantic love as an expression of our emotional or psychical needs (Clulow, 1993; Kernberg, 1995) rooted in our infantile experience.

So, whereas a social-constructionist reading of romantic love declares that it is not a biological or psychological fact, but a script which survives because of its capacities as a story for mutation, a psychoanalytic sociology of romantic love argues that it is a narrative that survives precisely because it speaks to the biological fact that we are object seeking from birth, a state of which the romantic narrative could be seen to be a psychological elaboration.

The romantic narrative can be read as promising lovers a refinding of the object (Freud, 1905) and a refinding of the sensory dimension in which our first object relations took place. A psychoanalytic sociology of romantic love could, for example, take Stern's description of affect attunement behaviours and correlate them with the discourse of romantic love (reading each others' minds, chemistry, wordless understanding) in order to understand the unconscious resonances of the narrative rooted in both biological and psychological facts. There are of course many ways in which to operationalise a psychosocial study of emotion. The point is that a psychoanalytic sociology of emotion argues for a complex interaction between our biological inheritance, its psychological elaboration and the social scripts of emotion which await us.

7.5   Conclusion

Giddens' work leaves us with the monadic individual of Western philosophy (the subject/object split) despite his expressed aim to challenge the dualistic thinking found in traditional sociology. Despite his preference for object relations psychoanalysis to post-structuralist emphases on language, Giddens' use of psychoanalysis, more firmly than Freud's, subordinates the id (emotion) to the ego (cognition). Love in the depressive position similarly represents Western concerns with rationality (the ego), individualisation (separation) and autonomy (self-possession). However, it is the dialectical nature of psychoanalysis (as outlined in Chapters 5 and 6) that subverts a one-sided concentration on rationality (the id), individualisation (the relational self) and autonomy (penetrative unconscious communication).

In object relations psychoanalysis, affective life is tied to mind, body, transitional phenomena, unconscious communication and discourse and this problematises love's status as a natural emotion waiting unproblematically to occur. Although it has been argued that an object relations approach to love can provide us with a more subtle understanding of what constitutes intimacy than Giddens' sociological account, his work is nevertheless interesting and invaluable. Giddens' work enables us to ground an object relations view of love in contemporary debates about culture, social change and new social formations. It offers a psychosocial approach to understanding love and intimacy, which Freud's or Klein's work alone cannot do.

This chapter has been shorter than previous chapters, because it is only intended to be illustrative of how we can bring the insights gained from the previous chapters into discursive dialogue (also demonstrated in these previous chapters). Moreover, in Chapters 9 and 10 insights from both psychoanalysis and sociology will be combined in order to understand the way in which people live at different levels of subjectivity that are not easily compartmentalised into two separate spheres of psyche and social.

Part III
Methods and Findings

8
A Psychosocial Approach to Narrative Studies and Reflexive Research

8.1 Introduction

I introduced Chapter 1 of this dissertation with a series of questions asking what romantic love means to us, what it promises and how we cathect it as an ideal. In order to answer some of the questions that were raised in the Introduction to Chapter 1, 'ways of seeing' romantic love from a sociological, feminist, existentialist,[1] Lacanian, cultural studies (post-structuralist), Freudian and object relations viewpoint were outlined. The guiding research question was whether these ways of seeing love[2] led to a view of love as possible or impossible. It was argued that object relations psychoanalysis could contain both possible and impossible views of (a reconceptualised) love in contrast to the other concepts of love that were reviewed, which tended towards a one-sided concentration on love as either quite straightforwardly possible or as tormentingly impossible.[3] However, the importance of a psychosocial way of seeing love was argued for, rather than a purely psychoanalytic or exclusively sociological explanation of love and its vicissitudes.

Although the theories that have been looked at might be deduced from personal experience and everyday observations of how people behave, think and feel when they are in love, they are not 'personal accounts' in any direct way (unmediated by theory).

By turning to everyday accounts of ideas about, and experiences of, love, romance, marriage, children, sex and so on we will be able to see if there is any 'fit' between the statements that can be deduced from Chapters 3 to 7 and everyday accounts of intimacy. However, these are illustrative interviews only[4] and have been carried out in order to highlight the ways in which we might be able to subject our theoretical interests and formulations to further scrutiny while at the same time demonstrating a psychosocial approach to both theory and method. In Chapter 2, it was explained that the broad aim of psychosocial studies is to avoid studying the individual in isolation from his/her society and vice versa and this will be the starting point from which the interview material that has been collected will be interpreted. A more specific inquiry will be focused on how love is conceptualised and whether it is believed to be possible.

Chapter 8 will provide a discussion of psychosocial approaches to biographical methods and Chapter 9 will detail the particular method used in this work. Chapter 10 will then discuss extracts from qualitative interviews about love undertaken with ten people of varying ages. This chapter will use extracts from the interviews in order to provide examples of methodological success, failure and differences in interpretive strategies (psychological, sociological and so on).

This chapter will first briefly discuss the place of biographical studies in sociology. It will introduce the difference between objective and interpretive approaches to biographical methods and point to the variety of methods that can qualify as interpretive. The increasing interest in the social sciences in narrative studies will be highlighted and its relevance to the psychosocial studies project explained. This chapter will briefly look at discursive or social-constructionist approaches to narrative studies and compare this to psychoanalytic and sociological approaches to narrative. What Denzin (1989a) refers to as the new life history approach (which partakes of both objective and interpretive methods) will be introduced and the version of psychosocial studies (and approaches to narrative) presented in this work will be placed within this tradition.[5] This chapter will conclude by detailing the similar methodological concerns which narrative studies and psychoanalytic observation methods share and it will emphasise the way in which this chapter has served to highlight the working assumptions which will inform the analysis of the interview material presented in Chapters 10 and 11.

8.2 Biographical studies in sociology

Denzin (1989a) explains that sociological biographical studies emerged in the 1920's,[6] but he points out that it has only recently begun to enjoy a rebirth in the 'human sciences'. Sociologists have, of course, always recognised the importance of studying micro constructions of reality and, in both psychoanalysis and sociology, we can see a shared interest in studying the single case. However, it was only in 1978 that a Biography and Sociology group was formed in the International Sociological Association and interestingly, this coincides with the years which marked the 'coming of age' for a sociology of emotion (see Chapter 2). What we can see in the above two formations is an emerging or increasing interest in psychosocial studies from within sociology itself and an interest in deconstructing the dualisms or working assumptions inherent in sociology.

However there are significant differences between sociological and psychoanalytic/psychosocial philosophies and methods. In sociology, for example, traditionally[7] the researcher's interest has not been in the psyche or in the psyche–society interface,[8] but more in people's individual experience/mediation of the macro (in Giddens' structuration theory, for example). As Denzin says 'lives belong not just to persons, but also to larger social collectivities, including societies, corporations, and, for some, the world system' (p. 29). 'The intent of the biographical project is' in this context 'to uncover the social, economic, cultural, structural and historical forces that shape, distort and otherwise alter problematic lived experience' (Denzin, p. 75).

As stated in Chapter 2, what this psychosocial approach[9] adds to the 'sociological imagination' is a theory of human nature and of the development of mind. This means that 'the intent of the *psychosocial* biographical project is to (also) uncover, or to address, the psychological, emotional, familial and unconscious forces and phantasies that shape, distort and otherwise alter problematic lived experience'.

Unlike a more traditionally conceived sociology, psychosocial studies does not state that if we can place individuals in their socio-historical context, then we will have the most significant facts about their life to hand (see Chapter 2). Rather, the 'forces that shape, distort and alter problematic lived experience' can be derived from our unconscious fantasy life as well as from our social, economic and structural life.

8.3 Narrative studies

Within the biographical method, there are two approaches to studying lives which Denzin (1989a) refers to as the interpretive and objective approaches (p. 49). The latter, Denzin says, work according to a set of criteria which includes 'norms of validity, reliability, truth, falsity, bias, data, hypotheses, theory, case representativeness and generalisability'. For example, sociologists can go to medical records and so on in order to verify their own interpretations and look for the 'real' subject in the text. Interpretive approaches, he explains, 'reject objective norms of evaluation and regard biographical materials from within a literary, fictional framework' (p. 49). The classic or objective approach, Denzin claims, conforms to the 'fallacies of presence' (Derrida, 1967–72) and is logocentric, phallocentric and ultimately masculinist. As Usher (1997) states:

> Social scientists located as they are in the modernist epistemological project, want to give 'reasoned', connected and totalising accounts. But ... the world they investigate and seek to explain is not one that can readily be reflected in their theories and accounts. It is, in other words, not organised naturally into disciplinary compartments. (p. 33)

The central assumption of the objective method (that a life can be unproblematically captured and represented in a text) is now, Denzin argues, open to question. Indeed, he says that the boundaries between the humanities and social sciences have become less clear and 'the golden age of empiricism in the social sciences is, if not over, waning' (Denzin, 1989a, p. 46). Thus, the social sciences are more humanistic or interpretive and social science writing is also, therefore, changing and becoming more essay-like and self-consciously reflective (ibid.).[10]

Denzin, for example, claims that society can now be seen as a text, a drama, a narrative production, a game, a series of speech acts, a carnival and so on. He also refers to a host of new theories from philosophy and literary criticism and cites such people as Derrida, Foucault, Lacan, Sartre, Barthes, Bakhtin, Baudrillard and Benjamin as representative of new streams of thought which have rendered the social sciences truly interdisciplinary.[11]

In Denzin's (1989b) chapter on 'The Biographical Method' (ch. 8) there are numerous examples of biographical material (diaries, letters, public archival records, autobiographies). There are different guidelines on how to gather and interpret biographical material (objective and interpretive methods) and there are different methods of analysing biographical texts. There therefore 'seems to be little consensus in the psychological, sociological, and anthropological literature on the form these guidelines should take' (p. 195).

However, a commonality of approach can perhaps be seen in the increasing interest that is shown in narrative methodologies as a viable alternative to 'objective' knowledge (Day Sclater, 1999, p. 116). Indeed, Denzin (2000) claims that we now 'live in narrative's moment' (p. xi).

Denzin (2000) describes narratives or stories in the following way:

> a story is an account involving the narration of a series of events in a plotted sequence which unfolds in time ... . A story has a beginning, middle and ending. Stories have basic structural features, including narrators, plots, settings, characters, crises and resolutions. (p. xi). The contention is that we are (either by nature or social convention) story tellers who need to impose narrative coherence on our experiences and that we are unable to live in Barthesian 'dialectical bliss' or Sartrean 'vertiginous freedom'.[12] Thus, there are many different types of narratives that theorists identify (illness narratives, romance narratives, coming-out narratives etc.) from which we may or may not diverge when ill, in love or 'coming out'.[13]

Narrative studies use, as Riessman (1993, p. 5) says, the story metaphor to draw attention to the way in which stories are meaning-making systems in contrast to a literal reporting of fact. This is why narrative studies draws a distinction between the 'lived life' and 'told story'. However, in narrative studies, to identify someone's life history as a 'story' is not pejorative (i.e. to associate it with lies). Rather it stresses the fact that we *create* narratives and meaning-making systems rather than literally report on bare facts, and it is for this reason that Denzin says that we have no direct access to experience, only to its 'storied representations' (ibid.).[14] That is, it is the way in which we rehearse or change the stories of our lives, daydream our fantasies into being or indeed dream, that can tell us something about the way in which we have constructed or challenged our self-identities and experiences of the wider social world.

The field of narrative studies is however, as Andrews *et al.* say, a wide one (p. 2) and their edited collection illustrates the wide variety of forms that narratives can take (interviews, films, memoirs) and the many methods available for analysing them.[15] One of its defining features, however, is that it does not suppose a dualism between self and society. Bradbury and Sclater (2000), for example, argue that 'one of the main strengths of narrative work must lie in its capacity to hold together sociological and psychological approaches, without recourse to the "figure/ground" configuration in which they are usually found' (p. 193).

Denzin also argues that the narrative turn forces the social sciences to develop new theories, new methods and new ways of talking about self and 1society (p. xiii) and it is described as addressing itself 'to the habitual dualisms of Western thought' (Bradbury and Sclater, 2000, p. 193). In this respect it can be classified as a methodological approach which is convergent with psychosocial studies more generally.

However, the way in which agency and structure, subjectivity and culture, or the psyche and social intersect is theorised in different ways.[16] Moreover, the ontological position which narrative approaches informed by post-structuralism (Squire, 2000a) assume is different to the ontological position which narrative studies informed by psychoanalysis assume (Hollway and Jefferson, 2000a) and these are different again to the ontological positions assumed by sociological uses of narrative studies (Wengraf, 2001). Whereas discursive approaches to narrative studies can be classified as interpretive, sociological approaches try to combine both objective and interpretive methods, as do psychoanalytic uses of narrative studies. The psychosocial approach presented in this work can be placed in the same tradition as Wengraf's and Hollway and Jefferson's to the extent that it partakes of objective and interpretive approaches in its philosophy of method.

This chapter will now very briefly outline the significant points in all three approaches (discursive or social constructionist, psychoanalytic and sociological) in order to highlight the way in which the psychosocial approach to narrative studies presented in this book shares some of the working assumptions of the above approaches, while also differing in some important respects from some of them.

8.4   Discursive approaches to narrative studies

Discursive approaches to narrative studies are interpretive approaches which represent a critique of positivist methods[17] and they involve critically questioning the epistemological tools with which we investigate the world.[18] This narrative studies approach is influenced by a post-structuralist view of language in which meaning is continually deferred, by the idea that objectivity and truth are categories which are themselves part of a particular discourse, by which we are inevitably 'penetrated' and by postmodern critiques of the grand narratives of Western philosophy.

Thus, from this narrative studies' viewpoint, the stories we tell about who we are, are told in relation to (and through) a set of competing discourses about being women, daughters, lovers and so on and represent our positionings in relation to them. Also, the form in which the story is told has to be placed in the context of a particular textual tradition and understood in terms of a language which is itself constitutive of meaning rather than just a relayer of it.

Derrida's (1972) position is that there is 'no clear window into the inner life of a person, for any window is always filtered through the glaze of language, signs, and the process of signification'. Derrida's position assumes that we are fully penetrated by the social world through language, and Denzin (2000) emphasises the prevalence of this approach in the social sciences by arguing that 'the linguistic and textual basis of knowledge about society is now privileged'.

What this means is that language constitutes the limit of our theoretical and empirical inquiry. That is, there is no access to the 'real' object of study outside of the terms in which we discursively describe and explain it. The ontological position that this discursive approach to narrative studies assumes is therefore relativist, rather than realist.

However, although the study of language is prioritised it is not assumed that it is easy to interpret what is meant when it is used. Since language is unstable, in flux and made up of traces of other signs and symbolic statements, 'there can never be a clear unambiguous statement of anything, including an intention or a meaning' (Denzin, 1989a, p. 14). 'The frontiers of a book (or other document)' Foucault tells us 'are never clear cut, because it is always caught up in a system of references to other books, other texts, other sentences: it is a node within a network' (in Malson, 2000, p. 159). The classic or objective approach to biographical studies would, in Barthes' terms, proceed as if there were no such theatre of speech and festival of meaning.

The subject is elusive from this viewpoint, because although we may try to appropriate the signifier 'I' as we speak, words, like the Lacanian mirror, will misrepresent as much as represent us. Denzin (1989a), for example, asks how we appropriate this pronoun 'I'. He argues that the pronoun 'I' does not contain someone's person-hood, it is an empty signifier (p. 21). For example, when asking Sam (an interviewee in her thirties) about her experiences of romance, we could hypothesise that I mistakenly searched for the 'real' Sam behind the ideological self that I thought she presented. Was I, for example in any danger of wanting Sam to talk to me from a position, or about an aspect of herself, which I assumed she had split-off (penetrated as I am by psychoanalytic discourses)? It could be that I found Sam's absolute refutation and 'ditching' of romance too harsh, too unconvincing or too rationalized, but was it my task to dig out what I might have assumed (quite incorrectly) to be the 'real truth'[19] of her story. For example, some of my questions do address the contradictions in Sam's story, as though I was looking for what Hollway and Jefferson (2000b, p. 137) refer to as a less unitary subject and a less coherent story or position.

However, when we read or listen to an interview for a second time, new meanings and associations to the story emerge and it might be tempting (and potentially infinite) to try and grasp the 'truer' reading as different layers of the narrative unfold. However, from a discourse-analytic viewpoint, whether by reading or listening to an interviewee's narrative, we are advised not to try to nail subjects down and in order to avoid this, discourse-analytic researchers look at the text as a story only. As Malson states 'discourse-analytic research ... takes discourse itself, rather than some putative "reality" assumed to be anterior to the text, as its object of study' (Malson, 2000, p. 152).

What discourse analysis reminds us of is that we cannot just hear the narrator's inner self, because his or her 'I' is in discourse:

> The self and its signifiers thus take on a double existence in the biographical text. First, they point inward to the text itself, where they are arranged within a system of narrative biographical discourse. Second, they point outward to this life that has been led by this writer or this subject. (p. 21)

The produced text, Denzin argues, is cluttered by the traces of the life of the 'real' person being written about (p. 26), but he implies that they cannot be reified or 'summed up'. To attempt to give a fixed meaning to the subject is, in this context, doomed. That is, we must question whether it is the subject's presence that we write into a paper or whether our interpretations decentre them out of it.

Discourse-analytic research (see Malson's 2000, p. 154 account of her method), as a methodological tool, does not therefore assume that texts only (if at all) represent the concrete presence of individuals, and it rejects materialist, essentialist and consensual readings of them. To deconstruct a reading of an interview would be, for example, playful, spontaneous and inconclusive and the meaning conferred on it would be found in the reader/writer interaction, rather than in the subject written about. Riesmann (1993), for example, says that the object of investigation for her is the story itself and that she is interested in the linguistic and cultural resources which people use.

Moreover, the form a life history takes may tell us as much about a particular textual tradition and social sciences canon as about the particular individual's life experiences being recounted. That is lives are constrained by the cultural writing practices of the time and they are spoken about in the context of a particular textual tradition. Moreover, questioning the forms that we use for telling the story of our own, or other peoples' lives, is important, because as the editors of Sage's Qualitative Research Methods Series state: 'As with any conventional form, the representational choices open to a writer are sometimes not seen as choices at all, such that degrees of freedom are lost, and a hardened or formula biography results' (Denzin 1989a, p. 5).

For example, the following question to Sarah is directive in asking 'If you can cast your mind back, could you tell me about when your first experiences of romantic love were?' I obviously looked for a beginning and thereby possibly set up the linear (masculine?) form in which Sarah's life history unfolded from the age of 16 to the present when she is in her mid-thirties. Is there a way to ask an opening question which does not direct interviewees to beginnings and thus allow less formulaic gestalts to emerge? Or is this the way memory works for most people? Lambek and Antze (1996) in *Tense Past*, for example, aim to 'imagine memory as practice, not as the pre-given object of our gaze'. They argue that the idea that stories have beginnings is an imported idea that goes unnoticed in the West.

The story as the only representational choice (with an end point or telos) was challenged by Sarah, however, as she contemplated the future of her present relationship by saying 'our goal is not to have too many goals, but to sort of enjoy the journey a bit more'.

8.4.1 The thematic links between theoretical approaches to love and intimacy and discursive approaches to narrative

In Chapter 3 we saw the way in which a social-constructionist or discursive position has influenced contemporary sociological understandings of love:

> Love, like all emotions, is not directly observable. We can, in the end, analyse only the ways in which it is talked and written about – the discourses around romantic love which circulate within our culture – but these, I would argue construct our experience and understanding of love. (Shibles, 1974, p. 32)

For example, Shibles states that we should not look within to find our emotions, but at our language which, he maintains, captivates us. This is akin to the sociological viewpoint expressed in Chapter 3 which tied romantic love to the advent of the novel. Thus, what might seem, as Sarsby said, to be 'uniquely personal and private' (our lives and loves) can be seen to be the product of the social. Thus, theoretical approaches to love and intimacy (as script, narrative or discourse) can inform the approach that we assume in our biographical methods.

However, since discourse assumes an instability of language it does not state that we are fully penetrated by the social in a one-dimensional way (see the 1980s critique of the second wave feminist condemnation of romance reading). As Day Sclater (1999) explains:

'Discourses cannot, ultimately, be determining, as they are always more or less open to contest and change, and oppositional discourses can and do emerge to challenge the dominant and privileged ones' (pp. 131–2).

As Sclater (1999) points out, 'discourses are said to produce signs and shape the meaning of reality and delimit what can be said, whilst providing the spaces – concepts, metaphors, models, analogies – for making new statements' (romance, for example, has contradictory meanings, see Chapter 3). That is, we can negotiate or resist our 'discursive positions'. In the following extract, Sam reflects on the position she occupied as a young woman powerfully hailed by the discourse of romance:

> S: And erm looking back on the person I was before, I do think, 'You sweet, trusting thing. What a joy you were to be around, and really it's a miracle that you erm didn't come a cropper a damn sight sooner.'
>
> I: Mm.
>
> S: Erm so it's like, you know, looking back with nostalgia at this, this sweet child, this, this woman who has nothing to do with me, and er sort of quite glad really that, that she's not around any more. Life would be a lot harder, otherwise I think I would have lost it [romance] anyway, it would have just been more gradual.

Sam resists the position of the romantic heroine and seems to be saying that this 'sweet thing' that she had tried to be was 'interpellated' and 'hailed' by the discourse of romance to her own detriment. (See Day Sclater's [1999] discussion of the concept of being 'hailed' by discourse.) Men who might want her to be that 'joy' for them again are therefore treated with caution and suspicion. As Malson explains in discourse analysis there is a particular interest with the effect of truth and or power produced by the use of a particular discourse.

As Malson argues, 'texts are analysed, not as a means of revealing the 'truth' about the speaker or writer (their attitudes, cognitions, traits or whatever), or about the events and experiences that they describe. Rather, texts are analysed in order to explicate the culturally specific discursive resources that have been drawn upon in order to produce a particular account of reality' (Malson, 2000, p. 153).

Hence, our focus, in this context should be on how a discourse of romantic love disempowered Sam and made Sarah circumspect about telling people that she met her partner through a dating agency. The stigma, for example, attached to the use of an agency is double edged. If it's for sex, it's 'shameful', and if it's because of loneliness it's 'shameful'. Sarah (another interviewee in her thirties) said that her friends wouldn't use a dating agency, because 'it's not the way to meet someone', thus the idea that there is a 'natural' way is challenged by the very existence of dating agencies:

> S: I don't know I think you' re supposed to meet someone like naturally as she calls it, through your, through having your life, you meet someone and bond with them, and that's how it happens. And most of the time that's how it is for people I guess. I wouldn't say going through that sort of process was not having your life, it's just another way of having your life for me.

Sarah refers to this idea that love happens 'naturally' as an idea which militates against her friend meeting someone, because love is here being likened to the blinding light, cupid's arrow, the bolt from the blue and so on all of which confers on us a sense of expectancy, waiting and finally passivity:

> S: And in some ways it's liberating because, you are not sitting there thinking, 'oh I am supposed to be in love with them', or 'have I fallen in love with them', or 'are we falling in love, love, love, love, love'. And you don't actually see the person, it is all very well, but there is such a thing as trying to get to know them really, without all the stuff. They tell you something, 'oh well that's alright because I'm in love with them ...', 'Oh well that's alright as well, because I'm in love with them.' The fact is that we weren't in love when we met, we didn't fall in love instantly, it wasn't love at first sight. And trust developed and, I don't know honesty. We have an honest relationship in some ways, although not completely. But, it is compared to some others, I think it is liberating in some ways the way we met.

In the above discussion of Sarah's interview, we can see the way in which she has been offered the signifier 'romantic love' and we can look at what it connotes (vitality, falsity), but we cannot assume that this meaning is fixed or transparent (or a window into Sarah's inner life).

Instead, we can use the text to look at cultural processes of signification (connecting up romantic love with, for example, cupid's arrow, predestination, love at first sight), but we cannot assume any stable meaning of the sign (signifier/signified relationship).

We can see interesting thematic links between theoretical approaches to love and intimacy described in Chapters 3–7 and biographical methods, because both (to some extent) assume that the other is elusive. In Chapter 4, for example, we saw Sartre's description of the elusiveness of the other and this is why, in 'Being and Nothingness' (1943) the Other is seen as a tormenting alienation.

Consequently, we might follow the shadow of meaning in a text or interview, as Barthes does in a Lover's Discourse, but my object of study will remain elusive and ungraspable. Even the act of speech 'Sartre says 'reveals to me the freedom (the transcendence) of the one who listens to me in silence' (1943, p. 374), so that we are to some extent beings who fade under discourse:

> Thus the 'meaning' of my expression always escapes me ... for lack of knowing what I actually express for the Other, I constitute my language as an incomplete phenomena of flight outside myself ... . The Other is always there, present and experienced as the one who gives to language its meaning. (Sartre, 1943, p. 373)

From Chapter 7, we might already be alerted to the importance of the textual traditions from which people tell the stories of their lives, since Giddens' thesis would suggest (as would Richards' 1997) that we are witnessing a new textual tradition and that a new genre or story is emerging (fashioned out of sociology, existentialism and psychoanalysis) for meaning-making in relationships. Hence, we could hypothesise that we will see less 'hardened' or formulaic narratives of love (and modes of writing in the social sciences).

In summary, these theoretical approaches to love and intimacy, and discursive approaches to narrative methods, demand a consideration of:

- language as the limit to methodological inquiry;
- language/speech as unstable, in flux and overdetermined;
- the other as elusive and the text as a joint production[20];
- subjectivity as discursive constructions[21] and multiple subject positions (see Malson, 2000, p. 150);
- the arguments in favour of concentrating on the text, rather than the production of it;

- the text as fragmentable, rather than a 'whole narrative' (Malson, 2000, p. 150)[22];
- the examination of one's own 'formulaic' mode of telling the story of the other's life.[23]

While these philosophical and methodological positions will be borne in mind, they will not necessarily be systematically adopted in the reading of the interview material in Chapters 10 and 11.

8.5 Sociological approaches to narrative studies

It might seem artificial to distinguish a sociological approach from a social-constructionist or discursive approach to narrative studies, because the latter is, broadly speaking, a sub-discipline of the former. Nevertheless, this chapter will briefly introduce the biographical narrative interpretive method (BNIM – Wengraf, 2001) in order to highlight a sociological approach that is psychosocial but not informed by post-structuralism or psychoanalysis. Also, Hollway and Jefferson's psycho-analytic method is an adaptation of BNIM and briefly outlining some of BNIM's defining features will help when referring to their work.

BNIM assumes, in contrast to Malson's (2000) discourse-analytic approach, a modernist notion of identity and a 'liberal humanist concern' (p. 155) with the individual and the core structure of their story.

It betrays a search for an objective[24] reading of the interview transcript in which the structure of a case or narrative is uncovered (rather than created by the hypothesising panel or researcher). The structure of the case refers to its core psychosocially produced meaning (it is deduced from a study of structure and agency). In psychoanalytic terms, the BNIM structure of the case is akin to the idea of a 'selected fact' or a latent meaning. O'Shaughnessy (1994) describes a selected fact in the following way: 'That fact which gives coherence and meaning to facts already known ... when the selected fact was interpreted the interpreta-tion was mutative and new possibilities then exist' (p. 944). The psychoanalytic deduction of a selected fact and the sociological identifi-cation of the structure of a case involve two very different processes, of course, but what we can see in both is a realist approach to their object of study.

BNIM's realist approach (they do search for the author and a real account of them) can also be seen in its contention that it is narrrative that best slips by our defences[25] which are better served by theories and arguments. Discursive sociology would not, of course, try to unearth a 'unifying author' or 'authentic autobiography' (see Malson, 2000). A narrative is described in a similar way to Denzin[26] and Wengraf and Chamberlayne hypothesise that when narrating (as opposed to arguing, evaluating, describing etc.) we are closest to our experience of what it is that we are recalling. In BNIM, the hypothesis is that people will reveal more of themselves in narrative.

BNIM therefore encourages researchers to ask their interviewees a 'single question aimed at inducing narrative' and it makes a distinction between narrative-pointed questions, narrative-permitting questions, open-ended questions, argument-pointed questions and so on. For example, in BNIM terms the opening question that Sam is asked ('tell me about your views on romantic love') is not a narrative-inducing question, but one which invites an evaluation or argument. By deliberately asking interviewees for a situation, event, happening, occasion or time we will, according to this method, be asking for narratives rather than descriptions, arguments, reports or evaluations[27] of experience.

When Sam explained that romance is not a 'way of loving in the long term, I don't, don't believe in it, no', we could, if following BNIM guidelines, have asked Sam to tell us about a situation, happening, event, incident or time when long-term love had clashed with romantic love. This would, BNIM hypotheses, have taken Sam closer to an experience of romantic love rather than a question which instead asked for a description ('what, what do you associate with romance?'). However, asking for a specific incident or event may be intrusive, since in the initial stages of an interview both participants might feel defended (see Hollway and Jefferson's concept of the 'defended subject') as they try to establish a narrative relationship[28] and settle into it.

Moreover, interviewees may pursue argumentative or evaluative lines of narrative as a way of defending themselves against the possible intrusions of an interviewer who wants to get closer to their experience (and pursues a fallacious sense of 'truth' in the manner Malson advises against). However, it is perhaps wrong to assume that these evaluative and argumentative modes of speech (in BNIM terms) are antithetical to experiential accounts, since they might be deduced from experience (rather than a defence against it).

The biographic-narrative interviewing method also discourages questions which ask about feelings,[29] because they invite self-evaluations rather than the recall of specific incidents and events. BNIM may be an inappropriate method therefore for a culture described as therapeutic or for a project that focuses on emotion. That is, our cultural 'system of relevancy' might not be conducive to narratives based only on situations, happenings, events and incidents at certain points in time. It is interesting to speculate on whether BNIM is more appropriate for people who were brought up in times in which an exploration of feeling states and psychic space was curtailed. Mrs Frost (a woman in her seventies), for example, began her interview by saying 'I don't suppose you're going to ask anything personal' although she knew the topics of interest were love, marriage and intimacy.

Mrs Frost (like Mrs Archer, also from the older group of interviewees), for example, never lost herself in a narrative in the way that all of the other interviewees did. In classic BNIM terms she did offer narratives, recalling a specific situation or event, unfolding over time:

F: But she's never er ... she's never married.

I: Hasn't she.

F: No. Well those days, when you look at it, we weren't so educated as the generations now.

I: Mm. Mm.

F: And erm she's got a very good job.

I: Right.

F: And course when her husband died, you know, I said to her ... she said, 'No, Mum, I've got a very good job and I'm quite happy at it.'

I: Mm.

F: Yeah. But he came home from work ... she said he came home from work one day. {pause} {laughs} It was this ... it was the good weather, and he s- he said to her, 'I'm going out and have a dig up the garden a bit', so she said, 'All right.' And he came in and he said, 'Phew', sat on a chair, so she said, 'Wait a minute and I'll get you a drink of water.' Before she got the glass of water he was dead.

F: No, he died young. But she's still on her own.

When Mrs Frost talked about her own husband and her daughter's husband dying, she did not refer to how they felt at all. This wasn't expected or judged to be odd in any way, but it is interesting to speculate on whether a factual or narrative report like this would have been told by Sam or Sarah, without a subsequent evaluation of it. The BNIM hypothesis, as we have already seen, would suggest that narratives in which a conversation is recalled and the weather is remembered and so on will take us closer to our experience of it, but narratives can also be vividly recalled without emotional content or experiential immediacy.

The BNIM approach to interviewing is characterised by a 'theoretical minimalism'[30] (see M.J. Rustin, 1989 on infant observation) and it recommends a kind of Rogerian 'biographical stance' (i.e., non-directive, facilitative support). BNIM advises its researchers not to console or give advice, interpret or intrude with their own life histories and to instead respect the gestalt[31] that their interviewees come up with.[32] They are advised only to keep to their interviewee's 'system of relevancy' and practice narrative[33] rather than pedagogic interviewing.[34] Otherwise they will be in danger of introducing a question in a system of relevancy that their interviewee does not understand.[35] However, some of the interviews with the older interviewees assumed a semi-structured nature and required the interviewer to give prompts and ask questions and we, therefore, have to ask when interviewees might be uncomfortable with non-intervention.

BNIM approaches the text of an interview by looking at the lived life (the biographical, chronological facts of that life)[36] and the told story. This method makes use of a consultancy panel (who do not know the story) to predict the form (evaluative, descriptive and so on) and content (children, marriage, work and so on) of a life on the basis of a small segment of transcript material that they are given.[37] BNIM then compares the panel's hypotheses with the life as it was lived and the story as it was told. This is not, they maintain, wild analysis, because the panel's predictions are based on an imaginative immersion in the life (as it is presented slowly unfolding). Events are, as Wengraf (2001) states, polysemic and a panel is more likely to predict the variety of meanings open to an interviewee than the solitary researcher.[38]

The contention is that although we may not always be in control of the lived life (bereavement, illness, employment), we are in control of the told story (as victims or survivors, for example) and BNIM is particularly interested in the congruence or incongruity between the facts of our lives and our interpretation of them.

The working assumptions that BNIM foregrounds demand a consideration of:

- the kind of opening question that is asked in an interview (for example, narrative inducing);
- the gestalt initially presented by the interviewee in response;
- whether to follow this gestalt thematically and sequentially or free associatively;
- the form in which an interviewee speaks (evaluative, argumentative, story telling);
- the form in which the interviewer speaks;

- how to present a case (with biographical 'facts' extracted and the text divided up into text sorts,[39] for example);
- whether different forms of speech are discernible in different historical periods (is contemporary culture a narrative-inducing one?);
- the use of panels and groups for testing the hypotheses we make;
- the question of whether the structure of a case exists.

8.6 Psychoanalytic approaches to narrative studies

Although 'Lines of Narrative' emphasises the psychosocial approach intrinsic to narrative studies, only one of the chapters explicitly uses psychoanalytic concepts in its method (Hollway and Jefferson) or in order to critically question the narrative studies method as a way of understanding human experience (Craib).[40]

This work will contribute to discussions of how psychoanalysis can be used in social research (see Hunt, 1989; M.J. Rustin, 1989; Craib, 1998, 2000; Day Sclater 1999; Hollway and Jefferson, 2000a; Rustin, 2000) and to discussions of how psychoanalysis can be used in order to critically question the narrative studies approach to understanding human experience (Craib, 2000). The distinctive contribution to these discussions will be in the use of the psychoanalytic observation methods (introduced in Chapter 2) for thinking about semi-structured or narrative interviewing.

The training in psychoanalytic observation methods at the Tavistock Clinic in London, as explained in Chapter 2, entails doing a two-year work-based observation, a two-year infant observation and a one-year young-child observation (in addition to reading psychoanalytic theory and child/developmental psychology). The infant observation course in particular is, as M.E. Rustin (1999) points out, mostly used as a pre-clinical course which plays a large part in how students are selected for child psychotherapy training. The infant observation work requires the observer to visit a family for one hour each week over a two-year period (the young-child observation requires the observer to visit a family for one hour each week over a one year period) in order to observe the emotional development of the infant in his/her family setting and observe their own role in this family constellation.

It is interesting to note that psychoanalytic and sociological methods share a similar concern with what is an appropriate biographical/observational stance, with how to move between primary material and established theory and with the idea that the interviewer/observer partly constitutes what is said/observed. Furthermore, there is a shared interest in making methods of interpretation explicit, with corroborative measures being used to check inferences made and with a critique of naively realist assumptions. Psychoanalytic (or infant) observation literature will therefore be referred to throughout in order to highlight the contribution it can make to a psychosocial approach to narrative studies.

However, the importation of psychoanalytic concepts into social research is not a straightforward matter. Squire (2000a), for example, explains that she is happy to use psychoanalysis metaphorically,[41] but that

> to claim to find HIV 'identities' or 'selves' being struggled with or negotiated in a consistent but unconscious way in these interviews, would require a careful formulation and justification of the interpretive procedure ... . To make a leap to the unconscious without such a formulation is to indulge in interpretive arrogance and unwarranted therapeutism, and to use academic authority to claim a vicarious psychoanalytic authority. (p. 203)

In the field of anthropology, Geertz similarly stresses the importance of the anthropologist focusing upon the informant's symbol systems rather than on trying to achieve communion in order to respect the resistance of the researched to an over-identifying fieldworker[42] and as a way of protecting the discipline of anthropology. Geertz refers to the anthropologist's task as one of understanding the semiotic means by which persons are defined, and he seems to be attempting to keep the anthropologist on the outside of their object of investigation and to encourage them to lay open their tools and methodological procedures. Thus, the ethnographer's task is to try to perceive what their 'informants' perceive with or by means of or through, and to relate this to the language of their academic community.

However, the symbol system which the psychoanalytic researcher is interested in could move them further on the inside of their research (and researched) than Geertz or Squire may be in favour of. Rustin (2000) explains that 'psychoanalysis moves between the phenomenological details of what patients say, as these are understood and interpreted by their analysts and more generalised concepts and classifications of states of mind' (p. 39).Hollway and Jefferson and Day Sclater similarly move between what their interviewees say and generalised concepts and classifications of states of mind.[43] What their psychosocial approach adds to this is a consideration of the sociological discursive positions that interviewees occupy and a psychoanalytic understanding of why certain social positions and discourses are assumed.

The psychoanalytic observer's/researcher's interpretations of infant observation/biographical data do therefore involve the use of concepts which refer to the mental states of others/oneself (in the former case this is after many years and as a preparation for clinical training).[44] Thus, there are important differences between biographical/psychoanalytic methods, because narrative analysis often takes as the object of investigation the story itself (as we saw in section 8.4).

A psychoanalytic concern with the concrete, 'real' person, may, therefore, sometimes be at odds with a post-structuralist reading of the disembodied text. In object relations psychoanalysis the language that people use is seen as a window into their inner life, however opaque this window might seem. That is, the text is seen as representative of a 'real' presence (or transitional space – see Day Sclater, 1998), but the notion of realism that is embraced here is nevertheless critical and informed by the above interpretive critiques of objective methods. As Hollway and Jefferson (2000a) explain: 'we think that, though it is far from transparent, there is a relationship between people's ambiguous representations and their experiences. This position is sometimes called critical realism' (p. 3).

However, because of the emphasis on discourse in narrative studies it often (as Day Sclater 1999 points out) fails to consider what is happening intrapsychically (or interpersonally) when people use discourse. Although narrative analysis usefully problematises the truth/fiction dichotomy, it therefore potentially leads to the 'death of the subject'. Malson writes interestingly about what kind of 'violence' might be done to authors via discourse analysis, because her own discourse analytic method involves chopping up a text to look at the discursive construction of anorexic and feminine subjectivities. However, she deconstructs this concern in order to expose it as a 'liberal humanist concern with the individual and her definitive story' (p. 155). 'It might' she says 'suggest a reinstalment of the self-knowing sovereign individual as originary and unifying author of her own authentic autobiography' (ibid.).

Malson therefore questions whether it makes sense to worry about the violence that is done to the author of a text by the fragmenting of it, because this conflicts with her position that the text is not indicative of a 'real' presence. Malson cannot therefore be concerned with 'attempting to identify any unifying authorial identity', because discourses, she says, do not originate from individual speakers. The objective of her work instead is to elucidate 'the cultural and discursive construction and regulation of truths, identities and experiences' (p. 156).

However, the danger with this narrative studies approach is that if the subject is seen to be so thoroughly penetrated by the social, then we are left with no way in which to speak about that which is meaningful because it is private, personal or internal. That is, although social discourses mediate our experiences, they may not fully constitute them. As Day Sclater (1999) points out there are 'profound psychological investments which people make in being 'hailed' by discourse; there is an affective dimension operating, involving both unconscious and conscious processes' (114).[45]

The aim of narrative studies, from a psychosocial perspective, is to focus on what Geertz calls the subject's 'symbol system' which they 'perceive with or by means of or through' and to think about the way in which external sociological factors might interact with internal psychic realities. From a psychosocial perspective, our questions might be: what are the psychological effects of, or investments in, social discourses? What are the psychological risks of developing a 'reflexive relation'[46] to dominant discourses of intimacy? We can, for example, look at the psychological subtext or covert meaning of a particular discourse and look at the psychological investments or benefits of assuming certain positions (romantic heroines or cynics, survivors or victims of love etc). We might ask, for example, why we can sometimes become trapped in a repetitive narrative imbued with *déjà vu* experiences and find that we need to unearth our unconscious memories (in feeling and of relating) in order to understand the manifest content of our lives.

8.6.1   Losing the plot

Psychoanalysis also alerts us to the fact that there is a fundamental difference between telling the story of our life (in which we may impose some order) and living through the sometimes messy, emotional reality of it in which centred meaning is lost, not because of the social discourses in which we grew up, but because of the emotional, relational dynamics which we have internalised and created.

What psychoanalytic theories of mind sometimes describe, for example, is an 'existential dizziness' (Freeman), vertigo (see Craib) or abjection (Squire, 2000b) when our ability to impose narrative order on experience breaks down. Mr Williams (an interviewee in his seventies), for example, refers to an aspect of his experience that could not be contained by narrative coherence:

> *W:* They were loading ... they was in bad condition to take to hospital ( ). They were just walking skeletons.
>
> *I:* Really?
>
> *W:* And it was the most pitiful sight
>
> *I:* Mm.
>
> *W:* I've ever ...
>
> *I:* Really?
>
> *W:* I've ever seen.
>
> *I:* Was that the worst part of it?
>
> *W:* It was horrible.
>
> *I:* Was it? Mm.
>
> *W:* It was atrocious itself. To think that people, that er humanity could do that to one another.
>
> *I:* Mm.
>
> *W:* And they was er ... he er he did ... not only did he do it to Jews, he was doing it to some of his own as well.
>
> *I:* Mm.
>
> *W:* And he done it ... Poles, don't matter who it was got in his way, went into them concentration camps.
>
> *I:* Mm.
>
> *W:* And they really were pitiful sights.
>
> *I:* Really?
>
> *W:* Some of them, they ... it took them all their time to stand up.
>
> *I:* Did it?
>
> *W:* And they were, well, they were just like walking skeletons.
>
> *I:* Mm.
>
> *W:* And when you've seen it, it ... you ... it ... you can ... you can never wipe it out of your mind.
>
> *I:* No.
>
> *W:* And they was, well ... {pause} (Reckon I) could write a book about some of the things (I've seen).
>
> *I:* Mm.
>
> *W:* That Belsen is one of the terriblest camps I've ever seen.
>
> *I:* That was the camp you went to was it, Belsen?
>
> *W:* Belsen.
>
> *I:* Yeah.

'There is', Craib argues, 'no cure for humanity and bad faith stories attempt to reduce our humanity: to reduce emotions to feelings, the things that we talk about in problem pages ... .' He adds 'what I think it is necessary to hold on to against the narratives I am criticising is the often incoherent height and depths of human experience and our ability to find as much of the human condition within ourselves as possible' (p. 73). Therapy is one of the ways in which our habitual narratives can be dramatically disrupted.

That is, our 'storied representations' of life may remove us (via a kind of secondary elaboration) from life's inherent challenge to narrative meaning or sense making[47]. It is interesting to think about the psychological function of narrative when there has been complete narrative breakdown (the death of Terry's wife was, for example, 'the biggest shock of his life') and Terry, Mrs Frost and Eddie all recalled the death of their spouse, for example, in narrative detail. Unlike the other widows, however, Terry had a religious narrative about why the 'God took away one angel (his wife) and gave him another angel (his granddaughter one year later).

However, according to Craib (2000), the social sciences might be guilty of Sartrean bad faith as narrative coherence and meaning are looked for when experience may resist the formal properties of a story with 'basic structural features, including narrators, plots, settings, characters, crises and resolutions' (see Denzin's definition above)[48]. Craib is referring to that which is unnarratable and this also relates to the points raised in Chapters 5 and 6 about the unconscious mind and the limits to what we can know. Furthermore, as Seale (2000) says 'the material life of the body precedes its narrative construction' (p. 36) and he thus points to the limits of narrative analysis with its emphasis on that which we socially construct.[49]

A psychosocial approach that is informed by psychoanalysis would encourage us to think about the extent to which we are free to invent our self stories, because we are not completely self-governing subjects in either a sociological or psychological sense[50]. However, because conventional narrative studies lacks a model of mind, it focuses on the social discourses that people draw on, without recourse to a language of psychological 'fact' (see Freud's and Klein's ontology outlined in Chapters 5 and 6) or emotional 'reality'[51] that might not be constituted by exclusively defined social factors.

8.6.2   Embodied encounters

What the emphasis on discourse also decentres is a concern with the embodied contact between two people and the non-verbal, unconscious communications (of the kind described by Stern – see Chapter 7) in an interview situation. It also decentres the importance of the physical setting in which interviews are carried out. The following, for example, is an extract from field notes on the atmosphere in a residential day care centre in which I interviewed Mrs Archer, Mrs Frost, Terry and Mr Williams (in their seventies and over):

'At the time, I reported feeling like a strange guest, who everybody was expecting. The atmosphere generally felt very intrusive and it was noisy outside of the interview room. At one point, a young male worker was staring through the window into the room and enjoying a joke with his co-workers. In the interview room, the phone or buzzer went off regularly. Each interviewee was brought and collected by somebody different and it felt as though my presence, the interviews and the interviewee's life history were not being respected or taken very seriously. This may not have been the case at all, of course, but it was not an easy atmosphere to walk into or work in.'

The centre itself seemed to be permeated by an air of waiting as many of the people sat in armchairs looking ahead or around the room or talking. It was, of course, a kind of social club for the elderly, but the quality of the social contact being offered did not seem to be very alive. What I was also very possibly affected by too was the reminder of death. This sounds terribly morbid, since one can be sprightly, alive and inspiring at any age (illness notwithstanding), but when interviewing people in their nineties who reminisce about past times, endings are necessarily in view too.

These factors alone gave these interviews a particular quality of awkwardness, poignancy and lack of focus. It is quite possible that I was 'thrown off course' by a combination of slightly infirm interviewees, uncontained staff and the prospect of life coming to its final years (in a rather undignified setting). Mabel, by contrast, lived at home with her daughter, son-in-law grandchildren and dogs and had her own living room, bathroom and bedroom in a light spacious house. This provided a different backdrop from which she could look backwards and forwards on life than Eddie's retirement home did, for example.

The way in which these external factors impinge on our states of mind and affect our ability to explore memory, psychic space and form relationships have to, of course, be borne in mind, because they are one of the many ways in which the psyche and social interact.

Denzin (1989a), however, argues that students of the biographical method must learn how to use strategies and techniques of literary interpretation, but he says nothing of the 'Doing of Life Histories' (Plummer, 1983) or about the emotional encounter between the two individuals in an interview situation. Psychoanalytic methods, however, prioritise an embodied, oral element which a literary interpretation of the written text cannot necessarily 'hear'.

For example, Some of Mrs Archer's children 'are very clever' as are Mrs Frost's and it is interesting to consider how an academic researcher is viewed by them. Is it assumed that an academic will understand doorstep cleaning, working with one's Dad on the rag and bone cart or not? Is the academic researcher positioned as privileged and unfamiliar with deprived, but not shameful material circumstances? It is unclear how an interviewer's class and educational background is communicated (via dialect, vocabulary and accent) and it is interesting to consider how interviewees are reflecting on these non-verbal cues. For example, Terry moves from recounting his views on cohabitation or marriage nowadays to noticing that he is being interviewed by somebody who does not wear a ring:

> *T:* Well of course now, it's ... I mean they're ... {clears throat} Well what can I say? Well they're going against everything really. They're, they're what I call flying in the face of God. I mean the Bible says the marriage bed is honourable and undefiled, but the bed of whoremongers – and it says that in the Bible – the bed of whoremongers shall be cursed for ever more.
>
> *I:* Mm.
>
> *T:* And I mean that's all they're doing now, they're ... they just go about, they don't think about marriage, love don't come into it. They, they just go and live with each other purely for sex. Well that's the way I see it anyway. That's the way a lot of other people see it as well.

Was I seen as a part of this generation of sexually hungry, narcissistic 'sinners'? Terry commented:

> *T:* I see you're not married.
>
> *I:* No, I'm not.
>
> *T:* No. {laughs}
>
> *I:* Not, not yet, no.
>
> *T:* Got a boyfriend?
>
> *I:* Mm.
>
> *T:* Good for you. Is he nice?
>
> *I:* He is, he's very nice.
>
> *T:* Good.
>
> *I:* Yeah. Yeah.

And did I perhaps try to court Terry's approval by saying 'not, not yet, no'? The important point is that psychoanalytically inflected psychosocial studies draws our attention to the emotional subtext of the interview situation and to the story told as a 'transitional phenomenon' belonging to both the interviewee and interviewer (see Day Sclater, 1998). That is, while both qualitative researchers and infant observers try to be non-interventionist, they are not passive. As Rustin (1997b) points out (in reference to Briggs' work), the infant observer is more likely to be a part of a triangular dynamic situation. For example, the infant observer can be the source of anxiety, reassurance, expertise, dependency and so on for the mother/family (ibid.). And this may be true for the qualitative researcher too, who is part of a dynamic dyadic situation. Although this non-verbal communication might not be the primary interest of one's project, it does, from a psychoanalytic viewpoint, inflect the interview itself, the remembering of it, its methodological 'success' and so on. It might also be, of course, unethical to marginalise the importance of the interpersonal process, since this will miss why many people participate in research projects. As Eddie said:

E: It makes you think, this business. See at my age, eighty-five, I'd given up ever thinking.
I: Mm.
E: But now, here, since you've been here, I've started to think.
I: Mm.

Eddie talked about being 'on his way to being a cabbage' before the interviews were conducted and thus thinking about embodied encounters, rather than disembodied text, also alerts us to the need for a sensitive handling of the end of an interview.

8.6.3 A meditative review of analytic work

Psychoanalytic methods encourage a 'meditative review of analytic work'[52] and this type of self-examination is also evident in psychoanalytically inflected social research. Usher (1997) says social research now demands 'not only an evaluation of outcomes, but a reflexive analysis of the research process and the place of the researcher within that' (p. 1) and psychosocial approaches to both theory and method are clearly in this tradition of reflexive analysis. Indeed, in order to provide some observations on the embodied encounters described above and on what we might latterly see as an unconscious response to, or relationship with, our work, we need to develop a self-reflexive approach to our object of study.

What we can see is that psychosocial approaches to narrative studies and reflexive research can demand a considerable degree of self-scrutiny in relation to one's psychic life, investments in academia and empirical/clinical work. Hence Hunt (1989) discusses the place of dreams in her research and Hollway and Jefferson (2000a) describes the way in which the transference dynamics between an interviewee and herself were permeated by her own unconscious relationship to the interviewee as a daughter figure. Hunt, and Hollway are, of course, trying to provide observations on transference and counter-transference issues in their research setting. Transference refers to the subject's projection of their own inner world into the research setting and counter-transference refers to the 'exploration of those elements in the observer's feeling state which seem to be determined by regular projections from family members (M.E. Rustin, 1989, p. 20) and, we might add, from interviewees. The counter-transference, however, may also refer to 'the intrusion of the observer's personal unconscious responses' (ibid.).

This focus on transference and counter-transference can provide very interesting insights into the research process, but it can also be used as a corroborative measure for checking the inferences that one has made. In the context of psychoanalytic observation methods Waddell (1988), for example, refers to Bion's idea of 'binocular vision' in order to explain that the infant observation method 'requires the observer to be as minutely cognisant of his or her own internal processes as of those of the subject of observation' (p. 314). This means that the observer needs to develop the capacity to look inward and outward simultaneously (ibid.) and we can see this being practised in psychosocial research.

As Geertz states, 'Once ethnographic texts begin to be looked at as well as through, once they are seen to be made, and made to persuade, those who make them have rather more to answer for' (1988). He argues that the ethnographer needs to be explicit about 'The Written About' and the 'Written To'[53]. Ethnographic papers, he says, 'look at least as much like romances as they do lab reports' (8) and it is for this reason that we need to make explicit the authorial voice which writes them. That is, an observational, biographical or ethnographic paper represents the construction of what Geertz calls a writerly identity with the researcher's own vocabulary and rhetoric and each needs to grasp what Geertz calls the 'signature dilemma' (p. 10). Hence, sociological and psychoanalytic methods show a similar concern (albeit from different perspectives) with the 'textualising, inscribing process' (Denzin, 1989a, p. 7).

8.6.4 The biographical task

Geertz defines the sociological task as one of 'grasping concepts that for another people, are experience-near, and to do so well enough to place them in illuminating connection with experience-distant concepts that theorists have fashioned to capture the general features of social life' (p. 38).

Similarly, when writing psychoanalytic observations, our task is to stay 'experience near' (Sandler and Sandler, 1994, p. 1001) and be vigilant about using literature or making interpretations which, although 'correct' (Harris Williams, 2000, p. 129), may also be very 'experience far'[54]. M.J. Rustin (1989), for example, says that 'readers are invited to assess the truthfulness of representations by reference to their own personal experience, and not only to the published findings of psychology' (p. 73). Geertz similarly invites his readership to judge the authenticity of an account by assessing to what extent it opens the consciousness of one group to life forms of another, inscribes the present and represents a 'vitality phrased'.

However, as explained in Chapter 2, Waddell (1988) maintains that the 'cataloguing language of developmental psychology and the metapsychology of analytic theory' (p. 313) are both in danger of erasing the 'language of insides'. The problem, she says, is how to bring these two languages together. Theories of infant development, she claims, speak the language of science and refer to the external world, whereas infant observation itself uses a language more akin to poetry, which tries to express the experience of the inner world. Whereas Waddell refers to poetry to describe the language of infant observations, Miller more generally uses literature. She argues that reading an infant observation report should be like the experience of reading a novel, where the story makes an impact in its own right, rather than being used to exemplify a theoretical point. She reminds us that Freud's case histories were likened to novels in such a way that although we knew about the author (in this case Freud) and the equivalent of his literary criticism (theories of the mind), these details did not detract from the case.

Waddell therefore uses Keats' notion of 'negative capability'as a way of expressing the caution that the observer must exercise when linking psychoanalytic interpretations to what has been observed. Symington (1986), for example, says that a theory means that a new thought cannot easily be born. He is explaining Bion's ideas, which explore the emotional and cognitive aspects of learning, and he writes about the way in which a thought has to be allowed to emerge. A thought cannot, he says, be forced into consciousness through artificial induction (p. 278).

The observer's role therefore requires that he or she can approach each observation without – to use Bion's (1970, p. 41) phrase – memory or desire.[55]

These observations on psychoanalytic method are very useful for thinking about narrative studies, because interview material also needs to be allowed to speak for itself and come alive without the constant intrusion of theoretical points. The question of how to move between 'experience near' and 'experience far' concepts is therefore common to both psychoanalytic and psychosocial methods.

As Craib (1998) explains, theory gives us a way of ordering the world and 'a way of avoiding confusion where confusion, or at least complexity actually exists'. Theory, Craib says, can be like a good interpretation or it can be barren (p. 139) and he says that when he engages in theory 'I am deploying a range of projections; I am not only acting rationally but bringing into play or even acting out a range of phantasies' (p. 140). Indeed, according to Craib, there is a theoretical id, demanding the immediate gratification of a totalising theory[56] and thus we can see the difficulty researchers might encounter in not being able to rush their material or omnipotently impose a structure upon it.

In this context, it is interesting to note that the observational stance is secured by the observer's efforts to prevent the observation from being 'clouded and distorted through preconception' (see Waddell, ibid.). This concern is evident in biographical work too. Anderson and Jack (1991), for example, use Reik's idea of listening with the 'third ear' in order to guide them in their own biographical stance:

> As a researcher, I have learned that critical areas demanding attention are frequently those where I think I already know what the woman is saying. This means that I am already appropriating what she says to an existing schema, and therefore I am no longer really listening to *her*. Rather, I am listening to how what she says fits into what I think I already know. (19)

However, the kind of appropriation that Jack writes about is, to some extent, inevitable. Nevertheless, 'listening with the third ear' or developing what Trowell and Rustin (1991) call an 'internal observer' (in the context of infant observation methods) may enable an interviewer to 'remain attentive to the moral dimension of interviewing' (see Anderson and Jack). That is, the philosophy which informs psychosocial (and infant observation) methods enables the researcher to remain attentive to questions of appropriation and intrusiveness.

8.7 Objective and interpretive approaches to narrative studies

Psychoanalytically inflected psychosocial methods can be thought of as belonging to what Denzin (1989a) refers to as the emergence of a new life history approach (p. 57), which attempts to bring the objective method in line with recent developments in narrative analysis, ethnomethodology, sociolinguistics, arguing that grounded theory is its aim. His own expressed aim is to combine a consideration of the 'metaphysics of presence',[57] with a 'commitment to the position that interpretive sociologists ... study real people who have real-life experiences in the real world' (p. 14). Similarly, Geertz argues that ethnomethodology is beset by the problem of realism, discourse and signature, but he nevertheless argues that although ethnomethodological reports represent 'imaginative writing', it is nonetheless, he says, 'imaginative writing about real people, in real places at real times' (p. 41). Likewise, the infant observation method is referred to as a 'literary enterprise', but one which is nevertheless 'committed to a high degree of literal accuracy' (M.J. Rustin, 1989). Psychoanalysis, for example, is beset with the methodological problem of subjectivity which undermines psychoanalytic researchers' attempts to provide a realist defence of the inferences made in their papers. In all of these interpretive methods,[58] we can therefore see a position which argues that although an infant observation, ethnomethodological or biographical paper or report is not seen as a complete fiction, neither can we be naïvely realist in our assumptions, because of the aforementioned philosophical critiques of positivist methods.

A realist ontology is one which assumes that the objects of our investigation have a reality independent of our awareness of them and it is therefore counterposed to relativism, which states that our mental/linguistic impressions of the world constitute its reality. If we assumed a relativist position, we would have to conclude that the observer, biographer or anthropologist and the paper that they produce could only tell us about their own perceptual/discursive reality. Geertz (1988) instead concludes that the ethnographic text is a work of the imagination which is less extravagant than Italian Opera and less methodical than quantum mechanics. It is, like the infant observation paper, 'imaginative writing about real people in real places at real times' (p. 41) and neither 'author saturated' nor 'author vacated' (p. 141). Nevertheless, Geertz concludes that the anthropologist's vocation is a literary one, because ethnographic descriptions, he says, are homemade and give us the 'describer's descriptions'. The anthropologist's task, according to Geertz is to

> demonstrate, or more exactly to demonstrate again, in different times
> and with different means, accounts of how others live that are pre-
> sented neither as tales about things that did not actually happen, nor
> as reports of measurable phenomena, produced by calculable forces.
> (p. 142)

Geertz does not lose recourse to the language of the real, but neither does he try to deploy a language of science to defend the validity of the ethnographer's texts.

Psychoanalytic theories and methods also both conform to, yet challenge, the scientific or objective, classic approach. That is, a psychoanalytic understanding of love *and* biographical methods is sensitive to some of the tenets of postmodernism (the ironising of 'Truth', certainty and rationality) despite its roots in the 'Age of Reason' (see Chapter 5). However, we can also see that psychoanalytic methods are very different from postmodern, discourse analytic methods. Psychoanalysis does, for example, betray a concern with the originating author and with a 'respectful' account of what they say (which involves more than a deconstruction of the social discourses that they occupy). The subject's language is not the limit of psychoanalytic inquiry, because there is a focus on an embodied encounter, transference/counter-transference issues and on unconscious meaning.

Nevertheless, psychoanalysis does share some interesting points of contact with more postmodern, interpretive methods (more so than BNIM does, for example). The assumptions that psychoanalysis makes (e.g., meaning and the subject are elusive, we live at different levels of subjectivity, the internal is not necessarily a reflection of the external and language is not transparent) means that psychoanalysis is implicitly critical of the classic, objective method and of its naïve realism[59].

These psychoanalytic reflections on method demand a consideration of:

- one's own biographical stance (as 'defended'[60] interviewee, for example);
- to what extent to focus on transference and counter-transference issues;
- to what extent to focus on the embodied encounter between inter-viewer and interviewee (how does the setting, a tender atmosphere, parapraxis, joke or awkward moment reflect on, or inflect, the told story?);
- how to achieve a 'vitality phrased' and bring the interviewee alive in memory and language;

- whether we can make interpretations about deep structures of personality on the basis of interviews;
- how to move between 'experience near' and 'experience far' concepts;
- how to bring general psychoanalytic understandings of the mind and object relations to my reading of these interviews (in order to think about the unconscious meanings of a discourse and/or investments in them);
- what claims we can make for the interpretations that we make;
- whether we should take our cue from narrative studies and take the story itself as the object of investigation;
- or, whether to argue for the status of our biographical work as 'imaginative writing', but about 'real people' (see Geertz) and which is committed to a 'high degree of literal accuracy' (see Rustin).

8.8   Conclusion

The philosophy of method that this psychosocial approach assumes broadly conforms to what Denzin refers to as 'the new life history approach' (i.e., it partakes of objective and interpretive approaches to narrative studies).

In Geertz's terms, the main aim is to 'grasp concepts that for another people, are experience-near, and to do so well enough to place them in illuminating connection with experience-distant concepts that theorists have fashioned to capture the general features of social life' (p. 38).

Since the interview material is only illustrative, the aims with respect to it are modest.[61] Although it will contribute to discussions about psychosocial approaches to narrative, a systematic method for analysing data psychosocially[62] will not be presented. This material will not be used to refute or support a hypothesis, because the sample has not been designed for that purpose and the method is exploratory, rather than systematic and definitive.

9
Personal Accounts of Love
Details of Method

9.1   Introduction

There are five aims related to the interview material:

1. to provide some discussion of the way the interview was conducted and unfolded (see Chapter 8;
2. to approach each interview without 'memory or desire'. In biographical narrative interpretive method (BNIM) terms the aim is to let the material's own gestalt emerge;[1]
3. to use selected aspects of the material in order to provide illustrative[2] comments on the statements deduced from Chapters 2–7 (views of love as possible, impossible and reconceptualised);
4. to argue for the importance of a psychoanalytic sociology of emotion or psychosocial way of seeing love (see Chapter 2);
5. to be explicit about the kinds of claims that are made in the light of the statements deduced from discursive, sociological and psychoanalytic approaches to the method discussed in Chapter 8.

9.2   The form of the interview

The interview was listened to and the transcript was read with the aim of letting its own gestalt or story emerge, before it was brought into dialogue with socio-cultural, existentialist and psychoanalytic conceptualisations of love.[3] In BNIM terms this is referred to as addressing the integrity of a case, before presenting what is of relevance to a particular research agenda or audience.

However, this cannot strictly be done 'without memory or desire', because interviewers inevitably use guidelines (from sociological and psychoanalytic approaches to method) in order to produce reflexive research.

Nevertheless, in order to prioritise a discussion of form, as well as content, the interviews were originally written up in the following way:

- first encounters
- summary of the told story
- the form of the interview
- theoretical analysis of the interview material.

The section entitled 'First encounters' provided commentary on the physical setting and atmosphere (see the extract from field notes in Chapter 8) with the aim of bringing the interviewee and the situation alive in memory and in the description of them.[4] The cue was taken from observational methods in which there is an attempt to immerse oneself back into the tenor of an hour, season or year in order to present a 'vitality rephrased' (see Geertz, 1988, Chapter 8). This meant that the text itself was not the limit of methodological inquiry.

The form of the interview used insights from discourse analysis, BNIM and psychoanalytic methods in order to provide commentary on the biographical stance (intrusive, confused, moved, defended and so on), the opening question asked (narrative permitting), the dominant mode of speech (evaluative or narrative based, for example), the interviewer's search for the real subject, the narrative relationship (see Duchet, 1981, 1991) and so on, all of which have been detailed in Chapter 8.

9.3 Theoretical statements and the interview material

Theoretical statements or hypotheses were deduced from Chapters 2–7 in order to look at the way in which the interviewees' reflections on love interact with or distribute themselves among the theoretical approaches to love discussed in those chapters. Forty-five statements were selected and they are listed below. These statements can, however, be condensed into the following three:

1. Romantic love is being deconstructed[5] and the question of whether love is possible or impossible is being struggled with.
2. A transformation of intimacy is occurring that is characterised by psychosocial reflexivity and de-traditionalised expectations from love and relationships.

3. A psychosocial interpretation of transcripts about love can address the weakness of an exclusively psychoanalytic or socio-cultural interpretive strategy.[6]

Each interview was read in the context of the above three hypotheses. The following statements provide a more detailed summary of the views expressed in Chapters 2–7 and some of them are referred to in Chapters 10 and 7 if they can be brought into a particularly illuminating or interesting dialogue with what interviewees have said. It is not the aim of Chapters 10 and 11 to systematically apply every deduced statement (listed below) to each interview.

9.3.1   Statements or hypotheses deduced from chapters 2–7

Chapter 2 – A psychosocial approach to emotional life

1. A psychosocial interpretation of transcripts about love can address the weakness of an exclusively psychoanalytic or socio-cultural interpretive strategy.
2. The psychosocial imagination is the 'intellectual common denominator of our times'.

Chapter 3 – Modern love: sociological approaches

1. Romantic love is based on premodern, religious ideas.
2. Romantic love is an enlightenment, modern conception of love.
3. Romantic love is destabilised by the conditions of modernity/late modernity.
4. Romantic love is a woman's enslavement.
5. Romantic love is impossible in a long-term relationship/marriage.
6. Romantic love is being replaced by the discourse/practice of confluent love and pure relating.
7. Romantic love is being revealed as an oppressive/enabling story masquerading as a natural emotion, life trajectory.

Chapter 4 – Love as bad faith: philosophical approaches

1. Romantic love exacerbates the culture of narcissism.
2. Romantic love aims to capture a consciousness.
3. Romantic love does not enable us to acknowledge the fact of contingency, freedom and separateness.
4. Romantic love denies one's own relative place in a world of others.
5. Romantic love aids bad faith.

6. Romantic love holds the seeds of its own destruction.
7. Romantic love is the antithesis of 'authentic' love.
8. Romantic love aims to put an end to one's own, and the other's, desire and lack.
9. Romantic love is antithetical to a courtly conception of love.
10. Romantic love denies that the self is a dramatic sequence.
11. Romantic love is constitutive of an imaginary world of misrepresentations and dialectical bliss.

Chapter 5 – Transference love: a Freudian way of seeing love

1. Romantic love is based on the pleasure principle.
2. Romantic love partakes of two principles of mental functioning (pleasure and reality).
3. Romantic love sublimates anarchic, sexual impulses.
4. Romantic love recalls the sensual experiences of infancy.
5. Romantic love catalyses childlike behaviours and feelings.
6. Romantic love is a transference love, recalling Oedipal conflicts.
7. Romantic love denies mourning, aloneness and solitude.
8. Romantic love exacerbates narcissistic tendencies.
9. Romantic love deposes the reality ego and the need for psychic work.
10. Romantic love is the antithesis of a 'mature' Freudian love.

Chapter 6 – Reparative love: a Kleinian approach

1. Romantic love recalls the mother/infant dyadic relationship.
2. Romantic love recalls Oedipal traumas.
3. Romantic love denies hate, sadism and frustration.
4. Romantic love denies psychic reality.
5. Romantic love is a split-off state of mind.
6. Romantic love promises a 'perfect internal world'.
7. Romantic love promises wordless, affective communion.
8. Romantic love is a turn towards the 'lifegiver' (see Symington, 1993).
9. Romantic love is the antithesis of 'depressive', reparative love.

Chapter 7 – Reflexive love: sociological and psychoanalytic insights

1. A psychosocial 'way of seeing' love addresses the existential, psychoanalytic and social nature of the self.
2. The sociological discourse of the pure relationship is complementary to the psychoanalytic discourse of reparative relating.
3. The discourse of the pure relationship is antithetical to the discourse of reparative relating.

9.4   Discursive, sociological and psychoanalytic approaches to method

When reflecting on the form and content of each interview and its relation to theory, the interpretations and claims that were made were referred to the discursive, sociological and psychoanalytic approaches to method, discussed in Chapter 8. The sociological approach described by BNIM, for example, was most useful for thinking about the 'doing of life histories' (Plummer (1983) – see Chapter 8). It has been helpful for deducing guidelines on how to analyse the form that an interview (see section 9.2) takes and on how to present material (with biographical 'facts' extracted and the text divided up into text sorts,[7] for example).

BNIM also, however, raises some interesting theoretical questions which can be used for interpreting data. For example, is narrative interviewing conducive to what Duchet calls a 'narrative relationship'? Are different forms of speech discernible in different historical periods (is this a narrative inducing culture?)? Should we consider using panels and groups for testing the hypotheses that we make? Can we access the structure of a case?

Discursive approaches to method do not refer to the embodied encounter, biographical stance or meditative review of analytic work involved in qualitative research in the same way that the psychoanalytic and sociological methods that have been described do. Discursive approaches to method are therefore most useful when thinking about the claims that are made for the interpretations that are offered (if, for example, they point to an internal world, beyond language). Sociological and discursive approaches to method are also particularly helpful for thinking about the social positions that people occupy and the social construction of love. Following the points highlighted for attention in Chapter 8, subjectivity, for example, was considered as a discursive construction, constituted by multiple subject positions. The analysis of the interview material was therefore attentive to the ways in which language/speech was unstable, in flux and over determined. Both discursive and psychoanalytic approaches to method see the other as elusive and the text as a joint production and reflections on this were provided. The emphasis on language as the limit to methodological inquiry was critically questioned, as was the argument in favour of concentrating on the text, rather than the production of it. The question of the extent to which a text is fragmented (for thinking about a particular research agenda), rather than treated as a 'whole narrative' was discussed. Finally, the discursive method encourages us to be conscious of our own 'formulaic' mode of telling the story of the other's life and this was borne in mind (as seen in Chapter 8).

Psychoanalytic approaches to method are useful for both the doing of life histories and the interpretation of data. The points that were attended to were concerned with whether it was possible to make interpretations about deep structures of personality on the basis of interviews. That is, how can we bring general psychoanalytic understandings of the mind and object relations to our reading of interviews (in order to think about the unconscious meanings of a discourse and investments in them)? We could, for example, take our cue from narrative studies and take the story itself as the object of investigation. Or, we could argue, as explained in Chapter 8, for the status of our biographical work as 'imaginative writing' about 'real people' (see Geertz, 1988), but committed to a 'high degree of literal accuracy' (see M.J. Rustin, 1989).

The interviews and the reading of them determined which methodological approach was most illuminating (discursive, sociological, psychoanalytic), but there was an attempt (albeit in general terms) to refer to the explanatory power of all three approaches for analysing the interview itself and presenting interpretations of it. The importance of a psychoanalytic sociology of emotion or psychosocial way of seeing love was argued for, because combining both approaches to method addressed the limitations of reducing a study of people and love to the status of a social construct and ahistorical mind/essentialism.

Like Hollway and Jefferson (2000a), each interview was approached with a psychoanalytic commitment to understanding subjectivity as informed by an a priori experience of anxiety and as being defended, as object seeking and relational and as constituted by unconscious dynamics.[8] This work had a simultaneous commitment to the position that subjectivity is constituted by the discourses that we occupy/resist (discourses of femininity, class, education, success etc.). Furthermore, the material conditions of our lives (which BNIM foregrounds) interact in dynamic ways with the discursive positions that we occupy and with the nature of the anxiety that might form our predominant orientation to the world and people (depressive or persecutory, for example). However, the fact that this work focused on emotion, meanings and relationships led, in some cases, to interviews in which very little was found out about the material conditions (jobs, education, housing etc.) of people's lives. Nevertheless, the macro structures in which people live were considered when it was possible to do so. Hence, a psychosocial approach involves looking at social structures, social discourses and models of mind with the aim of providing reflections on their complex interaction. This meant that the aim of this work was to provide a psychosocial explanation of an interviewee's view of love as possible, impossible or reconceptualised, or indeed, reluctance or inability to talk about it.

9.5   Sample

The variables to choose from in selecting a sample were numerous: age, gender, sexuality, ethnicity and so on. Age was the variable that was used to determine the sample which was chosen, because it gave the opportunity to think about the effect of the so-called de-traditionalisation process and the 'transformation of intimacy' regarding people's expectations of relationships/romance. Chapters 3–7 detail the deconstruction of romantic love in social/psychoanalytic theory and by looking at everyday accounts of love we can provide illustrative commentary on this theoretical questioning of love. The aim of the interviews was not to only, or exclusively, explore Giddens' thesis, but his work provided a platform from which to choose an appropriate sample.

Although qualitative interviews were judged to be an appropriate research tool for exploring the 'transformation of intimacy thesis', it was necessary to identify what year marked the transformation of intimacy and Giddens' citing of Rubin's (1989) study was used to do so. She interviewed a thousand heterosexual people in the United States aged between 18 and 48 about their sexual histories. She noticed a significant change in attitude between the 18-year-old interviewees and the post-forties age group. Rubin's 18-year-olds were born in 1971 and grew up in a consumer culture and so-called postmodern society[9] (and would now be 34), whereas Rubin's 48-year-olds would now be 64 and were born in 1941, growing up in the aftermath of the Second World War.[10]

The hypothesis was that if Giddens' thesis was accurate, then we would be able to see indications of the 'pure relationship' in the pre-forties' narratives of love and intimacy. However, as already stated in the Introduction to this chapter, there were five aims with respect to the interview material and testing the transformation of intimacy hypothesis was only one of them.

Four people in their thirties/early forties were interviewed and six people in their seventies/eighties were interviewed in order to look at what discourses of intimacy were drawn upon.

Sample	Pre-forties	Post-seventies
Male		Terry, Mr White, Eddie
Female	Sam, Sarah, Rachel, Zadie	Mrs Frost, Mrs Archer, Mabel

Sam lived with her partner, but had never married or had children.

Sarah lived alone, but was in a relationship. She had never married or had children.

Rachel lived with her partner and had two children. She had never married.

Zadie lived alone with her three children. She was divorced and in a new relationship.

Terry was widowed and had one child. He lived at home alone.

Mr Williams was widowed and lived at home alone. He did not have children.

Eddie was widowed and lived in a residential home. He did not have children.

Mrs Frost was widowed and lived at home alone. She had two children.

Mrs Archer was widowed and lived at home alone. She had one child.

Mabel was widowed and lived with her daughter, son-in-law and grandchildren.

Theoretical rather than random sampling was chosen, although as Day Sclater (1999) points out, this does not abandon a commitment to gener-alisability. Indeed, Denzin (1989b) argues that one single life history or small set of life histories can contribute towards an overall research enter-prise. That is, intrinsic to the biographical approach is the recognition that 'no two lives are the same, causal propositions will never be identical from case to case' (200), but that one study may contain 'propositions that per-tain to a total population' (Denzin). Moreover, as Day Sclater (1999) points out, these interviews can be placed in illuminating 'conversation' with one another (she cites Rosenweld's (1988) work in this context). Unfortunately, it wasn't possible to recruit men in the pre-forties age group in the time frame of the study. A comparison of cases was therefore com-plicated by a gender imbalance between the two age groups and by the role of memory in the older age group (discussed in Chapter 10).

The sample criteria were informed by age, gender and class,[11] because:

- The study was situated in the context of societal change since the Second World War. This allowed us to ask whether a discourse of pure/reparative relating was a result of internal maturational change or catalysed by socio-cultural change.
- Women are cited by Giddens as the 'underlabourers of modernity' (p. 200), both championing romantic love and replacing it with a new discourse of intimacy.[12] This allowed us to ask if reparative relat-ing was a gendered, feminised concept of intimacy.[13]
- Plummer (1983) offers us the choice of 'great', 'marginalised' or 'common' subjects, adding that they could be chosen, because they

are 'enculturalised'[14] or because they are non-analytic. This is a problematic demarcation, because people have different types of cultural skills, but the attempt was made to avoid choosing subjects who were well-informed (or likely to speak from) these debates about the possibility of love in psychosocial theory.[15] If the contemporary social conditions which sociologists and psychosocial theorists are describing are catalysing a new cultural discourse of intimacy (narcissistic, pure, reparative), then it should be identifiable beyond the confines of academic debate.

In choosing a sample informed by age, broadly speaking class, and gender there was an attempt to control some variables, but these were, as already stated, otherwise open illustrations of love/intimacy. Despite the similarities between some subjects in terms of age, class and gender, it was recognised that we live at different levels of subjectivity, are multipositioned in discourses, and that 'causal properties' cannot therefore be assumed to be the same from one life to another. Nevertheless, it was hoped that a three-way conversation could ensue among the cases themselves and among the cases, psychosocial theories of late modernity and ideal typologies of intimacy.

9.6   Ethics

As Plummer points out, the interviewer must be ready with an honest answer when asked about his/her motivations which 'will almost certainly include career and professional advantage side by side with some tangible political or moral concern for a problem' (p. 90).

All of the interviewees were told that their confidentiality would be protected, and none responded to the offer to send them a copy of the tape or transcript. Most of the interviewees seemed to enjoy telling their stories, but this was also, in a few cases, upsetting for them. Mr Williams, for example, spoke quietly and tearfully about his war experiences and it is therefore important to think carefully about how one listens, responds and ends an interview. I had completed two postgraduate courses at the Tavistock Clinic in London (trainings in self-awareness and communication skills) and had completed the BNIM training and I felt able to conduct these interviews professionally and sensitively, and to reflect carefully on my methodological mistakes. Discussing one's first encounters with an interviewee and the form of the interview at length is one way to engage in a 'meditative review of analytic work' which is mindful of the ethical implications of one's empirical work.

A self-reflexive approach to empirical work also offers the reader the chance to observe how a researcher occupies the 'biographical stance' and tries to learn from their methodological 'mistakes'.

Discourse analysis, also, however, alerts us to think carefully about the question of what academic theory 'does' to an interviewee's narrative, about what discourses interviewers are penetrated by and more generally about how the question of expertise and authority is negotiated when we analyse a text. Hence Chapter 8 provides a detailed discussion of discourse analytic, sociological and psychoanalytic approaches to method, all of which offer different perspectives on ethical practice in social research.

10
Love and War
Eighty-something Reflections on Romance

We have seen in Chapters 3–7 what sociological, psychological and philosophical approaches offer in answer to the question: 'what is this thing called love?. As explained in Chapter 9, three statements have been deduced from these ways of seeing love:

1. Romantic love is being deconstructed and the question of whether love is possible or impossible is being struggled with.
2. A transformation of intimacy is occurring that is characterised by psychosocial reflexivity and de-traditionalised expectations from love and relationships.
3. A psychosocial interpretation of transcripts about love can address the weakness of an exclusively psychoanalytic or socio-cultural interpretive strategy.[1]

The aim of this chapter is to present material from interviews carried out with six people who were born in the 1920s (and lived through two World Wars). As already stated, Terry, Mr Williams, Mrs Archer and Mrs Frost were interviewed in their day centres. Eddie was interviewed in his residential home and Mabel was interviewed at home. Extracts from these interviews will be presented in order to present some illustrations of love and in order to explore the three broadly conceived statements above.

In Chapter 11, extracts from interviews carried out with Sarah, Sam, Rachel and Zadie will be presented. They were born in the 1960s–70s and grew up in the conditions of 'late modernity' and in the context of a so-called de-traditionalised Western society. The material from the older people's interviews will be compared and contrasted with the material from the younger age group's interviews in the light of the three statements presented above.

10.1   The luxury of love

'What is this thing called love?' is not a question that the older people who were interviewed were preoccupied by. Although marriage and partnership was central to their lives, they did not subject their feelings for their partner, or the concept of love itself, to scrutiny. A preoccupation with the question of what love is, as we will see, clearly demarcates the two age groups interviewed.

Without exception, all of the older interviewees prioritised a discussion of marriage, scarcity, war and the death of a spouse when asked to talk about experiences of romance. None of the younger interviewees had experienced the death of a spouse or war and none had experienced rationing and the scarcity that the older age group had. The content of the older and younger age groups' narratives are therefore significantly different. Terry, Mr Williams and Eddie, for example, all began by detailing their work or war experience when asked about their experience of love and romance and none of them directly answered the question (about their experiences of relationships, marriage) straight away. Perhaps the question itself asked them something that in sociological terms was outside of their gendered system of relevancy (at least initially). This, however, was also true for Mrs Frost, Mrs Archer and Mabel who were from a similar generation, but occupied a different gender position.

What Mrs Archer and Mrs Frost emphasised (like all of the other older interviewees) was the material, structural conditions of their lives (low wages or unemployment, saving up for a marriage, etc.). Marriage itself was part of a material, structural or familial arrangement, rather than a romantic dream. Consider, for example, Mrs Frost's reflections on getting married after the death of her first husband:

I: Mm. Was it difficult getting married again, after? Was it difficult meeting someone?

F: No, I went out to work ( ). Mind you I didn't get married again till I was about thirty-seven.

I: Right.

F: I wouldn't ... I don't think I would have done it, but I wanted children.

Marriage represented leaving the family home (a female single person household being neither economically or morally possible), hence

Mabel recalls crying when her sister got married, because this meant that she would be leaving Mabel and her parents. Mabel got engaged to her husband Jack when she was 21, but she had to wait until she was 24 to marry him, because he had to financially support his mother:

> M: I mean erm it's just that I tell you I was engaged like over three years, and I did say to Jack er, 'The rate we're going on we're ne-we're never going to get married, Jack.' Er so er he, he broke down.
>
> I: Did he?
>
> M: He broke down, and said, 'Well don't say that, don't say that.' Erm I said, 'Well I, I do- I … it's the last thing I want, Jack, but,' I said, 'I don't wanna be engaged the rest of my life.' Erm but I did say to him, too, but he, he really broke down and that, and er in the end we were both crying. But erm er I did say to him, 'I tell you what Jack, if we don't hit it off,' cos I could see what was happening to my sister, I said erm, 'I'll never divorce you, Jack, but,' I said, 'I'd go into service.' He said, 'You're talking tommyrot,' he said, 'cos you'll never … we'll never split up.' 'Well,' I said, 'we say that but you never know, Jack.' So he, he said, 'We won't. I'd never let you go, I'd never let you go.' But as … no, no, no soft stuff. No, you know, no darling I … no darling this or darling that, no.
>
> I: No. Yeah.
>
> M: 'You can't do that, dear,' that's about it, you know. But that suited me, because I, I'm …
>
> I: That suited you?
>
> M: I'm not a … I don't like a lot of fuss.
>
> I: You don't?
>
> M: No.
>
> I: No.
>
> M: No. I mean erm it has to be the right person to cuddle me.
>
> I: Yeah.
>
> M: You know, else I, I, I …
>
> I: You don't like it?
>
> M: I clam up.
>
> I: Yeah.

Mabel is not hailed by a discourse of romance and marriage in a way that concerned second wave feminism (passivity, enslavement, emotional bondage). Her way of talking to Jack is, in fact, quite reality based and it is he who protests at the thought of love's depreciation (see Sartre, Chapter 4). But was this Mabel's intention, did women have to express their needs, (in Mabel's case to leave her family home), covertly?

However, the family home is not entirely left by early modern couples, because they often lived with their parents until they could afford to buy a house and they then cared for their elderly parents in their parents' old age. Eddie and Joy's married life was, for example, very intertwined with Joy's parents' life in a way that Sam's, Sarah's, Rachel's and Zadie's are not. The younger interviewees' stories of love sound quite isolated at points, because siblings and parents are not a part of their romantic narratives and their relationships do not unfold in the context of an extended family or shared community. Thus, the emphasis on talking (the notion of a modern need for 'intense disclosing intimacy' – Jamieson, 1998) might be explained by Berger and Kellner's (1964) observation that in the modern world we make our own romantic narratives by creating shared meanings, a shared reality. Indeed, according to Berger and Kellner the modern love affair is an isolated affair. However, for Sam and Sarah, female friends provide an important extended network and the idea that one's marriage partner is the 'significant other par excellence' (Berger and Kellner, 1964, p. 11) is called into question by their narratives of love. Interestingly, Eddie does question the wisdom of the exclusive tendencies of couples:

E: Well, you see, we did everything together really. I suppose it was a mistake really. We should have broadened our acquaintances really sometimes.

I: Mm.

And the men, in particular, (who were, and perhaps still are, less likely to forge intimate friendships) described themselves as 'going to pieces' when their wives died (Eddie was depressed for seven years, Mr Williams 'went to pieces' and Terry said that his wife's death was the 'biggest shock of his life' and was 'still terrible').

Mrs Frost, Mrs Archer and Mabel did not speak about how they felt when their husbands died and love was not mentioned by them romantically or derisively, or in terms that we might refer to as reparative. What is striking is that a discourse of intimacy isn't explicitly spoken about by any of them. The feminist movement and the 1960s transformation of intimacy perhaps didn't address their lives (when they were in their sixties and seventies), but they do not seem to have expected cupid's arrow to define their lives without these de-traditionalising influences. R. Collins (1972), for example, argues that 'in a situation where men control the economic world' a woman 'maximises her bargaining power by appearing both as attractive and inaccessible as possible' (p. 67). The dominant ideology of romantic love, in this context, is based on sexual repression in which sex and ideals of femininity are some of the 'goods' that women barter with. This might suggest that women of Mrs Frost's age would be more identified with romantic ideologies than women of Sam's age. However, contrary to the postulates of second wave feminism, Mrs Frost's material powerlessness did not lead her to harbour romantic fantasies but to think more pragmatically about arrangements for living.

Indeed, the women described quite assertive relationships with their husbands, within the confines of gender expectations. If there were a preferred discourse of intimacy to be deduced from their stories, it would have to be democratic and we cannot therefore simplistically assume that older women were interpellated by discourses of femininity, motherhood and marriage without resistance:

> A: Mm. {pause} Sometimes in the East End the husbands used to go out on the booze.
> I: Mm.
> A: And they used to set about their wives.
> I: Did they?
> A: My chap hit me once. He didn't hit me no more. Cos we were standing at the sink and he smacked me round the face. And I said, 'Oh.' You know, he was washing up.
> I: Mm.
> A: And I picked up a cup and I threw it at him.
> I: Did you?
> A: I didn't miss him, I cut his head down there. {laughs}
> I: And he never did it again?
> A: No, never hit me. Never.

Mrs Frost also proudly told a story about resistance and resilience, although it was not in the context of her relationships, but in the context of her class background. She recalled a vivid memory about being teased as the 'poor woodcutter's girl' and about tearing the coat of the stock broker's daughter who teased her at school. What seemed to be alive to Mrs Frost was her memory of her retaliation against the taunting school girl (who tried to shame her for selling firewood with her father), her cocoa and toast when she did the rounds with her Dad, her prematurely born daughter and so on. In the interview, she did not recall with the same animation her marriage, the quality of the relationships she had or how she felt when she lost two husbands. It may be that the quality of the intimacy that Mrs Frost shared with her husband, daughter, son, sisters and so on was very important to her, but it was not spoken about. Her sense of romance or her sense of verve, vitality and excitement (see Mitchell's, 2003, definition of romance) seemed to be associated with memories of family and with her childhood self:

F: I sometimes lay in bed and think of all them bits.
I: Do you? Remember them.
F: Yeah.
I: Yeah. They're nice stories.
F: You know, when I used to hear of people writing a book ...
I: Mm.

At the end of her interview, Mrs Frost said that she hoped that she hadn't been talking for too long and she said that 'it's nice to off load'. Her eyes were bright as she left the room and she winked saying 'I'll tell you what it's like being old next time'. Of course, what she raised here was crucially important to a comparison of age-based cases, because the younger interviewees were reflecting on present relationships and on their hopes for the future, but we cannot know if their preoccupations would be the same when they are Mrs Frost's age. As Mrs Archer said, 'there's nobody in the offing now', thus indicating perhaps that there was not enough promise or hope in the future that she could talk about:

A: And bombs was dropping out of the things (as they got burnt up). Uneventful.
I: Mm.
A: Happy enough. {laughs}
I: {laughs} Was it difficult bringing three kids up? Was that a lot of work?
A: I've always worked, so it didn't make much difference.
I: No.
A: I'd work now if anybody'd have me, though I'm too old.
I: Would you like to work?
A: Yes, why not?
I: Yeah.
A: Time seems long.

The future could not be 'colonised' by either work or love and this perception of what life now had to offer affected the form which the interview assumed.

This simple point might explain, to some extent, why the younger interviewees dwelt more on the felt emotional need for a securely attached or enlivening relationship, while the older interviewees (the women particularly perhaps) dwelt more on memories that validated or prioritised their independent identities (in the context of dependency as young women and dependency in old age), rather than more relational memories of restraint in courtships, infatuations and marriage.

Hence, the younger interviewees (despite growing up in de-traditionalised times) were more preoccupied by the question of romantic love (its real or illusory qualities) than their older counterparts. Since romance (historically) is linked to questions of self-definition, desire and hopes of being adored and transported, it is perhaps not something that is easily entertained when bombs drop, money is scarce and you or your partner might die in air raids or at war. Mrs Frost, for example, was separated from her husband for four years:

M: He went up and he was overseas four years and ten months.
I: Was he?
M: And I s- I ... and he came home for a month's leave and he went back on Christmas Eve.
I: Really? So you didn't see him all that time?
M: No.
I: What was that like?
M: I nearly fa- I nearly ... I nearly er passed out.
I: Did you?
M: Er because he went ... when we ... Mum and Dad and his brother and sister-in-law came with me to see him back on the train, and he walked down the platform and he never turned round.
I: Mm.
M: And I wrote to him and I said er, 'You, you never turned round when you ...' He said, 'If I'd have turned round I wouldn't have gone.' You know.
I: Mm.
M: Erm no, I was really lucky, I had a lovely partner, he was very good. Very good.

Interestingly, what emerges from all of the older interviewees' stories is an emphasis on being 'good to each other' in a marriage and on being thankful for having survived the war. A discourse of being good to each other was particularly evident in Mr Williams' narrative and he did not therefore dwell on romance either. He did, however, talk about his first wife 'as the first person he fell in love with' and said that he never 'wanted another woman' and that he was a virgin when he married (possibly like Terry). He might therefore have had expectations which are romantic (monogamy, consummation of a relationship via marriage, love as forever and ever), but he did not speak of great romantic expectations. Both Terry and Mr Williams suggested that their marriages were also friendships, but the kinds of marital friendships described were different to those described by Sam, Sarah, Rachel and Zadie, because they were not based on 'an intense disclosing intimacy' (Sam, Rachel and Zadie complained, because men can't do this).

Although Terry described his wife as an angel and said that he did marry for love, he also had a pragmatic view of marriage. He said that he and his fiancée were getting old (he was 29), that they wanted children and that he, or they, wanted a sexual relationship:

I: Right. Did it mean a lot to you to get married? Was marriage something you'd wanted for a long time, or ... ?

T: No, I hadn't wanted it for a long time, no. And I never thought about having my freedom, it was just that I'd been courting her and er as ... er I mean a lot of it er goes on today, but er it never happened between me and my wife, simply because she wouldn't let me. Er there was no free love.

I: No.

T: No, she would er ... she always insisted, 'That will come when we get married.'

I: Really?

T: Which I admire her for.

I: Yeah.

T: I admire her very much for that.

I: Yeah. And that was for two years then?

T: Two years, mm.

I: Before you got married.

T: Mm, and then I thought, 'Well er we must get married and er try and raise a family,' because I was thinking to myself, 'I'm twenty-nine now, I'm getting old.'

I: Mm.

T: But she was an angel. She was an angel.

Apart from Eddie, none of the older interviewees referred to experiences of falling in love, partnership or re-marriage after their spouses died. This was with the exception of Mrs Frost who re-married when she was 37, because her first husband suddenly died and she still wanted children. Otherwise, none of them spoke about having romantic longings (this does not mean that they did not have them, of course) or the need for a new life partner. Terry explained this by reference to his wife's spirit still being around and this belief would clearly have complicated 'serial monogamy' (if it had been desired by him), because the marriage vow was never, in one sense, broken.

That is, death parted Terry and his wife in material terms but not, in Terry's experience, in spiritual terms. For many 'modern' couples who do not have religious beliefs, children or grandchildren, the end of a long-term relationship can, by contrast, be absolute. Thus, the sociological contention is that 'expressive openness is undercut by fears of loss' (Hochschild, 1998, pp. 8–9):

> *T:* Laughing, she used to say to me er, 'If anything happened to me before it did you,' she said, 'would you get married again?' I used to say to her, 'Look, I've been married to you now for thirty-eight years.' She said, 'Yes.' I said, 'You don't think I'm gonna start all over again do you?' And I've never had any inclination whatever for another woman.
>
> *I:* No.
>
> *T:* No, none at all.

However, Eddie, unlike all of the other older interviewees, did want to re-experience love after Joy's death and his long depression, and he also wanted to dwell on what love meant. Romance for Eddie, like for some of the younger interviewees, seemed to represent hope and aliveness.

Eddie, for example, described being in love with Marjorie, his care worker at his residential home. He said that he was in love with her, but that she was 52 and he was 85, so it was platonic. When Joy died Eddie said that he lost his will to live and he said that he was depressed for the seven years he spent alone, before moving to the retirement home. It is here where he met his carer, Marjorie, who took an hour off after work to talk to him about why he was depressed. It was Marjorie he described loving thereafter and it is this empathic, maternal attention that he valued so much in her (repeating three times the story of her taking extra time to talk to him).

Although he referred to her as the 'most wonderful woman in the world', he also said 'there's no point', because she 'was his carer, living her own life'. His desire for an empathic partner ('I am', he said 'super emotional') clashed with his knowledge of reality, but Marjorie nevertheless seemed to be a symbol of hope for him and a means by which he could love again. So, he moved between describing their relationship in romantic terms (as 'involved', even if platonic) and recognising that she could not be a romantic partner:

E: What's happened since I met Marjorie, I've started to live again.
I: Have you?
E: I've got something that's interesting me.

Like Rachel (in Chapter 11), Eddie associated romance with growth and life, rather than closure and hopelessness (unlike Sam, for example, who unceremoniously 'ditches it'):

E: She er m- do you erm … Margaret bought me a CD of Maria Callas.
I: Oh yeah.
E: Oh, it's beautiful.
I: Really? Yeah.
E: I've, I've … she's taken it away to play, but …
I: Yeah.
E: Oh, it's er … well tell you the truth, when I sat on my bed listening to it, the tears were rolling down my face.
I: Really?
E: I know I'm super-emotional.
I: Mm.
E: I know that.
I: Mm.
E: But things happen that my, my eyes start to water. N- nothing …
I: Mm.
E: Nothing at all, nothing sad or anything like that.
I: Mm.
E: But er the circumstances seem sad to me, somehow. I suppose I've been so lucky all my life that I don't like to think of people who haven't had the same sort of luck as I have.

Love is linked to a romanticist appreciation of beauty, to transience, loss and gratitude, and here both Rachel and Eddie evoke a depressive view of love, which has some affinity with the romanticist sensibility of which love partakes. Although we can understand Eddie's romantic longing as expressive loneliness in his material, structural position (old age in Western capitalist society), this alone misses what romance might represent for him in terms of its life-giving potential.

However, Eddie said that when he was 18 and met Joy, he felt affection but not love, and that he wouldn't have known if he had loved her or not. He said that love grows if there are the right ingredients ('do you like the same things, each other's company and so on'). Love is not therefore seen as the result of cupid's arrow (or a thunderbolt), but as something that grows over time. Eddie was able to speculate on whether Joy was his absolute (he asked how he could know since he did not have any other girlfriends). Nevertheless, the absolute nature of marriage was a key question that he said you need to ask yourself ('could you spend the rest of your life with this person') in order to test your love. Like the other older interviewees, he did not therefore have a more contingent, confluent view of love, which Giddens urges us to confront and embrace. Rachel would also (from a different generation) have had difficulty with this relativist position, because for her, the appeal of love is in how indispensable it can make us feel.

Eddie said that Joy did not need to hear him say 'I love you' and that she did not tell him either. They took it for granted, he says, because they had been married for so long. They never considered divorce and were not therefore a generation of newly weds who could imagine the end of their relationship at the start of it (Hochschild's 1998 contention).

Unlike the other older interviewees, Eddie did want to think about how we might know when we love someone (a key question for many adolescents entering their first relationships) and about whether falling in love was the precondition for marriage for him. However, these were retrospective reflections prompted by the interview and Eddie did not describe being preoccupied by these questions when he was younger. This was in contrast to the younger interviewees for whom 'questions on the meaning of it all' and the 'old philosophical themes' (Beck and Beck-Gernsheim, 1995, p. 47) were at the centre of their personal lives.

10.2   Pragmatism and morality: sex

Giddens' thesis suggests that romantic love is being deconstructed by a younger generation of people. However, as we have seen, any romantic notion of a relationship is largely absent from Mrs Frost's, Mrs Archer's and Mabel's accounts of getting married. The kissing and cuddling of teenage years is referred to by them, but the passion or involvement with one's first loves is not (see Sam and Sarah's vivid recall of sexuality and romance in Chapter 11):

A: Yeah, I knew him at school. We used to stand on street corners and have a little waffle.

I: Did you?

A: Kissing and cuddling.

I: Mm.

A: Where there was a lamppost. Our mothers used to say to us, 'If you get in trouble you'll go to the workhouse.' That was their saying.

I: Was it? Mm.

A: ( ) she meant. {laughs}

I: Mm. And ...

A: They wanted to make sure you didn't have a baby.

Giddens' contention is that 'plastic sexuality' (freed from reproduction) is central to any transformation of intimacy and this clearly was not what women of Mrs Archer's generation experienced in the way that Sam and Sarah's generation do. As Mrs Archer explains:

A: But it's their mums and dads that put pressure on

I: Mm.

A: for you to get married.

I: And wasn't any pressure put on you then?

A: No.

I: No.

A: I married him of me own free will.

I: Did you?

A: I knew him at school, and he was the only one.

I: He was the only boyfriend you had, was he?

A: Mm.

I: Yeah.

A: And they all wanted that before marriage.

I: Did they?

A: Yes, they did. (Lines 42–64)

Mrs. Archer does not therefore see marriage as ordained, but as socially necessary. Terry similarly saw sex outside of marriage as also morally reprehensible and for the 'whoremonger' (though earlier on in the interview he referred to not being able to have pre-marital sex, because of his wife's refusal, not because of his own prohibitive conscience). Eddie similarly related his own views on pre-marital sex to his involvement in the Church and to societal mores:

> E: And er I must admit that a tremendous amount of my time was taken up, not in church, but with church affairs, and of course it was absolutely taboo wasn't it,
>
> I: Mm.
>
> E: to even talk about it.
>
> I: Mm.
>
> E: Not that we wanted to, because we spent all our lives out in the fresh air,

Interestingly, we can see the equation of sex (without love or marriage) to perversity, because it is perhaps cast as 'indoors and dirty', rather than open and fresh. Eddie is not, however 'sexless', he says 'far from it', but he questioned the quality of the emotional and sexual communication (and respect) in what Giddens calls 'episodic sexuality'. What we possibly see in Eddie and Terry's account is a Freudian view of masturbatory, pre-Oedipal sex and a Kleinian view of part-object perversity. It is marriage and partnership which therefore sublimates our more id-like, bestial natures and brings us closer to God and the angels. Reparative relating would not, of course, be conducive to part-object perversity, but neither is pure relating, despite its embrace of plastic, free sexuality. Indeed, Giddens' discourse of the pure relationship is informed by an ethics of (whole object) relating.

Terry's interview reminds us of the fact that the question of whether a new discourse of intimacy can arise has to be thought about in the context of one's religious beliefs. The democratisation of intimacy in Terry's view 'flies in the face of what the Bible says'. And thus a new discourse of intimacy has to be linked to a process of secularisation (in which the existential parameters of life are laid bare). Younger people with religious beliefs may, however, in some cases, have de-traditionalised expectations from love and intimacy, but this issue did not emerge in the younger interviewees' narratives of love.

Terry described his marriage to his wife as legitimating their sexual relationship since he was not 'allowed' to have sex with his wife before he was married to her. They were both Christians and this might support the view (Collins, 1972, p. 69) that the Church and marriage protected women from the uncommitted, but sexually hungry male. Terry's wife was 'admired' for her refusal of pre-marital sex and indeed Terry referred to her as an 'angel'. He said that she showed Christian compassion, she kept a clean home, she didn't drink or smoke and she provided Terry with clean shirts and so on:

I: What, what ... why? What do you remember ... what do you remember about when you met her?

T: Well not only looking after me, in other ways as well. I mean well we, we, we were walking out one night, or one afternoon if you like, and I saw this dirty scruffy tramp walking along, and I said to my wife, 'Look at him,' I said, 'the dirty sod.' My wife said to me, 'What you should be saying is there but for the grace of God go I.' She said, 'You never know what that man's been through.'

I: Mm.

T: And if she had ... in those days, if she had four shillings in her bag, which today would be er twenty pence, if somebody came by and they were hard up, she'd give them half of it.

I: Would she?

T: And then er as I say she never smoked, she never drank, she kept the place spotless.

I: Did she?

T: And all my underclothes were ... well all my washing, didn't matter what it was, it was always there clean and ready whenever I wanted it.

If we want to think about whether romantic, heterosexual relationships recall the mother–infant dyadic relationship we could say that there is some evidence of it here. Terry's wife could be seen as the gently chastising mother who kept him clean in body and mind. She could think about others and show concern and therefore perhaps represented something reparative. Of course, this is what partners in a relationship might take it in turns to offer to each other – mental, emotional and physical comfort or containment.

However, it is interesting to speculate on whether the discourse of the respectable/non-respectable working class/woman is evident in Terry's and Mrs Frost's interviews. Terry's first fiancée got pregnant by someone else and is 'the crafty cow' who tried to trap him via marriage, but his wife was described in more virginal terms.

Mrs Frost and Mrs Archer also condemned the consumption of alcohol which was (and still is) associated with sexual promiscuity and licentiousness. This was, however, more dangerous in their youth, because of the moral condemnation of pre-marital sex and the prospect of the workhouse for unmarried mothers.

Indeed, a striking difference between two of the young women (Sam, Sarah) and the older women is in their expectation about having children. Sam and Sarah are a part of a generation in which cohabitation is increasing, marriage decreasing, divorce increasing and having children later in life is the norm. Marriage, for example, is not Sarah's or Sam's ideal and Sarah only refers to children once. We could say, therefore, that Sarah adopts a sublimated generative identity (see Leff, 1993), which challenges the myth of the Woman as Mother.

10.3   Love and work

Although there are obvious gender divisions in the stories that the older interviewees present, the extent to which they are inequalities has to be questioned. Although Terry's job was important to him (he was a butcher in a factory), he did not seem to be omnipotently identified with a masculine position in which his own job had to be managerial, executive or an expression of strength (see Connell, 2000). There were, to some extent, more modest expectations from life/oneself and a gratitude for what he had already been given ('Oh, I've got many, many, blessings to be thankful for'). There was an admission of an 'egotistical' feeling when he saw his pies in the shop window, but he (like Mr Williams and Eddie) did not seem to be identified with a competitive work ethic.

Mabel and Mrs Frost also spoke proudly of their work, describing it as central to their own and their husband's lives. As Mrs Archer said:

A: It was all right. He worked when he could get work ... which is the thing in, in those days, if you had, had a good job.
I: Mm.

Mabel, in particular, spoke in great narrative detail about her work tasks and interestingly much more than she did the nuances of her relationships. Again, she evoked the image of an assertive relationship with Jack, who clearly didn't immediately understand a woman's need to work:

M: See, and I said to Jack, 'I'm gonna get ...' 'You're not, you're not.' I said, 'I'm going to get a job, Jack.' So he said, 'Do you owe anybody anything?' I said, 'No, I don't, I don't owe anybody anything.' Well he said, 'What are you worrying about, we've got next week's coming.' So I said, 'Well I don't care what you say, if a little one comes along what's gonna happen?' That's another tale I'll tell you.

In fact, she had described seeing her mother with money troubles and she said that she did not want to be in the same position as her. Nevertheless, it is interesting to note that she justified her wish to work by reference to maternal 'instincts', rather than to a more independently minded need to go out and work (which she said she loved). The times nevertheless dictated that Mrs Frost and Mrs Archer had less freedom than their daughters to live their lives outside of the institution of marriage. What this meant was that Mrs Frost did not question her husband's wish for her to be at home, while he was the breadwinner. She may also, however, have wanted to support her husband's need for some measure of 'respectability' as the provider (she described his childhood shame at living with an alcoholic mother):

I: Because when I got married {clears throat} my husband's one of those that … erm didn't believe in it (married women working).

I: Really?

F: No.

I: No.

F: He said, 'No,' he said, 'I'm married, I've got my own …' He had a very strict mother.

I: Right.

F: And when he got married he felt free.

I: Oh yeah.

F: You know.

I: Mm.

F: He said, 'In my house, with my mother and dad, you couldn't speak up.'

I: Mm.

F: No. So once he was married and he was

I: Mm.

F: free from all that … {pause}.

It is interesting to note that none of the younger interviewees spoke about work or about how work was a factor in their reflections on love and romance. All of the younger interviewees did work, but their work choices were not discussed in relation to their partners or in the context of their lives at all. The older interviewees all positioned work as central to the stories that they had to tell about love.

10.4   Love and war

What was also central to the older interviewees' love stories, as already stated, was their war experiences. The women endured long separations from their husbands, air raids and single parenting, and the men were also returning from war with experiences that prompted deep philosophical questions about humanity's capacity for destructiveness:

I: The only thing ... the only thing I used to think about ... you see I was on a Destroyer. I don't suppose you've ever heard of the Bismarck Battle have you?

I: I have, but not ... I don't really know anything about it.

T: No, well anyway, she was a ... she was a vast German battleship. Sunk our biggest battleship.

I: Right.

T: And er we, a little tiny Destroyer, went after her with torpedoes.

I: Right.

T: But then apart from that, a Destroyer mainly is used for submarine hunting, and you used to throw these depth charges over the side.

I: Mm.

T: You know what a depth charge is, do you? Well it's like a round barrel fixed to a long arm, and it contains about half a ton of explosive and you throw it over the side, well you don't throw it, it's mechanically thrown, sinks down to a certain depth and explodes. Well of course we had machinery on board where we could detect a submarine, and I used to stand on deck and I used to think to myself, 'My God, there's men down there in a steel tomb, and they're praying to the same God that I'm praying to.' That was the only ... I used to feel sorry for the enemy, put it that way.

I: Did you?

T: Yeah.

I: And how did you come to terms with it? Have you just thought, 'Well there's nothing I can do about it?' or ... ?

T: Well yeah, just ...

I: Cos you ... mm.

T: I thought, 'Well this is war. If er if we don't kill them then they're going to kill us.' Self-survival and that was it.

I: Yeah. Mm. And were you glad when it was over and you could go back home?

T: Oh, danced for joy.

I: Really?

T: Was in a cinema at Aberdeen. I was on a minesweeper then. We were in the cinema at Aberdeen watching a Bing Crosby film ( ), and it suddenly flashed up on the screen, 'The war in Europe is over, Germany has surrendered.' Oh, we went barmy.

I: Did you?

T: Went back on board ship. The skipper said, 'Right, Germany's surrendered.' He said, 'Now we've got Japan to deal with.' But they collapsed within a few months, so er that was great.

It is puzzling that identity crises are associated with more recent times when war must have catalysed quite radical existential questions about the meaning of life. It also raised quite pragmatic concerns. Eddie, for example, married for love at the time he said, but also because the war started and he wanted Joy to get a widow's pension if anything happened to him. And this sense of life's precariousness affected the wives who remained at home, as well as their husbands on the front line:

E: But I had quite a nice time really. And then of course when I came home the Blitz really started then, I mean when I ... when I went on my honeymoon when we got ... although we had to carry our gas masks round with us,

I: On your honeymoon?

E: there was nothing, nothing doing, but er directly after Dunkirk it really hotted up, you know, it was murder, there's no doubt about it.

I: And you told me last time you spent ninety days in the er air raid shelter?

E: In the air raid shelter, yeah.

The pure relationship, it has been argued earlier (see Chapter 3 and 7), is inflected by an existentialist emphasis on freedom, contingency and living in the present. It is interesting to speculate on whether these war experiences were conducive to this reflexive sensibility:

E: I said, 'But you girls have got to realise, really, that when Joy and I said goodbye in the morning, we never knew whether we were ... we were gonna see each other again.'

It could be argued that what Eddie and Joy experienced, due to material, structural (rather than fantasised) circumstances was an awareness of an obstacle to their love (money, parents, death), which could have catalysed a depressive and or persecutory fear of loss. But a persecutory, paranoid relationship or state of mind, is not what is described:

> *E:* But erm I often think really that ... I know it doesn't apply to everybody, but you see there are some people that, that they don't realise how lucky they are to have survived.
>
> *I:* Mm.
>
> *E:* Or h- or how grateful they (ought to be) to the people that made their survival possible.
>
> *I:* Mm.
>
> *E:* But we can't ... we don't talk about ... nobody wants to know. You start talking to people about the war they'll walk away. Good luck to them, I wouldn't wanna know.
>
> *I:* Mm.
>
> *E:* I, I don't wanna know about it.
>
> *I:* Mm.
>
> *E:* I'm, I'm pleased to think that erm I'm here. I lost a lot of good friends.

We might say that for Mr Williams, Terry and Eddie a new discourse of intimacy (about being good to one another, not assuming a victim position and thinking about those who are worse off) is catalysed by their war experience (rather than changes in gender expectations). Shortly after describing the way in which an Italian prisoner of war contravened certain rules, Mr Williams, for example, said:

> *W:* Well, at that moment I could have run a bayonet through him.
>
> *I:* Mm.
>
> *W:* That's how I felt. It wasn't that I had anything against anybody.
>
> *I:* Mm.
>
> *W:* War is a terrible thing.
>
> *I:* Mm.
>
> *W:* Sometimes you never know whether you might be actually harming your own brother.

We could use the concept of depressive concern to understand what Mr Williams is referring to when he is put in touch with his own propensity for destruction (and in Kleinian terms this awareness of love's adversary – hate is crucial to a more reality-based relationship). That is, a new discourse of intimacy can be catalysed by existential uncertainty and so on, which itself might undermine one's traditional habits and beliefs. Mrs Frost and Mr Williams, for example, have to endure long periods of separation from their partners and confront possible death. They do not, however, elaborate on this. We could imagine a situation in which these long separations might have catalysed a paranoid–schizoid persecutory response (as Zadie feels when out of touch with her partner for more than 24 hours – see Chapter 11), rather than a more depressive concern for the survival of a good object (in Kleinian terms). However, Mr Williams and Mrs Frost do not speak about being confronted by the potential destructiveness of sexual jealousy (though it was, Terry tells us, a time when trust was tested), which might be one consequence of overwhelming separation anxiety or by doubts in their partner's commitment to them.

Mr Williams' social experience (war) and emotional experience (humanity's destructiveness) possibly informed what he expected from his intimate relationships. Mr Williams questioned 'humanity's destructiveness' and he was perhaps closer to a Kleinian understanding of depressive concern than the younger interviewees who might use, on occasion, a new discourse of intimacy (the democratised relationship) in a defended, narcissistic manner. His story of love, however, was embedded in a narrative about world relations and a consideration of what people can do to one another, in contrast to the younger interviewees' accounts of individualised love. He spoke, for example, about how marriage could act to unite nationalities which might otherwise be at war, but it wasn't clear whether he had experienced the way in which war can be taken into one's personal life or whether marriage was the idealised (or merely modest) place where aggression was not supposed to feature.

A concern with the destructiveness that can colour intimate relations characterises sociological, philosophical and psychoanalytic reflections on love in different ways, but Mr Williams said that he didn't 'like to dwell on misfortune' and he said that 'you just have to think of people who are worse off than yourself'. He and his wife, for example, could not have children, but there was no sense of 'why me' and this was similar to the sentiments expressed by the older generation of people in the other interviews when they experienced hardship.

Although romantic love is not deconstructed by Mr Williams and some of the elements of a romantic narrative (courtship, marriage, long-term relationship, monogamy, exclusivity etc.) are evident in his experience of marriage, some elements of the pure relationship are perhaps discernible in the discourse of intimacy he uses (a sense of democratic rights and reciprocal pleasure). Nevertheless, despite there being a discourse of democratic rather than romantic relating (at least to some extent) in the older interviewees' narratives, there is not a search for the articulate therapeutic/reflexive self that characterises the model of intimacy to which the younger interviewees aspire.

Moreover, as we can see, Terry's and Mr Williams' views about love and marriage are not de-traditionalised and they do not analyse their own minds and emotional lives like the younger interviewees do. Indeed Terry, Eddie, Mr Williams, Mrs Frost, Mrs Archer and Mabel would all condemn some factors in the transformation of intimacy (the narcissistic, sexually saturated culture) and moreover, their languages of relating are embedded in socio-religious rather than psychosocial discourses.

Nevertheless, Terry's idea of love, for example, is linked to concern and gratitude, and we thus see thematic links between a Kleinian notion of concern and Christian compassion. The difference of course is that Kleinian concern is fuelled by a belief in how destructive of life and how perverse people can be. Terry is perhaps unforgiving, in this context (referring to whoremongers etc.), but his evocation of 'there but for the grace of God go I' shows some acknowledgement of the way in which loss, imperfection and destruction is a 'fate' which can befall all of us. Thus love is tied to gratitude in Terry's account, but not to socially transformed intimate relations and practices.

10.5   Reflexive love?

Luhmann (1986, p. 166), as already stated, argues that contemporary love relationships are modelled on the therapeutic couple. This, he maintains, is a kind of tyranny and false expectation. The 'illusion of authenticity/honesty' is one which, he argues, lovers should not expect to mirror. However, the younger interviewees' stories of love unfold with a high premium on honesty, psychological disclosure and emotional literacy.

Most of the older interviewees, however, referred to a certain kind of restraint when talking about their feelings with their partners. Mrs Frost, for example, referred to how long she waited before speaking to her husband about his alcoholic mother and his subsequent problems with his 'nerves'. Mrs Frost did not talk to her husband about it until his mother had died:

> *F:* And I s- I said to him, 'He never said anything.' Then, oh, years a-
> when his mother died, I said to him, 'You didn't have a happy
> childhood really, did you, John?' so he said, 'No. No', he said,
> 'I didn't.' So I said, 'Oh, I'm sorry,' I said. He said, 'I didn't know
> what a good home was like till I came into yours.'
>
> *I:* Really?
>
> *F:* And I saw how your mum and dad was.
>
> *I:* Really?
>
> *F:* Yeah.
>
> *I:* Oh.

Similarly, Mr Williams explained that his wife did not ask him about the
war (which he tearfully spoke about at length in the interview). The psychoanalytic 'archaeological dig' does not therefore seem to be a defining
characteristic of intimacy in the relationships that the older generation
of interviewees describe:

> *I:* Mm. And did you, did you talk to your wife about the war when
> you came back or did you decide not to talk about it?
>
> *W:* No, I never s- never about war, because I had enough of it when
> I was in it.
>
> *I:* Mm.
>
> *W:* And she never did fetch the subject up.
>
> *I:* Mm.
>
> *W:* And she understood, and she sort of erm ... she was a very er
> astute person, put it that way.
>
> *I:* Was she?

Although the reflexive project of self and the therapeutic sensibility
might be a late modern phenomenon, we cannot, of course, equate
'talk' about love, romance, feeling states with 'intimacy'. Nevertheless,
there is a different cultural expectation between the younger and older
interviewees in relation to being emotionally expressive, confessional
and articulate and the vehicle of self-realisation and self-expression
seems to be different for these two age groups.

Although it is difficult to know if Mrs Frost or Mrs Archer, for example, were more romantically inclined or expressive when they were
younger, they were clearly not living in times described as reflexive or
therapeutic.

The participants who people reality TV shows, chat shows and soaps in contemporary society may not have experienced anything as 'horrific' (or eventful) as the war that Mrs Archer referred to, but they and the audiences who watch them define their emotional lives as being of intrinsic interest. Mrs Archer, for example, often described her life as 'not very eventful' and it may be that hers, Mrs Frost's and Mr Williams' lives, the private world of emotion ('nerves', the horror of war, feelings about one's partner) were never defined as of intrinsic interest (what people felt or experienced in relationships, marriage etc.), and so Mrs Archer wonders what kind of 'narratives' she could offer. Also, Mrs Archer repeatedly said 'You've gotta get on with it' (life) which was possibly in opposition to 'talking about it'. Mrs Archer's impulse to narrate seemed to be curtailed by an equal impulse to 'get on with it and live'.

However, the cost of Mrs Archer's pragmatic view of life was that her own life was not defined as of intrinsic interest to anybody. Moreover, the prohibition on 'asking' (or exploring) personal questions might mean that other people are not intrinsically or internally seen as of interest. That is, if we all just 'have to get on with it', we might not reach out to 'each other's underlying mentalities' in the way that Stern (see Chapter 7) describes. That is, this fatalistic discourse might lead to isolating and unfulfilling relationships, because it might preclude the kind of deep attachment or rapport that can be experienced when trying to explore the subjectivity of the other.

Younger interviewees, by contrast, do seem to have more of a chance to define their lives and relationships (however uneventful in a material sense) as of interest, because of their material (occupational) and emotional (reflexive, therapeutic) resources.

Perhaps the injunction 'to get on with it' for the older generation who had witnessed the horrors of war is also a protective defence mechanism which aimed to contain that which could not be easily narrated ('the dizzying heights and depths of human experience' described by Craib (2000) – see Chapter 8).

Moreover, Mabel (like Mrs Archer, Mrs Frost, Terry, Mr Williams and Eddie) did not anticipate divorce and although this might have been constraining in some cases, none of the older interviewees describe suffering from the 'shivers of freedom', which Beck and Beck-Gernsheim (1995) argue torment (and empower) a younger generation of lovers:

> The consequence of ... structural changes in society is that for the first time large numbers of people are in a position to wonder about matters not directly connected with the daily grind of earning a

living. At the very moment when life becomes somewhat easier, questions on the meaning of it all can develop a new urgency. These are the old philosophical themes which now start to enter our private lives. (Beck and Beck-Gernsheim, 1995, p. 47)

It is also interesting to speculate on what the role of popular culture and the media is in expressing or provoking our romantic fantasies. Mabel, for example, referred to watching a programme on TV about adoption as a reflexive resource (advising her when it might be best to tell your child that he or she was adopted). It was, however, the only reference to the media she made, unlike the younger interviewees who referred to film, music, celebrities and literature as part of their exploration of what love and relationships ought to be ideally like. In contrast to this Mrs Archer, Mrs Frost, Mr Williams, Terry and Eddie referred to the beginning of cinema, but they did not have the 'oversupply of (media) options' (see Beck and Beck-Gernsheim, p. 7) available today.

10.6 Psychosocial interpretations

The older interviewees' stories, unlike the younger interviewees' narratives, were not characterised by emotional expressivity, self-reflexivity and a dialogical relationship with one's socio-cultural habitat. Their narratives of love were not therefore self-consciously psychosocial in the way that the younger narratives were. However, an emotionally expressive, discursively aware culture and narrative does not necessarily signify insight, compassion or knowledge and these reflections are not, therefore, meant to be value judgements. Perhaps what we see in these older peoples' interviews is a humble positioning of oneself in a world wider than the internal, psychological one. This might, in some cases, lead to a neglect of the psychological, but it shields one from the solipsistic world of narcissism. Perhaps war and death (or ageing) can lead to more of an appreciation of contingency, mortality and aloneness that deconstructs or overshadows more narcissistic romantic fantasies.

The older interviewees are more attentive to their societal circumstances than they are to their own states of mind and feeling and the psychosocial imagination is not, therefore, the 'intellectual common denominator of the times (Mills' 1959 term) for them. Nevertheless, a psychosocial interpretation of what they say and why is important, because we can speculate about the psychological effects of material circumstances, class or gender positions, ageing and the future, cultures of inhibition (as opposed to expression) and of a certain type (and benefit) of a fatalistic position.

The relevant psychosocial question[2] in this context is whether the socio-economic conditions in the older generations' youth were ones that encouraged an opening up of psychic space in which they could explore themselves and their relationships. Asking this question is not the same as speculating about their internal worlds, but it is a question that asks about how discursive positions and material circumstances might affect states of mind and the form that an interview takes.

11
Love and Peace
Thirty-something Reflections on Romance

In this chapter extracts from interviews carried out with members of the younger group will be discussed, and contrasted with the material from the older age group in relation to the three hypotheses presented in Chapter 10. To repeat, these are:

1 Romantic love is being deconstructed and a view of love as possible or impossible is being struggled with.
2. A transformation of intimacy is occurring that is characterised by psychosocial reflexivity and de-traditionalised expectations from love and relationships.
3. A psychosocial interpretation of transcripts about love can address the weakness of an exclusively psychoanalytic or socio-cultural interpretive strategy.

11.1 Deconstructing romance: love's inequalities

Like Mrs Archer, Sam immediately related romance and marriage to sex. Sam argued, quite simply, that romance is used as a way of sublimating sexual desire. She said that sexual desire for girls and women was complicated by their unappealing view of men as predatory, emotionally inarticulate and power hungry. Female sexual desire is also, of course, complicated by social norms which dictate that women should court desire, but not be the bearer of the gaze and of sexual hunger.

Sam did not, as a result, see romantic love as a modern, progressive form of love (the harbinger of the pure relationship),[1] and she was exasperated, she said, by the ideal of femininity that women had to live up to in romantic, heterosexual relationships. This ideal of femininity might be one that Zadie aspired to when she took four hours to get ready before going out with her partner, Pete. Men, as a result, Sam argued, have got much more reason to invest in romance, because the woman (as the symbol of romance) is the heroine who is beholden to keep her man's desires and fantasies alive:

> S: men want ... I mean in, in relation to that (romance), erm demureness with acceptable levels of vivacity and wit, erm good looks, virginity if at all possible, but not to be such a tedious bore that er breaking that virgin in would be terribly traumatic for either party. Erm I think men want contradictory stuff whereas women are thinking about what they, what they have to ditch in order to get what they actually want. I think men are terribly romantic.

And Sam pointed to an uneasiness that women may feel in relation to an imaginary sex symbol, which women must somehow resemble, compete with or envy. In the following extract, Sam, for example, described what her romantic fantasies coalesced around before she gave them up:

> S: being a f- er a far more beautiful version of who I was, erm with no spots and er felt comfortable in her clothes, and had fashionable clothes, erm being courted by erm terribly handsome men or more particularly very witty men who were leaders of men, who were men that I would be too scared to go for, erm being witty in response, erm being desired but not in an oppressive way. Erm just, just being adored really.

In this context (of beautiful romantic heroines) it is not surprisingly that Sarah said that she was relieved that her present partner (who she met through a dating agency) did not seek out a 'virile bandy woman'. Nevertheless, for their first meeting, she had 'blonde streaks' done and she described her dress sense as signalling that it 'is OK to have sexual feelings about me'. However, like Sam, she did not want to position herself only as the passive recipient of the male gaze. For example, she described her irritation at her partner's casual dress sense on their first date, as she herself dressed in a sexy way. Her disappointment seemed to be both gendered and class specific. 'David', by dressing casually, had not given Sarah the opportunity (permission?) to find him sexually attractive, because by dressing in an uncaring way, he did not position himself as an object of desire for Sarah's pleasure. Sarah was disempowered to the extent that David as she understood it 'didn't want to be a turn on'. However, on their second date, Sarah noticed that David had changed his footwear and she saw him bending down to tie his shoelace, and dust off his shoes, thus setting, for Sarah, the right signal. Sarah talked about this disempowering him and this was perhaps because she was now the bearer of the gaze and could be flattered by his efforts such as ironing his shirt. This then was part of Sarah's expectation of and pleasure from the romantic ritual. It was, for her, class specific, because for Sarah it was middle class men who dressed expensively, but scruffily, while her beginnings as a working class secretary recalled how both men and women dressed up in order to 'trap off'.

Traditional expectations and perceived transgressions were still evident in Sarah's story, however. When I asked Sarah how she 'got over' the end of one of the relationships she recalled, she answered:

S: Well only really through meeting someone else, and so sort of latching on to the next one. I just think it just sounds like a long list (laughter). Yeah.

I: And do you (S. continues to laugh) Well, they are, for us all (shared laughter)

I could not finish my sentence, because Sarah's laughter perhaps signalled some kind of uneasiness regarding her 'long list'. I tried to put her at ease by normalising this, making a generalisation to the effect that many people could cast their mind back on a 'long list'. However, in the older people's narratives the list was, in fact, very short (and women faced being called 'whoremongers', 'crafty cows' and the work-house if it was a long list). Nevertheless, these sexual mores were still exerting an influence on the younger interviewees. Thus, Sarah's unease or self-consciousness, at least, was an example of the way shame and embarrassment are emotions which can be used as mechanisms of social control or self-censorship (especially of women).

However, Sarah suggested that men are also oppressed by the representations of masculinity available to them, just as women are by the contradictory representations of a woman as 'Mother, Madonna and Whore' (to use Welldon's phrase, 1991). The fact that Sarah's partner could not tell her 'for a long, long time' that he was put off by a woman 'out for sex in a high speed way' perhaps reflects some anxiety about departing from the sexually insatiable, macho stereotype that Sam abhors.

The romantic narrative is, according to Sam, impossible to opera-tionalise in unequal heterosexual relationships (or more equal long-term relationships):

> S: I've never been in a relationship even with the one with the demon lover, where I didn't wake up one morning, look at them and think, 'Actually you bore me for quite a lot of the time.'

For Sam, a belief in romantic love is therefore something that we should grow out of just as we do when we stop believing in Santa Claus:

> S: I think that's … I think that's foolish, I think it's immature. It's the kind of yearnings we had when we were fourteen that, that we don't have now, or we don't live by them now. We wouldn't say, 'Until this happens this is not right.' We would say, 'It would be nice if this happened from time to time. I know it's not real, but enjoy it all the same.' But not put huge aspects of our life on hold for want of that feeling which isn't real.

The romantic narrative is an oppressive story to live one's life by, she thinks, but a good story once you realize that 'it is a load of hokum'. What we can see here is the idea that romance is a script, rather than a natural emotion, thunderbolt or blinding arrow that we are pierced by. And it is, according to Sam, a mistake to confuse the story for reality:

> S: Oh well, in relation to that, I mean there's something I read in Marie Claire shortly after that erm which they put in an advert, erm five women saying Elizabeth Bennett seeks her Mr Darcy and er Mr Darcy seeks Elizabeth Bennett. And er the most unlikely couples, you know, physically and, and emotionally and intellec-tually and verbally were, were photographed and were talking and they were all desperately disappointed with each other, quelle surprise, cos you shouldn't go looking for your Mr Darcy really.

However, she likened men to children who want to cling on to the idea that there is this magical, benevolent, gift bearer (the romantic heroine) who hopes for nothing in return for her emotional and aesthetic labour. Sam was angry at the masquerade that was expected of her (the sweet, sexually saturated, emotionally articulate, childlike, nurturing woman):

> S: But now we have other options, other expectations, and romance is incompatible with those, it's a kind of chain. Men have what they always had, and, and they want, they want that er …

I: And what, what is that?

S: The power. They still have the majority of the power, they, they have … a little tiny bit of it gets given to women, and they're up in arms about how the clock's going backwards, or the pendulum's swung to an opposite extreme. Erm and they want their … they want their women to be pretty and dainty and a professional career woman, but not as professional as them.

Sam's position can be described as social constructionist to the extent that she emphasised the ideological function of romance (the sublimation or domestication of sexual desire, the justification of sado-masochistic relationships, the obfuscation of the boredom experienced in long-term relationships, monogamy etc.). Sam had clearly (like Sarah and Rachel) been influenced by a feminist deconstruction of romantic love as 'the pivot of woman's oppression', but unlike Rachel, she did not rescue anything from the romantic narrative, apart from seeing it as a 'resource to be dipped into' occasionally. Sarah, Rachel and Zadie, like Sam, also deconstructed romantic love, but they expressed more nostalgia or fondness for the state of mind or feelings associated with it than Sam did:

R: I think the only other feeling that's close to romantic love that you feel for, you know, a boyfriend or girlfriend whatever, is with your child, and that feeling you have with them it's not usually when they're awake or anything, it's usually when they're fast asleep and you look at them and you think they're really cute and everything and you've got this connection with them that is … you wouldn't find anywhere else, that's unbreakable. That's … you can be suffused with the same sort of love. But that's not romantic love, but I think at least that feeling is somewhere else, not just with erm, you know, boyfriend or girlfriend.

11.2   Deconstructing romance: love's telepathy

Sarah's expectations from love were first challenged, she said, in her relationship with Tim, because he asked her to articulate her needs and thus work at being understood. Her former expectations from what love was supposed to bestow upon her rendered her passive as she waited for 'wordless understanding' (see Klein, 1963) with her partners. This is something that Sam disparagingly referred to as the desire to want things to be 'instinctively right', to 'click into place', which she found 'exasperatingly romantic'. Sarah's story, however, revealed how power-ful this desire for telepathy is:

> S: It was kind of like having expectations of maybe even concrete things they'd do, but not ever telling them, that that is what they're supposed to do. And then getting disappointed, because they didn't have telepathic ability or something, which is being generous to them, because sometimes they could have perhaps have had a bit more intuition than they did have, to be fair. But at times it was partly my responsibility I think.
>
> I: And why do you think you weren't telling them?
>
> S: I didn't realise that one could, or that perhaps one ought to. I sup-pose, I think I believed that they would just know, that if they were in love with me, that they would know. Otherwise they can't possibly love me, how could they love someone if they didn't know even these basic, basic things?
>
> I: And did that change with Tim?
>
> S: I began to think that perhaps it took more work than I had realised.

In Fromm's (1957) terms we could say that Sarah was beginning to 'stand' in love rather than expect to 'fall' into it. The idea that love is work is also much closer to Klein's concept of love, which is not, in fact, romantic. Sarah also described her discovery that sexual attraction might need working at too 'amazing'. That is, she discovered that neither sexual nor loving feelings are necessarily instantaneous or pre-ordained:

> S: Which was ridiculous ... now when I think about it, but at that time I didn't really have that concept that you could gradually fall for someone. So this was a big discovery. That feelings grew over time.

The passivity which a belief in romantic love (albeit seductive, charming and exasperating) confers on us (De Botton likens it to crystal ball gazing) is here discussed by Sarah:

> S: I think at the moment of splitting up with them or realising that things really weren't very good with them, I think then I probably thought that they really didn't have a clue. And I got very frustrated by it, I would say frustration was the key theme, and being disappointed and not really understanding why they

wouldn't want to know me or, why couldn't they just give me what I wanted, why couldn't they just make me feel nice, what was the problem? I think I just wanted to feel good, I think I just wanted to have a nice life, I don't think I had any concept that I could do anything about it myself, for quite a long time probably. I thought it just kind of happened when you were in love and then everything was all alright.

To want to be understood without talking (that is, lovers can read one another's thoughts) is to perhaps want what Winnicott refers to as the omnipotence (and relief) which a child might feel when a mother antic-ipates his/her needs without them needing to voice them. That is, in Barthes' (1978, p. 104) words, the lover wants the 'maternalism of infancy and the genitality of maturity' (see Chapter 4).

11.3 Deconstructing romance: taking a break from relationships

One of the things that clearly demarcated the two age groups was whether they had had an experience of serial monogamy and of being single as a life choice in-between two relationships. None of the older interviewees described more than one major relationship (with the exception of Mrs Frost who re-married after being widowed) or a situa-tion in which they could choose to be single in their youth. Sarah, however, described her first experience of being single as a turning point in self-definition and in shaping what she wanted from relationships:

S: Because what happened was that we (Sarah and a casual partner) were going to go out one night, and I went around to call for him and he didn't want to go, he was too low and we sat and watched telly and I remember sort of just sitting there and thinking I could be out, with some friends I'd met by then Deb, and Sue, who have now become good friends the last few years. I do remember thinking, like why am I here in some ways, so I think I did get lonely sometimes but I also began to perceive that you could be on your own. That nothing terrible happens, the sky doesn't fall in, the floor doesn't open, you know. I think it is around that time that I sort of began to think that, which I haven't sort of thought before really, properly.
I: How old were you then?

S: I was probably 20 something, er hang on 21–22–23–24, 25/26 maybe, yes.

I: Was that quite a sort of liberation to feel that?

S: It was and it was also frightening, because part of me also thought, well that's alright but obviously this is some kind of temporary state (laughter). So it is like going on holiday, it's nice to have your holiday, but I didn't seriously think at that point that I would be in that situation for a long, long time, not that I thought I was devilishly attractive particularly, but I didn't think that the people were, in general.

The theme of status is raised early on in Sarah's interview. She described her first relationship as 'almost for show', in order to have a 'boyfriend in public', and her second relationship gave her the one-upmanship she frankly talked about (over female housemates who didn't have a boyfriend to pick them up in a nice car and take them out for meals).

Interestingly, Storr (1988) observes that our society puts too high a premium on being in a relationship and suggests that having an active sexual/love life has become the contemporary hallmark of mental health. But Storr (1988) points out that many creative geniuses preferred and needed solitude, and he refers to the creative genius in order to show that solitude has its own reproductive qualities.

However, in Western society celibacy is still an oddity, as is choosing to live alone or not get married, or not to have a boyfriend or girlfriend and these normative assumptions clearly had a stronger impact on the older interviewees, but the younger interviewees also struggled with them. Sarah, for example, internalised these norms as a young woman and demonstrated her belonging to society by 'having a boyfriend in public'. The idea that a rich internal world may exist (Klein, 1963) despite external solitude is not easily countenanced in contemporary culture and neither was it yet an option for Sarah.

This is reminiscent of what De Botton (1993) refers to as a kind of romantic fatalism whereby we think that we must be destined to meet someone, and that this is life's end point or telos. Sarah's description of singledom as a holiday, therefore, implies that this break is merely an interruption on a journey to our lost half (or companion of some description). This echoes what Plato's character Aristophanes says in *The Symposium* (and which Freud echoes): we are only half a person without a soul mate with whom to unite. That is, somewhere, someone must be waiting to be completed by us (their lost half or right arm), just as much as we wait or search for them. Hence, it is very hard to consider singledom as anything other than a good or bad holiday, that is, a departure from the norm of coupledom or marriage. One can, of course, look at socio-economic and cultural reasons for this organisation of life, but a psychoanalytic explanation of the organisation of life around an axis of exclusive coupledom will focus on our entry into life as one half of a mother/father infant dyad and suggest that it is this union (and primary attachment figure and relationship) that we need to restore, in order to live an ontologically secure life.

However, Sarah is not willing to begin a relationship indiscriminately in order to assuage any uneasiness she has about being on her own. Importantly, she has a strong network of female friends, a factor which was equally important to Sam. Sarah remembered the night she stamped back home, feeling disappointed and angry, but she did not describe being despondent or hopeless. Thus, a sense of choice is what seems to have made this particular time of life significant:

I: So in that period of being on your own, did you have a sense of choice? Did it feel like choice then?

S: I don't recall meeting lots of blokes who were always asking me out, so in material terms I probably didn't have a huge choice. It wasn't like I was always being bombarded, you know. But I think I had perceived I could have made more effort, and that I wasn't really. I was quite happy to go and watch a video at somebody's house I didn't necessarily always feel who else is going to be there, will I meet anyone, I wasn't in that kind of state of mind.

Sarah described this period of her life as a growing up space, and referred to her past relationships as constituting 'silly choices'. She, therefore, said that she couldn't have done this growing up in a relationship, because she couldn't trust her choice of partner. The concept of projective identification allows us to surmise (not necessarily accurately) that one's choice of partner represents split-off aspects of oneself. Thus, being single allows one to perhaps take back one's projections and be unencumbered by another person's struggling sense of self. Sarah thus implies that there is a pleasant simplicity in just going to work, just being and doing what everyone else in the world does:

S: Umm ... Well I think also it just allows one to grow up a bit more really. I did a lot of growing up at university, but probably not enough, I am probably still quite immature by the age of 25 in some ways, it was probably quite nice to have that couple of years, just being and going to work. Doing what everyone else in the world does (laughter).

It's interesting that Sarah described this period as 'just being', and feels aligned with the world, perhaps in a way reminiscent of the way in which the older interviewees described their existential place in a world of work. Craib (1994) thinks that because we do not expect to encounter disappointments in our relationships, we suffer from a demanding need for intimacy, which work can actually offer us respite from. Berger and Kellner, writing over three decades before Craib also highlight the isolation of the nuclear family and the modern couple.

Does Sarah's 'just being and going to work' also recall Freud's view of love as a wild and furious master? Perhaps this period of Sarah's life can be seen as a kind of sublimation or latency period where other interests, other states of mind and worlds of work can be inhabited. In this context, we might also ask whether, despite their lack of material choices, some of the older interviewees had more mental space than some of the younger interviewees. Those like Zadie thought about their uncertain futures 24 hours a day, as she tried to understand her partner Pete's mind, desires and patterns of attachment.

Sarah's life, like Sam's and unlike, of course, the older interviewees' unfolded in the aftermath of the sixties ideas on free love and the feminist ideas of the seventies on equal love, ideas which filtered through in Sarah's education (Sam, Sarah and Rachel had all been to university, unlike the older interviewees who left school in their teenage years).

Hence Sarah described how when she became interested in feminism, she also dated two men at the same time (unbeknown to them). In this period of her life she had become, she said, more active and questioned her 'long list', the 'pick' she had, and why she had to passively accept this 'list' she never really wanted. Indeed, Sarah now asked herself why she was 'bothering' at all:

I: How did you start to want to leave the relationship? How did your feelings ... Can you remember your feelings changing, or what it felt like when they were changing.

S: Well, I ended up in a bit of a situation (laughter), it sounds awful, but I actually met someone else and dated both of them, for about three months and it was a nightmare, and at the end of it, the other one got very upset and just left, and umm I never told John about that really. Then I felt the guilt that I had was absolutely enormous. In the end I just didn't really want to go out with anyone, and around that time I was also becoming more interested in ideas of feminism, and associated ideas that I was learning due to courses and stuff I was doing. So I think I was probably beginning to question what I was doing anyway and why was I going out with any of them, and why bother

When I asked Sarah what attracted her to the man she dated at the same time as John, she said:

S: Umm (sigh) I don't know he just seemed very peaceful really, he was a bit of an old hippy really, and I think John wasn't. So it was to do with the new things I was finding out about love, more than anything. Yeah.

This described a different kind of masculinity from the 'man of the world' image that characterised her previous partners. This 'old hippy' also perhaps contrasted with Sarah's class background, John wasn't 'an old hippy', he represented 'nice cars', 'real restaurants', the 'proper', 'public' things Sarah may no longer have wanted or needed the comfort of. And she was also beginning to think about what *she* wanted and what *she* desired:

I: And did feminism take the place of relationships for a while then? Was that your experience when you were coming across those ideas?
S: No. I wouldn't say they took the place ... I think, I think they made me question my role in some relationships in a way that I hadn't before and umm ... I think at one point I thought I was getting harder to get to know or something, possibly. I suppose I assumed that the reaction to that would be very negative for most young men, and certainly somewhere like the University of Liverpool it probably was in reality. But I also think that I was finally trying to establish myself and wanted some space in some ways, which wasn't necessarily to do with those ideas, I don't know.

11.4   Deconstructing romance: love's past

Interestingly, Sam, Rachel and Zadie all understand their present need for love in terms of their childhoods. Although Mrs Frost referred to her husband's 'rotten childhood', she did not look at how this affected his attachment patterns or needs as an adult, and none of the older interviewees questioned their own ways of relating or choice of partner in terms of their childhoods. Thus, we can see the way in which the younger interviewees deconstructed the narrative of romance in both sociological (gender stereotypes, sexual sublimation, marriage vows and so on) and psychological (for example, transference love and the compulsion to repeat) terms (without, of course using these technical terms), thus showing how a transformation of intimacy is conducive to a psychosocial sensibility (and vice versa).

It would be wrong to assume, however, that a sociological and psychological deconstruction of romance was only the preserve of educated young people. Zadie, who did not go to university, like Sarah, Sam and Rachel (who did go to university) also tried to understand her partner's inaccessibility (and her own choices) in terms of gender and psychology.

Zadie said that romance was equated with 'showing your feelings' and risking being hurt and that Pete had 'put a lid on all that', because his wife had left him unexpectedly. The fact that Pete wouldn't show his feelings meant that 'it's like a battle all the time really. You, you then ... you never really know how they feel. You know, sort of ... well you're, you're left in a state of wondering'.

Zadie described herself as showing her feelings, but she also said that she too was defended against expressive openness (a characteristic of Giddens' 'confluent love'). It is life itself that had deconstructed romance or made Zadie temper her romantic hopes, because when you're 18 she said you: 'haven't been through what life throws at you, I suppose, and the ups and downs and the divorces and God knows what else'. Zadie seemed to veer between saying that she was different now (ready to 'start again'), but that 'it's not all plain sailing' despite her wishes (thus questioning the fully autonomous self assumed by a discourse of pure relating).

She said that she had 'stepped over' the 'insecurities and crap' of her past relationships, but she went on to describe a very insecure relationship with Pete. Her way of speaking and assessing her present position was therefore uncertain, just as her relationship was, thus confirming Beck and Beck-Gernsheim view of contemporary lovers (and reconstituted family life – Pete and Zadie both had children from first marriages) as plagued by doubts and uncertainty.

Although Zadie said that she was different now to how she was in relationships in the past, she nevertheless said that it's 'weird', because how she felt when she was 18 was no different to how she felt at 41. There is some reference here perhaps to emotion as always powerful and not necessarily subject to 'elocution lessons' (Phillips), and to an internal world in which our earlier blueprints for relating have retained their force and pull. In Zadie's story of what it felt like to be in a relationship (and it resisted narrative neatness), there was much more acknowledgement of a psychoanalytic view of relating than the confluent, pure, sociological view allows for. Zadie and Pete belonged to a generation for whom, we could argue, the transformation of intimacy has led to (persecutory?) wariness. Zadie's attempts at negotiating the terms of her and Pete's relationship, she said, have led to a 'roller coaster of a year' in which she thinks, she said, 24 hours a day about what is happening. However, one's efforts at depressive concern need to be understood as externally determined (by gender, the reality of the other's internal and external relating) and not only as the result of one's own psychic reality. However, in psychoanalytic, existentialist and sociological terms, even if the other is responsible for our relationship's lifelessness or persecutory quality, we are still left with the responsibility of choice if we stay in it (hence Zadie's annoyance at herself and Pete).

What Zadie describes is not a facilitative relationship in Giddens' sense nor a reparative one in a Kleinian sense, nor one which Zadie spoke about as ideal. However, her story does remind us of how difficult it can be to create and maintain relationships of concern, equality and altruism despite the proliferation of self-help books on the 'art of loving' (De Botton's 'romantic positivism'):

Z: Well the good days are I've got I suppose (some highly) positive feedback from him or erm {pause} petting a lot or whatever, you know. And the good ... the bad days are when he doesn't text me for several days, (he doesn't speak to me) and he seems to ... he just goes cold and then ... but erm and then, see then you think, 'I can't s- I handle this any more.' But it's a pattern with him now, I know it is. It's almost like if he gets ... {laughs} I don't ... I mean I don't know from a man's point of view, but when things are going well and it's almost like he's getting too close or he's starting to have some kind of feeling, then he cuts straight off, and he, he just holds back. He won't contact me for a bit and ... it's really weird.

Like Sam and Rachel, Zadie tried to understand her current relationship in terms of her past. She described her mother's and father's relationship as quite similar to her and Pete's relationship. Her Dad did not show his emotion, she said, and he was not particularly romantic about Christmas and New Years (they're just another day, he maintained) and as Zadie reflected on whether Pete would come to see her for Christmas, she tried to tell herself that perhaps her Dad was right. She described her first mother-in-law as emotionally distant and said that she 'never kissed or cuddled' her son (Zadie's first husband) or grandchildren (Zadie's children) and Pete was also described as 'cold'. Zadie said that she too was uncomfortable with 'kisses and cuddles', because she was embarrassed and scared of rejection. In her and Pete she therefore described two people who were 'keeping a lid' on their feelings. In psychoanalytic terms, we could say that this is perhaps a defence against separation anxiety and a simultaneous provocation if it:

> Z: Erm even if he only texts me, then that … I'm, I'm all right. If he doesn't, you know, it's like I just walk around like a sort of bear with a sore head and like an em – erm an empty feeling inside. So it's weird really. I'm only truly happy if I'm with him.

But because she could not securely be with Pete (or any of her previous partners), she said 'that what comes to mind is, is just … if you think of love is more or less heartache.' There seemed to be no end, for example, to Zadie guessing about whether Pete would commit to her, whether he would come for Christmas or New Year, whether he would move towards or away from her and to her wondering how she could play this game as best as she could.

Barthes (1978, p. 13) referred to the beloved as fugitive and the lover as in a state of perpetual waiting, but this was a very gendered problem in Zadie's case. She's 'on a chain', she said and 'it's yanked whenever he decides to yank'. This would be, from a second wave feminism point of view, the very bondage that romantic love traps women in. But Zadie wasn't only passive and captive. She was annoyed at her own choice and seemed to want to understand why she had attracted this type of man or relationship:

> Z: I went to a … actually recently went to a wedding and I was sitting beside my friend's husband, and he was talking to this other guy, and just sitting there and he was singing her praises so much, and how wonderful, and I thought, 'I hate you.'.

What romance therefore represented for Zadie was the good relationship that she could not find and because she couldn't, she struggled with the reality of it, but she questioned herself as much as the narrative of romance as a wish-fulfilment.

When it came to defining her attraction or love for Peter she said that it is 'something there that pulls me towards him, and it's just something right from the word go I thought was just meant to be'. Of course, we can be drawn to 'good' or 'bad objects' and relationships, and Zadie evoked something of the wordless communication that Stern (1985) foregrounds in his infancy studies, but that Giddens neglects in his rationally negotiated relationship. Zadie, was to some extent, struggling with the uncertainties about her self and her relationship and she was not completely self-present in the way Giddens describes. Of course, Lacan and Barthes would suggest that we never will be self-present and understand ourselves/the other in any complete way. Our frustrated desires are, from this viewpoint, our human lot, but accepting our incomplete, divided state can be done more sympathetically than perhaps Zadie's relationship with Pete allowed for. However, according to Mitchell (2003), although romance can make life feel imbued with importance, it is unstable – and this, he explains, is why many lovers sing the blues.

Zadie did not literally say that her relationship with Pete repeated her mother and father's pattern of relating, but it is interesting to note that she recalled their way of relating when recounting her own relationship with Pete. Rachel and Sam are perhaps more explicit in talking about how ghosts from the past affected their view of, and need, for love, but all of the younger interviewees shared an interest in 'the plethora of otherness in us' (Mitchell, p.81). Rachel, for example, related her passionate love with Adrian back to her own insecurity and 'massive hole' and to her need to feel special, and thus she spoke about love in relation to her internal world and its shadows (or radiance) from the past. She linked her own need for romantic love back to childhood deprivations and losses, and she wondered if romance was what we might call a transference love and substitute satisfaction:

R: I, I was just about to say that maybe, you know, the person who's feeling in love has got, has got to be susceptible to that, maybe they've got a special need, you know, in their life to feel special. But I can't even agree with myself on that, because too many people feel it, and I think you can't sort of say that everybody has got this pathological need

I: Mm.

R: to feel in love. Surely, I mean that it's just pleasant as well.

Although romance might have its pleasant side, for Sam it symbolized the violence of men, the passivity of women and the naivety and vulnerability of children. Mills and Boon are, she said, sado-masochistic, men are like children who need to be disabused of their fantasies and power, and trusting, childlike women need to grow up and defend themselves against their own fantasies.

Sam, however, did locate her own views about love in the context of her vulnerability as a child, perhaps explaining (to some extent) why she was despairing of the vulnerable positions women occupied in romantic narratives (in which they wait to be loved):

> S: There was, there was no, there was no love for me as a child. Erm there was violence erm and disappointment and fear, erm and I think I'll always crave love for, for that reason. You know, there are some people you recognise, no matter how much anybody loves them they can't love them enough, and that was certainly true of my father, but that was true for a reason. Nobody did and he carried it with him for ever. So I know what I want and I know when I'm not getting it. But I, I was loved by my mother as a child but I never felt it. Erm I know what I want for my child is, is unconditional love erm and, and again that freedom to be from a safe place, you can always come back to the safe place. But I didn't have that, erm so I craved it, but my requirements then as a child were so much more basic. Freedom from violence and freedom from fear that any kind of erm, you know, subtle nuances about the nature of the love that I required would have been so far ahead, based on the basic requirements that, that I had that weren't being met, that no I, I never really gave that any thought.
>
> I: Mm.
>
> S: You just know when something's a yearning and you, you can't have it, and er I yearned it but I, I didn't have it. So you, you don't get into erm levels of love or definitions of love, you just want some.

11.5   Defending romance

Mitchell (2003, p. 109) argues that the contemporary psychoanalytic ideal of mental health is one in which emotions are experienced vividly and intensely. There has been a move, he argues, from a prototype of health based on rationality, regulation and sublimation of feeling (a 'scientific' model) to an 'artistic' model of self-expression and self-exploration. The injunction to 'know thyself' is combined with 'express thyself' and 'explore thyself' (p.109), and this contemporary emphasis on vitality, creativity, authenticity (as well as safety and stability) makes romance, Mitchell argues, a viable adult experience (p. 140). Psychoanalysis casts a wary eye over the ideal of romantic love (see Chapters 5 and 6), and Mitchell's unusual defence of romance will be used in order to highlight the hopefulness it expresses and the reasons why we might yearn for some of its urgency.

Mitchell argues that the inability to romance oneself and the other is 'a defence against allowing oneself to become excited about one's potential and engaging others in a robust fashion' (2003, p. 110). Mitchell therefore defends the romantic sensibility (with a healthy capacity for episodic, passionate idealisation) against its detractors who would see it as regressive. Mitchell does add, however, that it is important to assess whether the idealisation of the other is in them (and unveils their masked/hidden qualities) or is an act of pure imagination.

In this context, it is interesting to note that Rachel, despite holding the sign of love up to scrutiny, equated it with something life-giving:

> R: Erm so I probably wouldn't be … I mean I'm probably misjudging, but I know a lot of erm … {pause} you know, I don't know, maybe I'm wrong, a lot of academic people would say that romantic love is a myth and it's probably a delusion and it's not good for you and such like. Where I, I, I think from that side, apart from just it feels nice, I think that side of feeling intense and aware is, is something positive to it.

For Rachel,[2] romantic love seemed to be the signifier of transformation (p. 14), what Bollas sees as the longed for re-experience of 'the transformational object relation' (p. 23). This object or relationship is believed to have the potential to transform one's total environment. What is sought is a deep subjective rapport with an object (a person, a painting, a poem, a symphony or natural landscape) and an uncanny sense of fusion with it. Hence she said:

> R: I suppose when you first get together all you want is to think how close you are and how alike you are. In fact, that's funny, I think when you do first get together with someone you really … well I erm, I suppose looking back, I, I, I would always be really pleased if erm if the bloke were to say, 'Oh we think really erm similarly on this,' so oh yeah, we've got this bond, and when you

find out you like the same sort of music, you feel really, 'Oh right, we were meant to be together.'

Rachel seemed to imply that the appreciation and awareness of transience (in an existentialist and psychoanalytic sense) was one of the ways to keep love alive and we might add that that depressive anxiety (concern, pining) might also be necessary to it (when we become aware of our own complacency in long-term relationships, passionless respect for our partner or bitter disappointments with them – see Mitchell, 2003, p. 27). Hence romantic love starts to go, Rachel said, 'when you stop discovering new things in each other' (p. 226). An awareness of separateness, and a feeling that you are still the 'chosen one' (p. 230) might she said, keep it alive:

> R: I remember erm seeing him (her partner) as a best man at a wedding er in a suit, which again is something different, because you live together you see each other in all your scruffy clothes and he'd never wear a suit, hardly ever, so there he is wearing a suit and sort of, I suppose, a position of ... a bit of authority, and so you have this sense of being proud of being with this person and erm ... but the main thing is is just seeing them as well it's not the person who didn't clean up properly today and that you feel really irritated with, erm ... {pause} so I think that is ... I think that is key to romantic love, is erm seeing that person as being separate from you, separate individual.

Mitchell argues that romance can give life a sense of robustness, purpose, excitement and it is something to be savoured and cultivated (p. 25), but he argues that we are interested in degrading romance for very good reasons (we may lose the other, be vulnerable and humiliated). Moreover, 'the sense of security, possession, ownership that often attends long-term relationships is partially a contrivance based on fantasies of permanence' (p. 44) which he maintains 'choke the richness out of life' (p. 24). Hence perhaps what Rachel described above is re-experiencing her partner anew and savouring this sense of him.

Mitchell asks how it is that primary relationships (rather than the thrill of the illicit) can feel so safe (p. 44) and he protests at 'how reductive of one's complexity and humanity, to have oneself made into a habit'. It is, Mitchell explains, the tension between our need for home, continuity and sameness and our contrary need for the uncanny, the unpredictable and inspiration that captures the essence of romantic love. For Rachel, however, although acknowledging contingency may

keep our love aflame, it must perform a double feat and not simultaneously move us out of the category of the other's absolute (an end to their
desire and freedom in Lacanian or Sartrean terms):

> R: Erm but definitely romantic love to me means that that ... the
> person in your life makes it clear to you that you're the most
> special to them, more than anybody, and you are more special
> than anybody's ever been. I would find it difficult to get with
> somebody who made it clear or didn't really ... made it clear that
> someone before you was more spe- was the love of their life,
> then you wouldn't be able to trust them. So it's definitely got to
> be this feeling of you're the ... you know, you're the closest to
> them than, than anybody else has ever been.

Romance for Sarah also involves accepting that fantasies of permanence
and security need to be challenged in order to keep romance alive ('I
don't think, I don't accept that people meet and never change, I just
don't think that is what happens really'). When asked whether her present relationship was romantic, she replied:

> S: Yes, it's because it's exclusive, so we have a life no one else can
> have, so it's partly about because I'm excluding everyone else, so
> if I'm excluding everyone else it's only because I'm including
> him, but he's including me, so I'm just a very special person,
> because I'm the only person in the world he includes. So it is actu-
> ally a one upmanship in a nasty sort of way, it's quite clever.
> I: So in that sense you think monogamy is really quite central to it?
> S: Well, not necessarily ... I think it is exclusive in the moment, and
> the moment could be a moment of having sex or it could be a
> moment where he smiles at me in a particular way in a room. So
> the thing is, it doesn't rule out not being monogamous, because
> he could have that with someone else. I wouldn't necessarily
> know, but I think it's become tied to monogamy for social reasons,
> and probably not so horrific for emotional reasons. It's probably
> quite difficult to smile at lots of people simultaneously, but I think
> it's the exclusivity, it's the knowledge that if he turns around from
> the kitchen and smiles at me, it's for me, it's not for anyone else.

Indeed Mitchell argues that monogamy dramatically increases our
dependence on the other, but that this need not necessarily lead to lifelessness or deadness with them, because in reality, love is not secure. For

Rachel, love's charm is in 'being the most special person in the world', hence monogamy is central to it, but one must be the most special person in the totality of the other's life, not only in brief moments. We must be, according to Rachel, unsurpassable, and she said that she was nostalgic for how urgent this kind of love felt:

> R: I think it has always meant that to me, even though the rational side of me can think, 'Well what does in love mean? What does it mean?' you know, you want to be dead special to somebody and you want to feel that erm really lovely feeling that you feel when you first get together with somebody, and is it just being egotistical or something? Erm I still would find it difficult to say erm that just having a companion and being content with somebody cos you get on well and, you know, more … was more of a friendship is as nice. I mean I can rationally say it is, but erm I don't think it's as strong a feeling. Maybe that's the emphasis on feeling rather than thinking.
>
> I: Mm. {pause}
>
> R: Erm yeah, it's difficult, isn't it. There's so many songs and all the, you know, literature and everything that's been inspired by romantic love to sort of rationalise it away, it's, it's difficult to do that really. Er yeah.

And Mitchell would counsel against rationalising feeling, because the quality of our relationships is, he says, central to the emotional quality of our lives, 'the very lifefulness of our lives, the texture, the tonal quality, the verve' (p. 26). Thus, Rachel is right to resist the cultural condemnation of romance, or more specifically the woman in love, as somehow damaged, unrealistic and narcissistic. If we try to eliminate excess, enigma and mystery from life, Mitchell argues, we will also lose eroticism and be left with passionless respect or bitter disappointment. Thus, Rachel's nostalgia for what she called the 'thunder and lightning of love' can be seen as a healthy wish to experience passionate idealisation in a long-term relationship:

> R: So another thing with romantic love is erm for me it's the opposite of just a fling, or just a purely sexual relationship, so you've … so I would have to feel that the, the few times that I've felt really in love that the, the erm … the physical side of your relationship is more passion and intense, passion-based and intense than sex. That when you've been with someone for a

long time, what to me can seem like the end of the ... your romantic love is when you- the physical side of your relationship becomes really erm mechanical and just, just something sexual, that it's got to carry something more with it, you've got to feel like it's a real moment of ... an intense moment rather than erm just a normal part of your life.

And even Sam, who was very critical of the promises of romance, hoped that she too could experience episodic passion in her present relationships:

S: Oh I, I think I think I ... my opinion is that, that people do (need love). I certainly do. Erm what I would hope for then is erm to at least occasionally admire the person that I'm with, to be proud of them and have them proud of me. Erm to be equals, to occasionally be surprised by them, to surprise them, for us both to be carrying on teaching each other stuff and learning ourselves. Humour erm and occ- occasionally, occasionally passionate sex. Erm kindness, erm tenderness, loyalty and creating stuff together and, and having the freedom to create stuff apart.

11.6   Reflexive love

What we can see from the discussion so far is that the younger interviewees have deconstructed romantic love and are struggling with dichotomous views of it as possible/impossible, desirable/undesirable, a social construction/an emotional reality, a substitute satisfaction/a real fulfilment and so on. They hold their relationships up to sociological and psychological scrutiny implicitly, if not explicitly, and clearly have expectations from their relationships and from themselves that are significantly different from their older counterparts. Although the older interviewees spoke about how structural conditions of their lives affected their marriage plans and marriages, they did not ask searching questions about their own psyches or their partner's psyche and thus they did not provide psychologically inflected commentary on their lives. Also, although they recounted their love lives in the context of a larger societal and world context (war), they did not overtly question the socio-cultural positions that they occupied (e.g., gender expectations). The younger interviewees varied in the extent to which they held the quality of their relationships and love ideals up to psychosocial scrutiny, but they all, to some extent, did speak about their life histories through what we might call a psychosocial lens.

Zadie, for example, was perhaps more willing to question her mind rather than her social, cultural and structural position in order to understand love. She said, for example, that a 'professional' would need to tell her why she couldn't trust men and she therefore showed an interest in thinking therapeutically or psychologically:

> Z: I think I should have ... I'd like to actually have been a {pause} psychiatrist.
>
> I: Mm.
>
> Z: To try and understand, but then again, I, I don't think anybody can understand.

Sam and Sarah also used a therapeutically inflected discourse (involving concepts of emotional expressivity, self-awareness and growth) when speaking about ideals of love. They both wanted their partners to be emotionally articulate, and they therefore had different expectations from the older interviewees who were more circumspect about exploring the emotional and psychological aspects of childhood, war or of their relationships.

Sam, for example, looked at her father's, her own and Gary's childhood in order to understand theirs and her own 'present act of love' (Theweleit, 1994). She wanted men to be more emotionally articulate (expressive), and she wanted her relationship to be based on knowledge (reality) rather than fantasy. She referred to a great deal of emotional work on herself and in her relationships but she also described being bitterly disappointed. There was anger in Sam's story, because, she said, Gary did not want to grow psychologically or emotionally:

> I: He doesn't?
>
> S: No. Or not ... or in such a small way and I've got to clap every small development, and I just think, 'Sod off, I did this with less support ten years ago. Erm do you, do you want a rosette every time you make a tiny progression.' And erm the fact that I still have to translate so much for him.
>
> I: In terms er ... feelings, what you feel?
>
> S: Mm. And also his, you know, it's, it's like translating stuff for a child or articulating stuff for a child, and it's boring.
>
> I: Mm. And is ... does that ... is that because he's not ... he ... is it the case that he, he's trying to grow, or that he can't, or that he's not trying?
>
> S: I don't believe anybody can't, erm unless they have a learning difficulty, erm or unless they're so fundamentally damaged by

their life experiences that it's not something they can afford to do. Erm I think he's damaged, I think he knows that he's damaged, and I think his stop/start approach to dealing with that is erm he hasn't got all the time in the world, either for us or for himself. You, you are long time dead and you're not alive for very long, and you're only alive once, and he doesn't seize the moment in any respect. And he doesn't occupy his own space, and I hate that. It's not er ... it's the antithesis of the, the first two men that I er started fancying, who more than occupied their own space. I mean some men occupy all their space, all their woman's space and other people's space besides. I'm a woman who tries to occupy her own space, I find it very difficult to be with a man who doesn't, erm it's quite boring really. It's er unrewarding.

Sam and Sarah seemed to hope for a relationship which could provide a facilitating environment for the 'reflexive project of self'. Sam and Sarah's teenage hopes for a kind of telepathic love or love as a reified external attribute seemed to be replaced by a discourse of the dynamic relationship, which denotes an active interaction or art (as described by Fromm).

Sarah was perhaps more hopeful about gender expectations being challenged than Sam. She did, for example, speak assertively about one of her partners being on *her* level and *her* finding him interesting and *him* being available to be loved. She did not, therefore, only locate the importance of this relationship in terms of her own narcissistic need for recognition (see Freud's discussion of the woman/narcissist in love, 1914) and the man's omnipotent need for control. Interestingly, for Sarah, it was two men in her life who encouraged her to talk about her feelings and express her opinions, thus showing that the 'transformation of intimacy' also involves a challenge to gendered stereotypes. Hence, in Sarah's story we see masculinities, rather than one homogenous masculinity:

S: ... and his whole view (Tim's), he kind of assumed I would know things that he wouldn't know and stuff, that was a huge thing, because, especially some of the younger blokes maybe, it always played big games, the whole point was that they knew more than me. So it was a kind of big change.

I: What you felt more empowered.

S: Yes.

I: Yes.

S: Yes. Yes.

I: In what sort of way, what were you supposed to know?

S: That I would have views and opinions and I would wish to discuss our relationship and have assertive demands about what I would and wouldn't want. I would have to get some positions quickly (shared laughter).

Although there was a call for more emotional literacy and intelligence in the younger interviewees' narratives of love, they also recognised the limits to the reflexive project of self. That is, Sarah, Rachel and Zadie referred to their inability to 'rationalise away emotion'and it is this kind of psychoanalytic insight (into the world of the id, desire, primary process or fantasy) which perhaps enabled them to take a more critical look at questions of morality and right and wrong conduct. Hence Sarah described having an affair with somebody who was already in a relationship in the following way:

I: So you could isolate your relationship with him then?

S: Yes. Yes. The reality was him as I knew him, not her.

I: Do you think you would be able to do that now?

S: Possibly, but I don't know. I think if you are swept up in strong feelings it is more easy to compartmentalise things than it first would appear. So I would like to think that I would sort of think about things a bit more. If that happened again, if that scenario arose I would want to be a bit more clear about what I thought I was doing. I would be less casual about it perhaps, but I don't know really, I would like to think that I would do the right thing 'morally' whatever that is, but I also think one doesn't in life. I think it is very difficult to ... these things happen, and I know I'd be mad at the partner I am with now, if he went out with someone else. I know it would kill me, I know it would, I know I would lie down and cry about it for a long, long time, but in the end I think it is very hard, these things do happen. They do, people do and, we shouldn't, but we do. I don't know. It's all sorts, like trying to rationalise it, isn't it. I don't think it is very easy to rationalise strong feelings, I think if you've got them you've got them, however much your intellect says that it shouldn't matter, and it does matter, because you feel it somehow.

There were, however, limits to the transformations of intimacy occurring for these young women. None of them, for example, questioned their own heterosexuality and for most of them monogamy was not optional. There were also differences between them in the extent to which their hopes or expectations were de-traditionalised. Zadie, for example, did not question her own gender identity (in the way that Sam did), but she was de-traditionalised to the extent that she lived alone for six years (although, as for Sarah, this was like a holiday one returned from and not a final destination).

Sam, Sarah, Rachel and Zadie may have shared a psychosocial approach to understanding love, but the accent fell upon the psyche and social in different ways in their stories. Sam's views, for example, were more inflected by a socio-cultural way of seeing love rather than a psychoanalytic or psychological way of understanding love. Indeed, Sam would perhaps have been quite exasperated by an ahistorical view of love and love relations. Her story suggested that it was men who needed to make reparation and do psychic work and her views could be used to support a critique of reparative relating as lacking any understanding of the social nature of love and relating. A psychosocial discourse of intimacy therefore carries different meaning in different narratives. However, what the younger interviewees shared, in broad terms, was a sociologically and psychologically inflected interpretation of their intimate life, thus demarcating this age group's discourses of intimacy from the more socio-religious discourses of intimacy drawn upon by the older interviewees.

11.7 Psychosocial interpretations

As stated in Chapter 2, the emergence of psychosocial studies (and the sociology of emotion) is expressive (and constitutive) of cultural changes in which the personal becomes political (see second wave 1970's feminism), everyday life is psychologised (see the 'triumph of the therapeutic', Rieff 1966) and the postmodern challenge to Cartesian rationalism and enlightenment 'truths' (Lyotard, 1984; Derrida, 1967–72) led to a reconfiguration in the social sciences (in which sociology tried to address its neglect of the mind/emotion and psychology more fully addressed a study of society in its study of the mind). It is perhaps not surprising then that we see a psychosocial interrogation of love, relationships and the self in these younger interviewees' narratives.

Thus, we could use this interview material to say speculatively that contemporary socio-cultural conditions have 'encouraged individuals to open up psychic space in an attempt to explore oneself and one's relationships' (Craib, 1994, p. 173) thus supporting Giddens' 'transformation of intimacy' thesis and Richards' 'therapeutic culture hypothesis'.

However, this would have to be done very tentatively, because drawing upon therapeutic and social-constructionist discourses of intimacy can lead to the possibility of 'bad faith narratives' (Craib, 2000) or narrative foreclosure (Freeman, 2000), in which one prescriptive discourse of intimacy is replaced by another which similarly limits the bounds of what it is possible to think or say.

However, what we can see from these stories is that the possibility or reality of romance is being deconstructed and a new discourse of intimacy or attenuated version of romance is emerging. These reworked concepts of love can be understood by reference to existentialist, psychoanalytic and sociological 'ways of seeing' love that were outlined in Chapters 3–7, thus allowing for an understanding of love as a play between our social, psychic and existential selves.

Part IV
Conclusion

12
Conclusion

This work has argued for the importance of a psychoanalytic, object relations view of love, but only if it is placed in a dialectical relation with socio-cultural theory. That is, it has argued for the importance of a psychosocial study of emotion.

Two very broadly conceived questions have been asked:

- Is love possible in sociological and psychological theory?
- Why should, and how can, love be studied as a psychosocial phenomenon?

In answer to question one, we have seen that romantic love has been deconstructed and rendered suspect in socio-cultural, existentialist and psychoanalytic theory. The question of whether this deconstruction of love is symptomatic of the conditions of late modernity (evident in everyday living and academic and clinical debate) has been explored.

Although romantic love is not seen as a realistic form of love, the theories that have been presented give us an insight into why romance remains compelling in novels and films as an everyday aspiration and as a way of anticipating the future. For example, from a socio-cultural viewpoint, romantic love is our cultural script, expressive of a contradictory intellectual and political lineage. It is a discourse of love into which we are born and by which we are penetrated. From an existentialist perspective romantic love is seen to be compelling, because it saves us from a feeling of instrumentality and aloneness. According to Lacanian psychoanalysis, romantic love is seductive because it promises to close the door to our insatiable desires and inaccessible needs. From object relations psychoanalysis we learn that romantic love is compelling because it recalls the exclusivity, need and passion of infancy and childhood.

Nevertheless, this needy, passionate love is not seen as reality based from any of the perspectives discussed, and from contemporary socio-logy and object relations psychoanalysis we have seen alternative mod-els of love which can replace or attenuate the emotionally driven nature of romance. However, romantic love is expressive of powerful needs for recognition, hope and closeness which cannot be dismissed (in theory or in everyday life). These are love's high but not necessarily impossible hopes, and they have an important place in a re-conceptualised view of love – as possible, as romantic, but not as sublime or redemptive.

It has been argued that an object relations view of love presents a more multi-layered understanding of the meanings of love than views which concentrate on only one of love's defining features – a type of emo-tion, sexual impulse, linguistic construct, psychological and existential defence, game or social construction. It has been concluded that, because of its own dynamic and dialectical view of the mind, object relations psychoanalysis presents a view of love as possible, but:

1. not idealised (in contrast to its popular exaltation);
2. nor subject to rational negotiation (as in the pure relationship);
3. nor blind to the narcissistic, inauthentic, illusory dimensions of love (as highlighted by views of love as despairingly or ironically impossible);
4. nor unaware of the myriad meanings that might be condensed in the signifier of love for any one person.

From a psychoanalytic viewpoint love is possible and moreover necessary to mental health and well-being. However, the love it argues for is one in which the tantalising but unrealisable promises of romance are acknowledged as impossible for all of the reasons outlined in socio-cultural, philosophical and psychoanalytic theory. This does not, how-ever, leave us with an anaemic, rational view of love, because the love that has been outlined is informed by psychoanalytic insights into our impassioned need for intimacy and attachment from infancy to adulthood. This need for love cannot, however, be idealised because from a psychoanalytic viewpoint, we have an equal propensity for destructiveness and blind narcissism.

However, in arguing for the strength of an object relations contribu-tion to our understanding of love it is important to be mindful of this 'tradition's risk of moralism and intellectual rigidity' (see M.J. Rustin, 1995, p. 243). Moreover, object relations theory does not pose a dialectical relation between our capacities for love and our socio-cultural, discursive and structural positions in life, which mediate and determine how we love and what we understand love to be. Conjoining a sociological and psychoanalytic approach to understanding love can aid our understanding of how intimate relations are formed or damaged in the context of our material, structural and socio-cultural lives. Indeed, it has been argued that we have to analyse how social and psychic factors combine in order to understand why any one person might see love as possible, impossible or transformed.

In order to look at how love could be studied psychosocially at the level of theoretical elaboration, we can see that three forms of psychosocial analysis have been operationalised: psychoanalytic application (to the discourse of romantic love), critique (of possible and impossible views of love and ideal typologies of intimacy) and discursive dialogue (object relations psychoanalysis 'converses' with socio-cultural, existentialist and Lacanian psychoanalysis).

In order to look at how love could be studied psychosocially in the empirical realm, a psychosocial method was developed that was influenced by discursive, sociological and psychoanalytic approaches to narrative studies. The philosophy of this method was influenced by objective and interpretive approaches to narrative studies and contributed towards the development of a 'new life history approach'. The question of whether romantic love was being deconstructed was asked and the interviews carried out were compared and contrasted in terms of their form and content.

It was argued that there was more evidence of a new discourse of love as possible in the younger interviewees' stories, thus substantiating Giddens' claim that a transformation of intimacy is occurring. However, although the older interviewees do not deconstruct romantic love in the same self-referential or psychosocial way that younger interviewees do, their material, structural and cultural circumstances are not conducive to an idealisation of romantic love either. That is, as demonstrated in Chapters 10 and 11, in some cases, it was the younger interviewees who were more preoccupied with romantic love than the older interviewees.

This challenges any strict notion that it is the conditions of *late* modernity that necessarily facilitate a disengagement from romantic love or act as the catalyst for the emergence of a new discourse of intimacy. That is, one's socio-cultural context may be conducive to a suspicious or critical questioning of romantic love, but one's psychic investments in the discourse of romance (see Rachel and Zadie) may make it hard to declare love to be impossible. That is, there is a complex interaction between one's psychic and social self, and it is by analysing this dynamic interplay that we can understand why romantic love is deconstructed and speculate on what this deconstruction, disinterest or preoccupation with love means for an interviewee.

It has been explained that a psychosocial analysis is committed to analysing the dialectical relationship between the individual and society at the level of lived experience and at the level of theoretical elaboration. A psychosocial study of emotion is therefore committed to understanding love as a play between our social, existential and psychoanalytic selves. That is, there is a complex interaction between our structural, discursive and psychological positions that a psychosocial analysis of love highlights, in contrast to an exclusively defined socio-cultural or psychoanalytic analysis.

However, by working across too many disciplinary boundaries, we have at times been dealing with incommensurable discourses and logical inconsistencies. For example, some of the theories of love discussed were expressive of an anti-essentialist, postmodern or social-constructionist position, and some represented humanist, modernist and essentialist positions. Moreover, academic rules of theorising and clinical psychoanalysis represent two different modes of knowledge generation (literary-observational/quasi-scientific) and it was argued that the social science/humanities researcher, who is working with psychoanalysis, might be led (like the infant observer) by the very terms of their studies to develop a particular kind of reflexive relation to their work. These tensions in conceptual and empirical psychosocial research have been discussed in order to clarify what the possibilities, limits and different forms this new disciplinary paradigm might assume.

It is not the aim here to provide a definitive conclusion to the question of what love means. Although a set of statements about love are presented and a psychoanalytic psychosocial study of emotion is argued for in this book, it is worth paying heed to Barthes' warning that it would be 'monstrous' to produce a theory of love, and that we should instead look for its affirmation; what people say and do in its name. As Phillips (1995, p.xvi), states, 'no one language has a monopoly on our ignorance' and theoretical maps are always smaller than the ground beneath our feet. It is thus helpful to think of this work as an exploration of the sociological, psychoanalytic and everyday attempt to 'give love words'.[1] However, as with Jackson's (1993) sociologist,[2] an intellectual understanding of love does not relieve us of the pain and pleasures of living through the vicissitudes of it.

Notes

1 The Demise of Romantic Love?

1. The title of Berman's 1983 book on modernity.
2. 'Love in the Age of Psychoanalysis' was the title of a conference at the University of Sheffield.

2 A Psychosocial Approach to Emotional Life

1. In chapters 2–6 he explains why.
2. However, he does not think that art can provide us with the intellectual clarity required for understanding the link between private troubles and public issues and their relief, despite the fact that 'art does express such feelings and often focuses them – at its best with dramatic sharpness' (p. 18). With the advent of a more humanistic sociology, the artist, Mills maintains, might benefit from a social science made 'sprightly by the sociological imagination' (p. 18).
3. Although he does trace versions of sociology which have given more 'scope to agency'.
4. The lived life refers to the 'hard' facts (age, sex, siblings, occupation, residence etc.) of our lives, whereas the told story refers to our interpretation of them.
5. 'It is not true', as Ernest Jones asserts, 'that man's chief enemy and danger is his own unruly nature and the dark forces pent up in him.' (Mills, 1959, p. 13).
6. We need to define what kind of psychosocial studies we are doing. This involves being clear about how we have appropriated the use of the words psyche and social. In this work, the appropriation of the word social is much more socio-cultural rather than socio-economic, for example (though this is sometimes an artificial separation). What this means is that this work does not necessarily put a materialist analysis of emotional life first, but rather a more anthropological, cultural approach (this does not mean that it is insensitive to the importance of a materialist analysis and the way in which this can be an indispensable tool for understanding the lives and theories that we study).
7. See Hochschild, 1998.
8. See Newton, 1998; Crossley, 1998.
9. See Hochschild's (1998) reference to the sociology of emotion as a 'way of seeing' (drawing on Berger, 1972).
10. However, as already stated, the discourse of object relations psychoanalysis has not been deconstructed to reveal its own historical relativity.
11. See Glaser and Strauss, 1967.
12. Hence, this theoretical work is a form of discursive dialogue, application and critique, rather than 'grounded theory'. However, the theories of intimacy which will be analysed could be said to be inductively formed (see a realist defence of object relations psychoanalysis – M.J. Rustin 1999 and Bell 1999, and Giddens' 1992 use of empirical sociological data to support his thesis).

13. O' Shaughnessy (1994, p. 942) refers to this quote from the United Kingdom psychoanalyst, W. Bion in order to describe her own self-reflexive return to her clinical material.

14. The training at the Tavistock Clinic in London in psychoanalytic observation methods (an accredited MA course) entails doing a two-year work-based observation, a two-year infant-observation and a one-year young-child observation (in addition to reading psychoanalytic theory and child/developmental psychology). The infant observation course in particular is, as M.E. Rustin (1999) points out, mostly used as a pre-clinical course which plays a large part in how students are selected for child psychotherapy training. The infant observation work requires the observer to visit a family for one hour each week over a two-year period (the young- child observation requires the observer to visit a family for one hour each week over a one-year period) in order to observe the emotional development of the infant in his/her family setting and observe their own role in this family constellation.

15. Craib, 1998, p. 145.

16. We are, as Craib (1998) points out, acting out a range of defences when theorising. That is, our intellectual pursuits are always personal, albeit to varying degrees.

17. See Brown, J. (forthcoming) in *'Reflexivity in the Research Process: Psychoanalytic Observations'* for a discussion of this.

18. Giddens (1992) model of ideal-typical relating.

3   Modern Love: Sociological Approaches

1. Rylance (1994, p. 117) refers to Barthes' work on love as offering a 'reservoir or thesaurus' of the lover's being. The lover's discourse is, Barthes (1978, p. 67) argues a 'festival of meaning'.

2. Sociology does not, unlike psychoanalysis, have a theory of human nature which informs its explanation of why love stories have existed for centuries.

3. The term 'romantic love' can be seen as an instance of condensation (dreamwork) in which a single signifier conceals or holds a variety of meanings.

4. Euphoric, hopeful, agitated, manic etc.

5. Monogamy, marriage etc.

6. The individual ways in which people impose narrative coherence on experience and life.

7. Complex power/knowledge relations embedded in languages of love.

8. See Hochschild's (1998) demonstration of a sociological 'way of seeing' love.

9. Margaret Rustin's first name is included in order to differentiate references to her work from references to Michael Rustin's work.

10. Subjecting the study of love to academic modes of argumentation is also in danger of this. That is, the form which this book must take is partly dictated by a specifically Western philosophical/academic tradition.

11. The origins of our modern conception of love, according to many theorists.

12. However, the process of individualisation did not begin in the eighteenth century. Gusdorf (1980), for example, explains that the conscious awareness of the singularity of each life is the product of a specific civilisation, for which St Augustine's *Confessions* provides us with a very early beginning

(p. 29). Moreover, Davies (1997) traces humanism (individual will, rational consciousness, authenticity of individual speech etc.) from ancient Greece through to the Renaissance and then through to eighteenth-century Europe.

13. We will then be able to see the way in which romantic love incorporates this, while also being defined by different social practices and by a different philosophical heritage (rationalism).

14. That the doctrines of the Catharist religion find expression in the myth of courtly love.

15. However, the letters of Abelard and Heloise do not depict a courtly, chaste love or the loss of self.

16. De Rougemont is not a sociologist, but more of a social/cultural historian. His work is being used in order to describe the phenomenology of courtly love and in order, in later chapters, to see how this is expressed in romantic love and to see whether the phenomenology of romance differs from courtly love.

17. Is this what we most often see in 'popular' depictions of romantic love? Is this why many love stories end at the point of sexual consummation or death?

18. De Rougemont argues that courtly love prefigures romanticism.

19. See Stendhal's (1822) 'On thunderbolts' in *Love* in this respect.

20. Day (1996, 164) says that the Romantic poets also enjoyed their own despair (especially after the collapse of the French Revolution).

21. Romeo and Juliet is, De Rougemont argues, a resuscitation of this myth. It also dramatises the transgression of social/moral codes of conduct and draws a link between passion and death. See M.J. Rustin's (1991) use of Bion when reading Shakespeare's play, in which Rustin claims that what it really dramatises is a failure of thinking.

22. Women are ambiguous symbols (the earth and the eternal), according to De Rougemont.

23. The story can be likened to a spiritual training according to De Rougemont.

24. Hamilton in the (1951) 'Introduction' to *The Symposium* explains that this dialogue cannot be exactly dated. He says that it was composed between 416 and 385 BC.

25. Freud (1930) refers to the impossibility of us falling out of life.

26. See Chasseguet-Smirgel's (1985) discussion of a narcissistic need to deny our instincts and messy anality.

27. Rustin M.J. (1991) points to the fact that Romeo and Juliet takes place over five days. Their love therefore escapes the chronological reality of time (love's depreciation, according to Barthes, 1978, p. 24) and the subsequent 'haltings of ambivalence' (Phillips, 1994, p. 40).

28. This is, as already stated, often missing from socio-historical accounts of love.

29. Hence Freud referred to our 'cauldron of seething excitations' (1923) and Klein to the 'death in our hearts', leading Phillips (1995, p. xii) to conclude that we are born with an excess of feeling and are too much for ourselves.

30. 'To which the rejoinder of the aesthete can be: If this is "real" then let's make something else' (Phillips, 1994, p. 40 speaking of the psychoanalytic offering of a romance of disillusionment).

31. Sarsby accuses Stone (1977) of having a denigratory view of sixteenth-century peasant life. She criticises a view of history which champions the urban middle classes as the vanguardists of romantic love and of 'civilisation'.

32. Both Day and Davies refer to an upsurge in radical feeling at this time, represented by both enlightenment ideals and romanticism.
33. Nevertheless, Berman writes that in contrast to twentieth-century thinking it is a voice that 'knows pain and dread, but *believes in its power to come through*' (p. 23).
34. Sarsby questions the extent to which the private sphere afforded women a space for self-realisation.
35. Ibid., p. 4. Contemporary sociologists would argue that we are no longer protected from the 'existential parameters of life' (Giddens) or 'the shivers of freedom' (Beck and Beck-Gernsheim, p. 5).
36. However, Collins (1972) argues that the 'first approximation to the private-household economy structure appeared in the cities of the Roman empire, and its here that the major love ideal is found as well, contained in Christianity' (p. 69).
37. Hence, for Giddens it is the harbinger of the 'pure relationship'.
38. This is also, of course, when psychoanalysis emerges.
39. Hendrick, 1992, p. 17.
40. However, Collins (1972) argues that the 'early expression of the romantic love ideal has been obscured historically because of the decline of urban Rome and the reruralisation of European society until approximately the fifteenth century AD' (p. 70).
41. From a sociological point of view its emergence is co-terminous with the advent of the novel (see Watt (1957), Stone, Giddens, etc.).
42. This is what the discourse of romantic love supposedly expresses, but this does not mean that actual marriage choices did represent a sense of self-possession and individuation. The interview material in Chapters 9 and 10 does not reveal this kind of freedom of choice, although questions of self-definition are preoccupying ones for the younger interviewees particularly.
43. Sarsby argues that marriages were still based on rational calculations and not on finer feeling and free choice. The companionate marriage, she says, did not replace a consideration of rank.
44. This is also class-specific according to Newton (1998, p. 71) who discusses the early English Industrial Period: 'The distinguishing trait of people according to good society, is calm imperturbable quiet ... they eat in quiet, move in quiet, live in quiet, and lose their wife or even their money in quiet'. Newton argues, however, that there is an informalisation of emotion codes as power inequalities become less marked.
45. Zeldin (1994) on the whole agrees with this view of women, applauding their salons of the seventeenth century until they became 'boorish' and obsessed with class. Indeed, according to Zeldin, women's autobiographies are the most original part of contemporary literature (p. 19) in contrast to official history which, he says, is 'stuffed with the names of Generals, rather than conversationalists'.
46. Newton (1998) cites Elias in order to demonstrate that the desire for the managed heart was determined by courtly society, which Rousseau reacted against (courtly rationality, suppression of feeling). Newton points out that the courtier performed emotional labour as a matter of course (p. 268) and he therefore criticises Hochschild for citing the managed heart as a twentieth-century phenomenon.

47. Working-class women, he states, were in the 'least favorable position to use the feminine ideal' (p. 72), but that they protected themselves by use of the categories of 'loose' and 'respectable' women. In Chapter 10, we will see that the working-class women who were interviewed were not preoccupied by the ideology of romantic love, but they all refer to their own sexual inaccessibility before marriage.

48. See Goleman (1996) on emotional intelligence.

49. However, in the 1980s Radway and other feminist writers argued that romance was a narrative of refusal and hope, rather than a measure of women's gullibility (Greer). Although 1980s feminists recognise Sarsby's point that there is an inherent contradiction in the idea of men and women falling in love, due to a structured inequality of need, Radway and other feminist writers see more utopian moments in women reading romances. Moreover, critics like Jackson (1993) argue that the position of second wave feminists reveals a naïve assumption that a purer love freed from ideology is possible. That is, they assume a humanist discourse of whole selves.

50. See Rylance's (1994, pp. 111, 118) analysis of the dialectical nature of Barthes' work.

51. The future is colonised, we might argue, by unconscious narratives.

52. For Giddens, modernity is associated with the socialisation of the natural world (p. 34). 'Nature', he says, has become dominated by socially organised systems and 'plastic sexuality' is sexuality freed or severed from its tie with reproduction.

53. Even though we are dependent on forces which elude our grasp. Indeed, it is this paradox which gives the individualist ethic its ironic twist.

54. It was apparently referred to as 'the *Gone with the Wind* of its generation' (p. 600). However, 'the undisputed champion' financially is, according to Kramer, '*Gone with the Wind*' when the price of a ticket for *Titanic* is adjusted to 1939 standards.

55. However, the establishment of this private world of love makes extreme demands on its 'participants' and Craib (1994) refers to a demanding intimacy from which we might seek release. Tweedie (1979), in a less sympathetic vein, bitingly refers to 'dwarfish twosomes' and 'shrinking couples'.

56. Richards (1989c) claims that we all live the metropolitan life whether urban dwellers or not (globalisation, TV etc.).

57. Some sociological statistics ('Britain Uncovered', *The Observer*, 18 March, 2001, 'The Singles Issue', *The Observer*, 5 November 2000), could be used to suggest that we might indeed be doing this – the rise of the single person is apparently the greatest social phenomena of our time (see Collins, 2001; Gibson, 2001; Dennison, 2000).

58. What they are therefore particularly interested in is how the love story that is 'always already written' (42) is transformed by lovers. This is particularly interesting, they imply, because we now have the opportunity of writing or imagining another story.

4   Love as Bad Faith: Philosophical Approaches

1. The section in *Being and Nothingness* entitled 'First Attitude Toward Others: Love, Language, Masochism' from Chapter 3 is a useful summary of Sartre's view of love.

2. Salecl analyses Wharton's *The Age of Innocence* as a story about love in which there is no 'utilitarian demand' (p. 20). This section will mainly use Salecl's 1994 edited collection and Sarup's (1992) book in order to provide an overview of a Lacanian way of looking at love.

3. See Sarup's (1992) overview of Lacan's work.

4. Sarup (1992, p. 129) describes courtly love as a love of the impossible. From a Lacanian point of view, 'courtly love is an altogether refined way of making up for the absence of sexual relation by pretending that it is we who put an obstacle to it' (Sarup quoting Lacan).

5. The *Crying Game* tells a story in which the IRA capture a black army British soldier. Fergus (one of the IRA captors) befriends the army soldier who asks him to go and see Dil (his girlfriend) for him after his death. Fergus does this, but falls in love with Dil, who, unbeknown to him, is a transvestite. The love between Dil and Fergus is therefore marked by impossibility, because Fergus inadvertently killed her lover and because Dil is a man. Nevertheless, the film depicts their love as enduring and tender (Fergus goes to prison for Dil when 'she' kills some IRA members in revenge).

6. She also develops Brooks' argument (the detail of this discussion of melodrama is not relevant for the purpose of this chapter).

7. As with Sartre and Lacan, the aim is to provide a 'broad brush' summary of Barthes' way of seeing love. For an overview of his way of understanding love Rylances' 1994 text and Barthes' 1978 *A Lover's Discourse* have been used. Rylance refers to Barthes' discourse on love as a 'thesaurus of the lover's being' (p. 117).

8. Rylance (p. 103) places *A Lover's Discourse* in the final stage of Barthes' career. It comprises, he says, three books – *Roland Barthes* by Roland Barthes (1975), *A Lover's Discourse* (1978) and *Camera Lucida* (1980).

9. It is, for this reason, difficult to situate Barthes in a possible/impossible paradigm. This is also true of contemporary, post-structuralist feminism, but the extent to which both deconstruct humanist or essentialist discourses of love, qualifies them as presenting 'impossible' views of romantic love.

10. Phillips' texts are similarly enigmatic.

11. See Plato's (427–347 BC) *The Symposium*.

12. Rylance (p. 118) argues that loving is, in this respect, an unethical activity, from Barthes' point of view.

5   Transference Love: A Freudian Approach

1. Symington writes about an infant's primary decision to turn towards its objects as representative of an impulse towards life and creativity. That is, the infant/adult has to take some responsibility for whether he/she has turned towards the lifegiver (the relational world) or has not (and remained essentially narcissistic).

2. Here love does begin to look like the 'magic answer' (see Sartre's observation that this is what we want), but it is a complex achievement.

3. It is never definitively overcome.

4. Bettelheim (1983) points out that the word 'ego' is in danger of 'leaving reality behind' (p. 54). That is, it 'reeks of erudition precisely when it should

emanate vitality' (ibid.). When I refer to the reality ego throughout, it is worth bearing in mind Bettelheim's criticisms of the English translation of Freud's work, because of the emotional response it potentially provokes (distancing, alienating). The reality ego is not a reified entity, but one aspect of 'me'.

5. Freud/Klein did not try to derive an ethics from their ontologies, but instead purported to describe reality as it is (godless, destructive, object seeking). An ethics is, however, implied (instinctual renunciation, reparation).

6. Klein's work develops (and changes) Freud's work and also therefore inherits this tension between science and art. However, her work is less constrained by the 'project for a scientific psychology'.

7. The 'Age of Reason' refers to the Enlightenment period in the eighteenth century. Day comments that *L'Encyclopedie* (1751–72) was one of 'the great monuments of the French Enlightenment and helped to lay the intellectual foundations of the Revolution' (p. 6).

8. The Frankfurt School, of course, deconstructed the rhetoric of enlightenment (Western rationality) in order to reveal its own irrationality and intellectual dogma.

9. And in this context we can understand Elam's (1992) point (referred to in Chapter 4) that romantic literature is an anachronism for enlightenment thinking, which counterposed romantic literature to real learning.

10. Elam points out, however, that it is women who are identified with romance and romantic literature and that it is they who are identified with symbols of excess, going beyond the dictates of reality and realism. As explained in Chapter 4, this is because 'within the terms of this realism, affective disturbance is merely the effect of excessive feminine sentiment', and the 'woman' becomes the historical sign of uncertainty (p. 111).

11. Although as Chapter 3 explains, the concept of romantic love, if not the practice in its name, represents an attenuation of amour passion.

12. Internal honesty is, however, hard to achieve, because it entails a knowledge of our own narcissism, irrationality, destructiveness etc. The 'thinking self' (see Craib, 1994) is, therefore, essentially also the 'disappointed self'; hence the centrality of the concept of loss from Freud through to Klein (mourning, depressive anxiety).

13. Freud's 1911 paper provides us with a hypothesis about the psychological response to our biological inheritance (our 'premature' birth) and it is less constrained by his early quantitative view of the mind than some of his other papers (1914, for example).

14. Stern (1985), for example, describes the infant who becomes 'glassy eyed' and stares through/past the person who might be intrusively coming into their field of vision.

15. Secondary narcissism occurs specifically in response to a 'disappointment in love' and is more fully described in 1917. Primary narcissism can be thought of as a defence against helplessness or as an experientially a priori state of mind/being.

16. Hence, in 1925, anxiety is reconceptualised as a response to danger instead of a need for the cathartic release of instinctual tension. Birth trauma is described as the prototype of anxiety and we can thus see Freud's work pre-empting psychoanalytic work on separation anxiety (see Quinodoz, 1993). In 1923, Freud says that to the developing ego, living means the same as

being loved, first by our parents and then by our own conscience and self-observing super-ego (p. 400).

17. The work of developmental psychologists like Stern (1985), Trevarthen (1980) etc. challenges this view of the 'autistic' infant. Kleinian psychoanalysis also argues that the infant is object seeking/related from birth.

18. Although narcissism can lead to a pseudo-independence or, in infant-observation terms, a second skin formation (see Bick, 1968). That is, when the infant is not held or contained by their carer, they develop a second skin (muscular rigidity etc.) in order to hold themselves together.

19. Although there may be reality-based ways of protecting one's narcissism (working towards one's ego-ideal, for example, see Chasseguet-Smirgel, 1985).

20. See the link to courtly love (as an ideal) and the Catharist religion.

21. The title of Meltzer's (1973) book.

22. Satyamurti's (2000) poem, 'Muse' evokes part-object sex:

> Don't let's welcome love
> in the sweaty horizontals of the bed
> not that again. Enough
> of being stapled to the sheets
> disposing surplus limbs.

23. Hence, according to Meltzer (1988), the apprehension of beauty (originally the mother and her breasts, eyes, voice etc.) contains in its very nature the apprehension of the possibility of its destruction.

24. Freud said that 'germs' of sexual impulses are present in newborns (p. 92), but Klein more fully states that sexual life begins in infancy.

25. Meltzer (1988), for example, explains this by saying that there is a struggle in the mind between aesthetic sensibilities and forces of philistinism, puritanism, cynicism and perversity.

26. A mishandling of the child's sexual curiosity can consequently lead to a permanent injury to his/her instinct for knowledge.

27. Indeed, the id is 'the source of our vital energy, without which life itself could not continue' (Bettelheim, p. 62).

28. Oedipus' parents (the King and Queen of Thebes) have been warned by an oracle that Oedipus (their child) is fated to murder his father and they maim his feet and send him away to be killed. He is rescued and raised by the King and Queen of Corinth, but he is told one day that they are not his parents. He consults the oracle in order to discover the truth and flees Corinth upon hearing the oracle declare that he will kill his own father. On his travels, Oedipus unwittingly kills a stranger (his father) at a crossroads, but thereafter answers the riddle of the Sphinx who bars entry to Thebes. He is rewarded by being made King of Thebes and marries the Queen (his mother). When a plague descends on the city for the unavenged murder of the King, Oedipus tries to find out who the murderer is. His mother commits suicide upon finding out the truth and Oedipus blinds himself, because he cannot bear to see what he has done.

29. But he states that many people do not know how to love another with affection and passion simultaneously: 'The whole sphere of love in such people remains divided in the two directions personified in art as sacred and profane (or animal) love. Where they love they do not desire and where they

desire they cannot love' (1912b, p. 251). A healthy or mature object relation in Freudian psychoanalysis is not therefore courtly (i.e. chaste) or guiltily embarrassed about the sexual relation. If, however, aggressive/sexual conflicts with our parents were not resolved, later relationships may bring quite unconscious, childlike feelings (guilt, excitement, rivalry, revulsion etc.) to the fore.

30. Although Phillips (1997) also writes in praise of the child's promiscuous attention span.

31. However, when we are thrust back into this maelstrom of Oedipal desire, jealousy, displacement etc. we may be more driven to repair our narcissistic wound by being competitively seductive rather than by re-experiencing disappointment however educative an experience disappointment (see Craib, 1994) might be.

32. Since all finding is a refinding (1905), Freud could be accused of saying that 'the love affect has no particular existence of its own. That sexual satisfaction, the release of tensions, is oriented to earlier occurrences, and the present act of love is just a feeble imitation?'. Theweleit (1994) comments 'a little sad, this sort of love' (p. 17).

33. Similarly, King Lear blinds himself when he cannot bear to see the destruction which his own narcissism has led to.

34. Bettelheim claims that the tale dramatises the fact that we have to 'overcome tremendous inner resistance against recognising the truth' (p. 30).

35. Steiner (1985) reads the Oedipus complex as a warning against 'turning a blind eye' and he looks at each character in the play and argues that everyone of them knew what was happening, but pretended not to.

36. In Freud's 1911–13 paper the lover is noticeably female, but in 1912, Freud does refer to the male patient too.

37. Which denotes passivity (see Fromm's *The Art of Loving* in which he writes about 'standing' in love).

38. Transference love is an attempt to, for example, destroy the doctor's authority by bringing him down to the level of a lover while also gaining 'all of the other promised advantages incidental to the satisfaction of love' (Freud, 1911–13b, p. 163). It is therefore according to Freud a stubborn, impetuous refusal to accept the doctor's treatment. Indeed, 'Genuine love, we would say, would make her docile and intensify her readiness to solve the problems of her case, simply because the man she was in love with expected it of her' (ibid.).

39. 'Confluent love' is predicated on self-reflexivity.

40. For Giddens, however, self-reflexivity is self-evidently good (benign), but Freud can be used to alert us to the fact that self-observation can also be the 'harbinger' of a persecuting self-consciousness.

41. We re-find the dynamic of our early object relations.

42. Identification precedes object choice, according to Freud, because the infant is a priori narcissistically fused with their parent/carer.

43. This is not a study of filial love, but psychoanalysis shows us that adult psychosexual love cannot be understood without reference to our families.

44. We may also gain insight into the ways in which, at any one time, the feeling/thoughtful state to which we attach the word love can be aroused by any number of things: a momentary idealisation, a reality-based admiration, a visceral 'chemical attraction', an emotional fit, a surge of gratitude etc. That is, insight necessarily problematises our understanding of love.

45. Hence, Phillips (1995, p. 7) says that it is the post-Freudian Freud (the friend of ambiguity) who tells us that we can search for good ways of bearing our incompleteness, rather than searching for wholeness.

46. Day (1996), although not writing from a psychoanaytic perspective, concludes that the Romantics exalted their own powers of perception over and above nature 'herself'.

47. Hence, Craib (1994) bemoans the fact that (as he sees it) it is 'Freud the Romantic' who has gained popular appeal to the exclusion of 'Freud the Rationalist'.

48. The notion of the transcendent in both romantic love and romanticism can be read as an attempt to turn towards what Symington (1993) calls the life-giver. What Meltzer points out, however, is that 'the apprehension of beauty contains in its very nature the apprehension of the possibility of its destruction' (p. 6).

49. Romance may symbolise the mitigation of hate by a love, which is not born from splitting, projection and idealisation.

50. Although romantic love is supposed to represent an attenuation of amour passion; hence it is the 'harbinger' of the pure relationship.

6 Reparative Love: A Kleinian Approach

1. In order to understand Klein's concept of 'love in the depressive position', this chapter will primarily refer to her 1935, 1940 and 1946 papers. In 1935, Klein shows the connection between the infantile depressive position and manic-depressive states and in her 1940 paper she draws out the similarities between the depressive position and normal mourning. In 1946 we are more fully introduced to her concept of the paranoid-schizoid position.

2. In Greene's *The End of the Affair* (1951), for example, 'Maurice' eventually realises that it is his own suspicious mind that made him unable to love, but the obstacle to love is often portrayed as external to us (which it sometimes is, of course).

3. As already stated, Craib (1994) argues for the importance of a 'thinking self'.

4. See Ainsworth *et al.*, 1978.

5. Trowell, J. and Rustin, M. (1991) pp. 233–45.

6. Craib's work has the tone of an 'optimism of the spirit' (see Berman ch. 3), but it does not hold out hopes for a 'pure' relationship.

7. Stern is particularly evocative when describing the perceptual, affective world of the non-verbal infant and some of the ways in which these experiences are described are helpful for thinking about the 'interpersonal world of love'. Stern uses dance and colour as metaphors for thinking about the ways in which we feel another's presence.

7 Reflexive Love: Sociological and Psychoanalytic Insights

1. Stern's (1985) work and the work of the Tavistock Marital Studies Institute provide empirical examples of what is constitutive of intersubjectivity and 'psychic intimacy' (Stern, p. 126) from infancy through to adulthood.

2. Giddens' model of relationships does not lend itself to lovers becoming 'frantic epistemologists' (Phillips, 1994), because his reflexive project of self

focuses on the individual's search for self-identity, rather than an intrusive search for the kernel of the other's identity.

3. See Mills' point that art may not have the intellectual clarity required for linking private troubles and public issues. He does, however, argue that artists, poets etc. 'have often been the major, and only, formulators of private troubles and even of public issues' (p. 18). See Chapter 2.

4. It is interesting to read Zeldin's (1994) work on the 'art of conversation' in this context. He asks what words are used for (to reach out or to bully, for example).

8 A Psychosocial Approach to Narrative Studies and Reflexive Research

1. These loosely correspond to psychological and sociological ways of seeing love. As already stated, although Sartre's ontology is not a psychological theory, the idea that life is essentially without an a priori meaning does lead to a psychological response (anxiety).

2. As, for example, a social construction (sociology), an oppressive ideology (second wave feminism), a democratic gesture (contemporary 'psychosocial' sociology), bad faith (existentialism), an end to desire (Lacanian psychoanalysis), a festival of meaning (post-structuralism), a degradation of the ego (Freudian psychoanalysis) or a denial of psychic reality (Kleinian psychoanalysis).

3. And some viewpoints did not lend themselves very easily to this possible/ impossible positioning.

4. As stated in Chapter 2 this theoretical work is a form of discursive dialogue, application and critique, rather than 'grounded theory'.

5. It will demonstrate the way in which psychoanalytic observation methods also qualify as belonging to a new life history approach to method.

6. He argues that the birth of qualitative sociology began with Weber's work on verstehen and method, but he dates the life history method back to the 1920's sociological work at the University of Chicago on interpretive, interactionist approaches to studying social phenomena (pp. 8–13).

7. The discipline of sociology, and the character of the social sciences more generally, are changing (see Chamberlayne *et al.*, 2000, p. 8 for an account of the 'turn to subjectivity' in sociology).

8. Models of the mind are not often referred to in narrative studies either, although there is a focus, for example, on agency and subjectivity.

9. There are, as explained in Chapter 2, many versions of psychosocial studies.

10. As Andrews *et al.* (2000) furthermore point out:

Just as the social sciences were discovering the importance of 'subjectivity', the humanities were starting to celebrate the advantages of 'objectivity' – the application of formal concepts and methods to cultural artefacts of all kinds. One can see this process as a kind of reintegration of the sciences and humanities, after a long post-Enlightenment period in which they were sharply counterposed (2).

11. We can see that the identity crises supposedly characteristic of late modern society (see Chapter 3) are matched by disciplinary crises or transformations.

12. See Craib's (2000) discussion of narratives as bad faith.
13. Squire (2000c) writes about the way in which an HIV narrative may centre on gender, disempowerment, poverty, marginality, relationship success or failure etc. rather than symptom recognition, diagnosis, treatment, management or cure. Radway's 'Reading the Romance' was more useful for her work on HIV, for example, than life narratives for women and HIV.
14. Similarly, in Kleinian psychoanalysis any strict demarcation between the internal/external is seen to be difficult to achieve, because of the way in which our phfantasies imbue the external with our own unconscious dynamics. (Nevertheless, there is a commitment to achieving a more realistic, less projective view of the world.)
15. The three sections of their book centre on the interconnection between narrative and culture, narrative and life history, and narrative and discourse.
16. Squire (2000), for example, states that the narrative studies viewpoint takes a 'top-down' perspective on narrative which leads to a 'sustained attention to the cultural locus (Denzin, 1989, p. 3) of stories'.
17. They are different from ethnographic studies more generally, because they do not view language as a transparent medium (see Riessman, p. 4). Moreover, in ethnographic studies the emphasis is on the event recounted rather than the form etc. in which it is recounted.
18. See the interesting parallels between debates in clinical psychoanalysis about 'what is a clinical fact' (Tuckett, 1994) and the questioning of the 'truth' status of biographical material.
19. See the way in which the discourse-analytic approach advises researchers to avoid doing this.
20. Malson notes that she makes a choice about what other texts refer to and about what questions to ask her interviewees. Thus, the text is not a 'whole' narrative spoken by the interviewee.
21. We are 'interpellated' or hailed by a variety of discourses (see Malson, 2000, p. 157).
22. See Malson's (p. 155) concern about 'chopping up' the interview narratives to reveal discursive constructions and thus losing the whole narrative (though she questions if there is, in fact, a 'whole' narrative). She recognises that discourse analysis does not necessarily consider the plot, structure, style and temporal dimensions of an interview. Narratives can, Squire (2000) explains, de-emphasise language (p. 205). She prefers to think of narrative as genre, rather than as a property of human psychology, for example.
23. 'Research interviews constitute a very particular interactional context' (Malson, 2000, p. 157).
24. It combines objective (what are the facts of our lives) and interpretive (how do we interpret them) approaches.
25. Craib (2000) challenges this view of narrative.
26. Wengraf and Chamberlayne refer to Labov's description of a narrative (abstract, orientation, complicating action, climax, resolution and evaluation). The fairy story is presented as a classic narrative.
27. Thus, we can think about whether interviewees tend to speak in a largely argumentative, evaluative or descriptive mode.
28. Duchet's description of a 'real narrative' does not prioritise the emergence of a definitive or exhausted life history or any particular use of theory. Her

definition of a real narrative refers to whether a story, which is dependent upon the quality of the exchange between two people, has in fact, emerged at all.

The production of a *real narrative* implies that the interviewee has been able to organise the information conveyed by (his) memory in such a way as to give it coherence and significance. In other words, the interaction scheme governing the exchange has succeeded in overdetermining the communication frame of the interview so that a narrative relationship has been established in which the set of questions and answers refers not to the questionnaire prepared by the historian but to the narrative itself (1981, p. 91).

29. To limit oneself to narrative inducing questions in a psychoanalytic infant observation, for example, would be inadvisable, because it involves an exploration of emotional development.

30. Although, as we can see, their approach is theory-laden.

31. Indeed, they are asked to itemise this gestalt and only ask questions which follow it thematically and sequentially, at least in the initial stages of interviewing. In later stages, they are 'allowed' to ask questions which do not respect this gestalt. (This chapter will not describe this method in full, because it is extremely detailed.)

32. A psychoanalytic viewpoint would alert us to the unconsciously communicated gestalt that we might hear in contrast to the one that is manifestly narrated.

33. Stories may pull us out of experience and always asking for a sequence, happening, event, incident and time (in order to induce narrative) can lead to a very artificial interview which prevents the researcher from using their own intuition.

34. To this extent the method is already prescribing the gestalt of the interview.

35. To what extent we can control what is understood or misunderstood is questionable (especially if we factor in unconscious communication and a discourse-analytic approach).

36. They extract the 'hard' facts of life and create a one page 'biographical data chronology'.

37. They look at the biographical data chronology and make predictions about it and at the told story and do the same. For a detailed account of this method, see Wengraf (2001).

38. The panel acts as a kind of corroborative measure checking the interpretations researchers make. It is similar (in this respect) to the psychoanalytic infant-observation seminar group to which infant observers take their infant observation reports for discussion.

39. In BNIM terms these are form (description, argument, report, narrative, evaluation)/speaker/topic.

40. Although Freeman's (2000) chapter shares some of Craib's concerns.

41. Chamberlayne *et al.* (2000), in a similar way, point out that psychoanalysis can be seen as producing or offering a 'more coherent and personally acceptable narrative' (p. 8) to people rather than being seen as a means of discovering truth.

42. By way of contrast it is interesting to consider Houzel's (1999) point that the psychoanalytic observer needs to be receptive at the perceptual level, receptive at the empathic and emotional level and also unconsciously receptive via

analysing the counter-transference (p. 44). The fieldworker, Geertz argues, however, has to be perceptive, but not magical or 'a walking miracle of empathy and tact'.

43. Although Day Sclater (1999) focuses on the psychological effects of certain discourses and is more wary of making interpretations about deep structures of personality.

44. However, in the context of a sociological method, it is understandable that many researchers see it as inappropriate to try to make interpretations about deep structures of personality after only limited contact with an interviewee. Moreover, these kinds of interpretation are only tentatively approached in the infant observation method (it largely represents a training in *self*-awareness – see M.J. Rustin, 1989, p. 63) after two years of supervised, weekly contact.

45. Day Sclater (1999) uses Lacan's concept of desire to explain why we might try to identify ourselves with particular discourses and thus 'make good the lack inherent in subjectivity' (p. 114).

46. See M.J. Rustin's (1997) work on social exclusion and the subject's reflexive relation to discourses which have, for example, made single parenthood into a contemporary social issue. He also refers to a 'reflexivity deficit' amongst unemployed graduates (p. 5).

47. Psychoanalysis foregrounds 'narrative impossibility' (e.g., primary process thinking), while simultaneously searching for narrative meaning or containment.

48. Freeman (2000) also writes about the danger of 'narrative foreclosure' and writes about the importance of a process of desocialisation.

49. Not all, but many people working under the rubric of narrative studies assume a social-constructionist position.

50. Psychoanalysis does, however, confer on us responsibility for the meaning which we have ascribed to our lives.

51. For example, in psychoanalytic terms, an a priori experience of separation anxiety.

52. O'Shaughnessy (1994) refers to this quote from Bion in order to describe her own self-reflexive return to her clinical material (p. 942).

53. This is similar to Plummer's point about interviewers being aware of their own motivations and career aspirations when they interview people and write about their lives.

54. O'Shaughnessy (1994) makes a distinction between observed and clinical facts, stating that while observed facts may be correct, they do not speak to the immediate emotional realities between analyst and patient (clinical facts).

55. Spence (1994, p. 920) argues that cases need to be written from the bottom up, rather than top down and he maintains that the long-term health of psychoanalysis is dependent upon this 'steady accumulation of bald facts' (ibid.). The 'thick description' account refers to the way in which a clinician clarifies the 'interactive procedures of inference from observational material to theoretical constructs' (Rustin, 1997c, p. 106).

56. In this context, Craib (1998, p. 140) says that we could try to respect (or remind ourselves of) the following 'rules of theorising':

   1. avoid wishful thinking;
   2. avoid monistic assumptions and explanations;

3. try to argue intelligibly;
4. avoid logical hatchet work;
5. maintain a respect for available evidence.

57. Derrida's critique of a naïve view of the text as representative of a real presence.
58. There are, of course, fundamental differences between these sociological/ psychoanalytic methods.
59. Similarly, the psychoanalytic concept of the self that has been argued for is not naïvely realist (it partakes of the reality and pleasure principle – see Chapter 5 and Chapter 6). The task for the observant self is to disentangle that which is projected from that which is not (the interpretive from the objective).
60. See Hollway and Jefferson's (2000a) use of the idea of the 'defended subject' in their interpretation of interview data.
61. That is, this work will not be producing new, grounded theory. However, psychoanalytic and sociological theories of love will be brought into dialogue and debate with 'grounded', everyday accounts of love. This work is therefore interested in a grounded, as well as conceptual psychosocial study (though this work is largely conceptual, rather than empirically generated).
62. By contrast, see Hollway and Jefferson's (2000a) *Doing Qualitative Research Differently: Free Association, Narrative and the Interview Method*. This is a book devoted to questions of method.

9 Personal Accounts of Love: Details of Method

1. As already stated, this is, to some extent, impossible. However, the material was not immediately read (explicitly) in the context of theoretical statements. Instead, emerging themes from the interview material were brought into dialogue with the theoretical positions outlined in Chapters 3–7.
2. The theories of love that have been outlined are critically evaluated in some case discussions, but the use of these interviews is illustrative and exploratory (i.e. how and why do we interpret life experience psychosocially and how does one's psychosocial position or subjectivity affect one's discourse/experience of love). This material is not used in order to provide a robust evaluation of a socio-cultural, philosophical or psychoanalytic view of love, because the aim has been to demonstrate that an understanding of love benefits from a psychosocial analysis which can combine elements of all three in various ways (depending on the material).
3. Some interviewees reflect at length on the phenomenology of love, or speak about love largely as an ideology, while others speak exclusively about their current partner and relationship and some do not speak freely about love and relationships at all. These differences need to be discussed before the interviews are 'used' for thinking about the theoretical discussion of love presented so far.
4. See Geertz (1988), Waddell (1988), Miller (1989) and M.J. Rustin (1989) in Chapter 8 on how to write in such a way that the story makes an impact in its own right.

5. As one or more of; a contradictory concept; a social construction; an act of bad faith; an end' to lack, desire and uncertainty; a bittersweet theatre of meaning; a degradation of the reality ego and a denial of psychic reality.

6. The first two statements are hypotheses about the world, whereas the third statement is a hypothesis about method.

7. In BNIM terms these are form (description, argument, report, narrative, evaluation)/speaker/topic.

8. Hence, Hollway and Jefferson (2000b) focus on 'where a less unitary and rational subject erupts through attempts at a coherent story' (p. 137).

9. See the significance of 1975 as a turning point in social theory (postmodernism, feminism, therapeutic culture).

10. This sample did not exactly match Rubin's. The two age groups were, however, clearly demarcated by choosing people in their thirties/early forties and people in their seventies/eighties in order to look at processes of de-traditionalisation and views about, and experiences of, love. Rubin's study suggests that growing up after 1971 was conducive to a critical questioning of one's own sexuality and so on, but this critical questioning can be backdated. The 1960s, for example, would be one obvious time when a questioning of identity and process of de-traditionalisation was occurring in the UK. It is therefore difficult to pinpoint a year that represents an exact turning point in a socio-cultural transformation of intimacy. We would have to conduct more interviews in order to be more precise about the turning point period, but this was not the aim of this study.

11. People were not strictly chosen on the basis of class, but the majority of the interviewees did have working-class childhoods or lives. The class profile of the interviewees was perhaps influenced by approaching a public sector residential home in a particular part of a UK city. The method of snowballing (asking people who were known to recommend people they knew) also drew on my working-class background and friends. This study does not, however, prioritise a discussion of the links between new discourses of love and class.

12. Gay relationships are also cited as examples of the pure de-traditionalised relationship.

13. According to the primary material Giddens based his analyses on, boys are still unable 'to speak of love in narrative form' in contrast to the 'professional novelist of the girl' (p. 49).

14. He defines this as fully aware, deeply involved and informed of their cultural world.

15. It may be that these intellectual debates are constituted by changes in popular culture, individual beliefs and practices. Sociologists, for example, do provide us with empirical data on changing social formations (divorce, re-marriage, cohabitation, single person homes) and it is this data (Rubin's 1989 study etc.) on which Giddens' thesis rests.

10   Love and War: Eighty-something Reflections on Romance

1. The first two statements are hypotheses about the world, whereas the third statement is a hypothesis about method.

2. Craib (1998) argues that psychoanalysis can be used to explore whether particular socio-economic conditions are conducive to self/relational exploration.

11   Love and Peace: Thirty-something Reflections on Romance

1. See Sarsby's (1983) critique of the sociological view of romance as tied to individualisation and choice.
2. For a more detailed discussion of Rachel's views of love, see Brown, 2005.

Conclusion

1. This phrase is taken from Judd, D. (1995). To Give Sorrow Words: Working with a Dying Child.
2. Who falls in love ('even' sociologists do) despite his/her intellectual scrutiny of it.

References

Ainsworth, M., Blehar, M.C., Watess, E. and Wall, S. (1978) *Patterns of Attachment: A Psychological Study of the Strange Situation*, Hillsdale, NJ: Lawrence Erlbaum.

Alvarez, A. (1992) *Live Company: Psychoanalytic Psychotherapy with Autistic, Borderline, Deprived and Abused Children*, London: Routledge.

Anderson, K. and Jack, D. (1991) 'Learning to Listen: The Feminist Practice of Oral History Interview Techniques and Analyses', in Gluck, S. and Patai, D. (eds) *Women's Words: The Feminist Practice of Oral History*, London: Routledge.

Andrews, M., Day Sclater, S., Squire, C. and Treacher, A. (2000) *Lines of Narrative*, London: Routledge.

Audard, C. and Grosz, S. (2000) (Organisers) 'Recognition: Psychoanalysis and the Politics of Identity' Conference (4 June), The Institute of Psychoanalysis and the Forum of European Philosophy.

Bak, R.C. (1973) 'Being in Love and Object Loss', *International Journal of Psycho-Analysis*, 54.

Barfood, D. (ed.) (2002) *The Ship of Thought: Essays on Psychoanalysis and Learning*, London: Karnac.

Barthes, Roland [1978] (1990) *A Lover's Discourse: Fragments*, Harmondsworth: Penguin.

Beauvoir, S. de [1949] (1989) *The Second Sex*, London: Vintage Books.

Beck, U. and Beck-Gernsheim, E. (1995) *The Normal Chaos of Love*, Oxford: Polity.

Beebe, B. (1998) 'Infant-Parent Psychotherapy'. Tape recording: Tavistock Clinic Library.

Bell, D. (1999) 'Introduction: Psychoanalysis, A Body of Knowledge of Mind and Human Culture', in Bell, D. (ed.) *Psychoanalysis and Culture: A Kleinian Perspective*, London: Duckworth, pp. 1–24.

Bendelow, G. and Williams, S. (1998) 'Introduction' in *Emotions in Social Life: Mapping the Sociological Terrain*, pp. xv–xxx, London: Routledge.

Benjamin, J. (1988) *The Bonds of Love*, London: Virago.

Berger (1972) *Ways of Seeing*, London: BBC.

Berger, J. and Kellner, P. (1964) 'Marriage and the Construction of Reality', in *Diogenes*, 46, pp. 1–24.

Bergmann, M.S. (1987) *The Anatomy of Loving*, New York: Columbia University Press.

Berman, M. (1983) *All That Is Solid Melts into Air: The Experience of Modernity*, London: Verso.

Bertilsson, M. (1991) 'Love's Labour Lost? A Sociological View', in Featherstone, Mike, Hepworth, Mike and Turner, Bryan S. (eds) *The Body: Social Processes and Cultural Theory*, London: Sage, pp. 297–324.

Bettelheim, B [1983] (1991) *Freud and Man's Soul*, Alfred Knopf; Harmondsworth: Penguin.

Bick, E. (1968) 'The Experience of the Skin in Early Object Relations', *International Journal of Psycho-Analysis*, 49, pp. 484–6.

Bion, W. [1970] (1984) *Attention and Interpretation*, Tavistock; London: Karnac Books.

Bollas, C. (1992) *Being a Character*, London: Routledge.

Boston, M. (1987) 'Splitting Image? The Child Observed and the Child Within', British Psychological Society, paper presented to the Medical and Psychotherapy Section.

Botton, A.de, [1993] (1994) *Essays in Love*, London: Picador.

Botton, A. de, (2000) *The Consolations of Philosophy*, London: Penguin Books.

Bradbury, P. and Day Sclater, S. (2000) Conclusion in Andrews, M., Day Sclater, S., Squire, C. and Treacher, A. (eds) *Lines of Narrative*, London: Routledge, pp. 193–8.

Brown, J. (2000) 'What is a Psychoanalytic Sociology of Emotion?', *Psychoanalytic Studies*, 2, No. 1, pp. 35–49.

Brown, J. (2005) 'The Compelling Nature of Romantic Love: A Psychosocial Approach', *Psychoanalysis, Culture and Society*, 10, pp. 23–43.

Brown, J. (2006) 'Reflexivity in the Research Process: Psychoanalytic Observations', *The International Journal of Social Research Methodology: Theory and Practice*.

Brown, J. and Day Sclater, S. (1999) 'Divorce: A Psychodynamic Perspective', in Day Sclater, S. and Piper, C. (eds) *Undercurrents of Divorce*, Aldershot: Ashgate, pp. 145–60.

Brunner, J. (1994) *Freud and The Politics of Psychoanalysis*, Oxford: Blackwell.

Butterworth, G. (1991) 'Theory of Mind', *British Journal of Developmental Psychology*, 9, pp. 1–4.

Chamberlayne, P., Bornat, J. and Wengraf, T. (2000) *The Turn to Biographical Methods in Social Science: Comparative Issues and Examples*, London: Routledge.

Chasseguet-Smirgel, J. (1985) *The Ego Ideal*, New York: Norton.

Chasseguet-Smirgel, J. and Grunberger, B. (1986) *Freud or Reich*, London: Yale University Press.

Clarke, S. (2003) *Social Theory, Psychoanalysis and Racism*, Basingstoke: Palgrave.

Clulow, C. (ed.) (1993) *Rethinking Marriage: Public and Private Perspectives*, London: Karnac Books.

Collins, R. (1972) 'A Conflict Theory of Sexual Stratification', in Dreitzel, H. P. (ed.) *Family, Marriage, and the Struggle of the Sexes*, Recent Sociology No. 4, London: Macmillan, pp. 55–64.

Colman, W. (1993) 'Fidelity As a Moral Achievement', in Clulow, C. (ed.) *Rethinking Marriage: Public and Private Perspectives*, London: Karnac, pp. 71–93.

Coltart, N. (1992) *Slouching Towards Bethlehem...And Further Psychoanalytic Explorations*, London: Free Association Books.

Connell, R.W. (2000) *The Men and the Boys*, Cambridge: Polity Press.

Copjec, J. (1994) 'The Cogito, the Unconscious and the Invention of Crying', in Salecl, R. Lacan and Love 'New Formations: A Journal of Culture, Theory, Politics', No. 23, London: Lawrence and Wishart, pp. 1–12.

Craib, I. (1994) *The Importance of Disappointment*, London: Routledge.

Craib, I. (1995) 'Some Comments on the Sociology of Emotions', *Sociology: The Journal of the British Sociological Association*, 29, 1, February 1995, pp. 155–8.

Craib, I. (1998) *Experiencing Identity*, London: Sage.

Craib, I. (2000) ' Narratives as Bad Faith', in Andrews, M., Day Sclater, S., Squire, C. and Treacher, A. (eds) *Lines of Narrative*, London: Routledge, pp. 64–74.

Crossley, N. (1998) 'Emotion and Communicative Action: Habermas, Linguistic Philosophy and Existentialism', in Bendelow, G. and Williams, S. J. (ed.) *Emotions in Social Life: Critical Themes and Contemporary Issues*, London: Routledge, pp. 16–38.

Davies, T. (1997) *Humanism*, London: Routledge.

Day, A. (1996) *Romanticism*, London: Routledge.

Day Sclater, S. (1998) 'Creating the Self: Stories as Transitional Phenomena', *Auto/Biography*, 6, pp. 85–92.

Day Sclater, S. (1999) *Divorce: A Psychosocial Perspective*, Aldershot: Ashgate.

Dennison, S. (ed.) (2000) 'The Singles Issue' in *Life: The Observer*, 5 November.

Denzin, N. (1989a) *Interpretive Biography*, London: Sage.

Denzin, N. (1989b) *The Research Act*, Upper Saddle River, NJ: Prentice Hall.

Denzin, N. (2000) 'Foreword', in Andrews, M., Day Sclater, S., Squire, C. and Treacher, A. (eds) *Lines of Narrative*, London: Routledge, pp. xi–xiii.

Derrida, J. (1967–72) *Writing and Difference*, Chicago, IL: University of Chicago Press.

Duchet, C-M (1991) 'Narrative Structures, Social Models and Symbolic Representation', in Gluck, S. and Patai, D. (eds) *Women's Words: The Feminist Practice of Oral History*, London: Routledge, pp. 87–98.

Elam, D. (1992) *Romancing the Postmodern*, London: Routledge.

Finlay, O. and Gough, B. (2003) *Reflexivity: A Practical Guide for Researchers in Health and Social Sciences*, London: Blackwell.

Firestone, S. (1972) *The Dialectic of Sex*, London: Paladin.

Fonagy, P. and Target, M. (1997) 'Attachment and Reflective Function: Their Role in Self-organisation', *Development and Psychopathology*, 9, pp. 679–700.

Foucault, M. (1976) *The History of Sexuality: An Introduction*, London: Penguin.

Freeman, M. (2000) 'When the Story's Over: Narrative Foreclosure and the Possibility of Self-renewal', in Andrews, M., Day Sclater, S., Squire, C. and Treacher, A. (eds) *Lines of Narrative*, London: Routledge, pp. 81–91.

Freud, S. [1900] (1997) *The Interpretation of Dreams*, Ware: Wordsworths Classics of World Literature.

Freud, S. [1905] (1991) *Three Essays on the Theory of Sexuality*, 7, Harmondsworth: Penguin.

Freud, S. [1911a] (1991) *Formulations on the Two Principles of Mental Functioning*, The Penguin Freud Library, 11, Harmondsworth: Penguin.

Freud, S. (1911b–1913b) *Observations on Transference Love*, Standard Edition XII, London: Hogarth Press.

Freud, S. (1912a) *The Dynamics of Transference: Series on Technique*, Standard Edition XII, London: Hogarth Press.

Freud, S. [1912b] (1991) *On the Universal Tendency to Debasement in the Sphere of Love*, The Penguin Freud Library, 7, Harmondsworth: Penguin.

Freud, S. [1914] (1991) *On Narcissism: An Introduction*, The Penguin Freud Library, 11, Harmondsworth: Penguin.

Freud, S. [1915a] (1991) *Instincts and their Vicissitudes*, The Penguin Freud Library, 11, Harmondsworth: Penguin.

Freud, S. [1917] (1991) *Mourning and Melancholia*, The Penguin Freud Library, 11, Harmondsworth: Penguin.

Freud, S. [1920] (1991) *Beyond the Pleasure Principle*, The Penguin Freud Library, 11, Harmondsworth: Penguin.

Freud, S. [1921] (1985) *'Being in Love and Hypnosis'*, in *Group Psychology and the Analysis of the Ego*, Pelican Freud Library, 12, Harmondsworth: Penguin.

Freud, S. [1923] (1991) *The Ego and the Id*, The Penguin Freud Library, 11, Harmondsworth: Penguin.

Freud, S. (1925) *Inhibitions, Symptoms and Anxiety*, Standard Edition XX, London: Hogarth Press.

Freud, S. [1927] (1985) *The Future of an Illusion*, Pelican Freud Library, 12, Harmondsworth: Penguin.

Freud, S. [1930] (1985) *Civilisation and its Discontents*, Pelican Freud Library, 12, Harmondsworth: Penguin.

Fromm, E. [1942] (1989) *The Fear of Freedom*, London: Ark (an imprint of Routledge).

Fromm, E. (1957) *The Art of Loving*, London: Allen and Unwin.

Frosh, Stephen (1991) *Identity Crisis: Modernity, Psychoanalysis and the Self*, London: Macmillan.

Gay, P. (1986) *The Tender Passion*, Oxford: Oxford University Press.

Geertz, C. (1988) *Works and Lives: The Anthropologist as Author*, Cambridge: Polity Press.

Gibson, F. (2001) 'No Strings Attached' in 'Britain Uncovered',*The Observer*, 18 March.

Giddens, A. (1992) *The Transformation of Intimacy*, Oxford: Blackwell.

Glaser, B.G. and Strauss, A. L. (1967) *The Discovery of Grounded Theory: Strategies for Qualitative Research*, New York: Aldine.

Goethe, W.V. [1808] (1986) Faust, London: Penguin.

Goleman, D. (1996) *Emotional Intelligence: Why It Can Matter More than I.Q.*, London: Bloomsbury.

Gough, B. (2003) 'Deconstructing Reflexivity', in Finlay, L. and Gough, B. (eds) *Reflexivity: A Practical Guide for Researchers in Health and Social Sciences*, Oxford: Blackwell, pp. 21–35.

Greene, G. (1951) *The End of the Affair*, London: Vintage (2001).

Greer, G. (1970) *The Female Eunuch*, London: Paladin.

Gusdorf, G. (1980) 'Conditions and Limits of Autobiography' in J. Olney (ed.) *Autobiography: Essays Theoretical and Critical*, Princeton, NJ: Princeton University Press, pp. 28–48.

Hamilton, V. [1982] (1993) *Narcissus and Oedipus: The Children of Psychoanalysis*, London: Routledge and Kegan Paul; Karnac.

Hamilton, W. [1951] (1975) 'Introduction' to Plato's *The Symposium*, London: Penguin (first translated in 1951).

Harris Williams, M. (2000) 'Psychoanalysis: An Art or a Science? A Review of the Implications of the Theory of Bion and Meltzer', *The British Journal of Psychotherapy*, 16, 2, Winter 1999, pp. 127–35.

Hatfield, E. and Rapson, R.L. (1996) *Love and Sex: Cross-Cultural Perspectives*, Hemel Hempstead: Simon and Schuster.

Heaney, S. (1980) *Preoocupations: Selected Prose 1968–1978*, London: Faber.

Hendrick, S. and Hendrick, C. (1992) *Romantic Love*, London: Sage.

Hochschild, A.R. (1983) *The Managed Heart: The Commercialisation of Human Feeling*, Berkeley, CA: University of California Press.

Hochschild, A.R (1998) 'The sociology of emotion as a way of seeing' in Bendelow, G. and Williams, S.J. (1998) (ed.) *Emotions in Social Life: Critical Themes and Contemporary Issues*, London: Routledge, pp. 3–15.

Hoggett, P. (1992) *Partisans in an Uncertain World: The Psychoanalysis of Engagement*, London: Free Association Books.

Hollway, W. and Jefferson, T. (2000a) *Doing Qualitative Research Differently: Free Association, Narrative and the Interview Method*, London: Sage.

Hollway, W. and Jefferson, T. (2000b) 'Narrative, Discourse and the Unconscious: The Case of Tommy', in Andrews, M., Day Sclater, S., Squire, C. and Treacher, A. (eds) *Lines of Narrative*, London: Routledge, pp. 136–49.

Houzel, D. (1999) 'A Therapeutic Application of Infant Observation and its Teaching to Seminars in Work Discussions', *The International Journal of Infant Observation and its Applications*, 2, 3, June, pp. 42—54.

Hunt, J. (1989) *Psychoanalytic Aspects of Fieldwork*, London: Sage.

Hunt, C. (2002) 'Psychological Problems of Writer Identity: Towards a Horneyan Understanding', in Barfood, D. (ed.) *The Ship of Thought: Essays on Psychoanalysis and Learning*, London: Karnac, pp. 175–92.

Jackson, Stevi (1993) 'Even Sociologists Fall in Love: An Exploration in the Sociology of Emotions', *Sociology*, 27, 2, 201–20.

Jamieson, L. (1998) *Intimacy: Personal Relationships in Modern Societies*, Oxford: Polity.

Judd, D. (1995) *Give Sorrow Words: Working with a Dying Child*, New York: Haworth Press.

Kernberg, O. (1995) *Love Relations: Normality and Pathology*, New Haven, CT and London: Yale University Press.

Klein, M. [1932] (1989) 'The Sexual Activities of Children', in *The Psycho-Analysis of Children*, London: Virago Press, pp. 111–22.

Klein, M. [1935] (1975) 'A Contribution to the Psychogenesis of Manic-depressive States', in *Love, Guilt and Reparation*, London: Hogarth Press, pp. 262–89.

Klein, M. [1940] (1975) 'Mourning and Its Relation to Manic-depressive States', in *Love, Guilt and Reparation*, London: Hogarth Press, pp. 344–69.

Klien, M. [1946] (1975) 'Notes on Some Schiziod Mechanisms', in *Envy and Gratitude*, London: Hogarth Press, pp. 1–24.

Klien, M. [1963] (1975) 'On the Sense of Loneliness', in *Envy and Gratitude*, London: Hogarth Press, pp. 300–13.

Kramer, P. (1998) 'Women First: "Titanic"' (1997) Action–Adventure Films and Hollywood's Female Audience', in *Historical Journal of Flim Radio and Television*, 18, 4, pp. 599–618.

Kristeva, J. (1987) *Tales of Love*, New York: Columbia University Press.

Laing, R.D. [1959] (1975) *The Divided Self*, London: Pelican.

Lambek, M. and Antze, P. (1996) *Tense Past*, London: Routledge.

Lasch, C. (1984) *The Minimal Self: Psychic Survival in Troubled Times*, New York: Norton.

Lear, J. (1990) *Love and its Place in Nature: A Philosophical Interpretation of Freudian Psychoanalysis*, London: Faber.

Leff, J.R. (1993) *Pregnancy: The Inside Story*, London: Sheldon Press.

Luhmann, N. (1986) *Love as Passion: The Codification of Intimacy*, Oxford: Polity.

Lyotard, J-F (1984) *The Postmodern Condition: A Report on Knowledge*, Manchester: Manchester University Press.

Main, M. (1991) 'Metacognitive Knowledge, Metacognitive Monitoring, and Individual Differences in Attachment Organisation during Childhood', in Parkes et al, *Attachment Across the Lifecycle*, London: Routledge, pp. 139–52.

Main, T. (1967) 'Knowledge, Learning and Freedom from Thought', in Day, L. and Pringle. P. (ed.) (2001) *Reflective Enquiry into Therapeutic Institutions*, London: Karnac, pp. 1–22.

Malson, H. (2000) Fictional(ising) Identity? Ontological Assumptions and Methodological Productions of ('Anorexic') Subjectivities', in Andrews, M., Day Sclater, S., Squire, C. and Treacher, A. (eds) *Lines of Narrative*, London: Routledge, pp. 150–63.

Marcuse, H. (1969) *Eros and Civilisation*, London: Sphere.

Mc Dougall, J. (1986) *Theatres of the Mind*, London: Free Association Books.

Meltzer, D. (1973) *Sexual States of Mind*, Scotland: Clunie Press.

Meltzer, D. (1988) *The Apprehension of Beauty*, Scotland: Clunie Press.

Meltzer, D. (1990) *The Psychoanalytical Process*, Scotland: Clunie Press.

Mestrovic, S.G. (1997) *Postemotional Society*, London: Sage.

Miller, J-A, Rustin, M.E. Rustin, M.J. and Shuttleworth, J. (eds)(1988) *Freud's Papers on Technique: The Seminar of Jaques Lacan Book I* (trans. John Forrester), New York: W.W. Norton & Company.

Miller, L, Rustin, M.E. Rustin, M.J. and Shuttleworth, J. (1989) 'Introduction' in Miller, L. et al, (eds) *Closely Observed Infants*, London: Duckworth, pp. 1–4.

Mills, [1959] (1967) *The Sociological Imagination*, Oxford: Oxford University Press.

Mitchell, S. (2003) *Can Love Last? The Fate of Romance Over Time*. New York: W. W. Norton & Company.

Modleski, T. (1982) *Loving with a Vengeance: Mass-produced Fantasies for Women*, London: Routledge.

Moi, T. (1990) *Feminist Theory and Simone de Beauvoir*, Oxford: Blackwell.

Mollon, Phil (1993) *The Fragile Self: The Stucture of Narcissistic Disturbance*, London: Macmillan.

Newton, T. (1998) 'The Socio-genesis of Emotion: A Historical Sociology?', in Bendelow, G. and Williams, S. J. (ed.) *Emotions in Social Life: Critical Themes and Contemporary Issues*, London: Routledge, pp. 60–80.

O'Shaughnessy, E. (1994) 'What is a Clinical Fact?', *The International Journal of Psycho-Analysis*, 75, Part 5/6, pp. 939–49.

Pearce, L. and Stacey, J. (1995) *Romance Revisited*, London: Lawrence and Wishart.

Phillips, A. (1994) *On Flirtation*, London: Faber.

Phillips, A. (1995) *Terrors and Experts*, London: Faber and Faber.

Phillips, A. (1997) *Monogamy*, London: Faber and Faber.

Plato, (427–347 BC) *The Symposium*, London: Penguin (1975).

Plummer, K. (1983) *Documents of Life: An Introduction to the Problems and Literature of a Humanistic Method*. London: Allen and Unwin.

Price, H. (2000) 'Being Happy is What Matters Most: A Look at Two High-achieving Girls', *Psychoanalytic Studies*, 2, 1, pp. 51–65.

Proctor, B., Cutcliffe, J.R., and Butterworth, T. (eds) *Fundamental Themes in Clinical Supervision*, London: Routledge.

Quinodoz, J. M. (1993) *The Taming of Solitude: Separation Anxiety in Psychoanalysis*, London: Routledge.

Radway, J. (1984) *Reading the Romance*, Chapel Hill, NC: The University of North Carolina Press.

Richards, B. (1989a) *Images of Freud: Cultural Responses to Psychoanalysis*, London: Dent.

Richards, B. (1997) 'Popular Culture', in Kennard, D. and Small, N. (ed.) *Living Together*, London: Quartet Books, pp. 73–98.

Richards, B. (2000a) *Psychosocial Studies: Some Historical Notes*', available at www.psychosocial studies.org.uk (accessed December 2000).

Richards, B. (2000b) 'An Anatomy of Envy', in *Psychoanalytic Studies*,.2., 1, March, pp. 65–77.

Richards, B. and Brown, J. (2002) 'The Therapeutic Culture Hypothesis: A Critical Discussion', in Johansson, T. and Sernhede, O. (eds) *Lifestyle, Desire and Politics: Contemporary Identities*, Gothenberg: Daidalos, pp. 97–114.

Rieff, P. [1966] (1983) *The Triumph of the Therapeutic*, Harmondsworth: Penguin.

Riessman, C. (1993) *Narrative Analysis*, London: Sage.

Rose, N. (1990) *Governing The Soul*, London: Routledge.

Rougemont, D. de (1983) *Love in the Western World*, Princeton, NJ: Princeton University.

Rustin, M. (1991) *The Good Society and The Inner World*, London: Verso.

Rustin, M. (1997) 'From Individual Life Histories to Sociological Understanding: A Preliminary Report from the Social Strategies in Risk Societies Research Project' *Conference of the European Sociological Association*, August 27–29, University of Essex.

Rustin, M. (2000) 'Reflections on the Biographical Turn in Social Science', in Chamberlayne, P., Bornat, J. and Wengraf, T.(eds) *The Turn to Biographical Methods in Social Science: comparative issues and examples*, London: Routledge, pp. 33–52.

Rustin, M.E. (1989) 'Encountering Primitive Anxieties', in Miller, L. *et al* (eds) *Closely Observed Infants*, London: Duckworth, pp. 7–21.

Rustin, M.E. (1999) 'The Training of Child Psychotherapists at the Tavistock Clinic: Philosophy and Practice', *Psychoanalytic Inquiry: A Topical Journal for Mental Health Professionals*, 19, 2, pp. 125–42.

Rustin, M.J. (1989) 'Observing Infants: Reflections on Method', in Miller *et al*, (eds) *Closely Observed Infants*, London: Duckworth, pp. 52–78.

Rustin, M.J. (1997a) 'Give Me a Consulting Room…', The *British Journal of Psychotherapy*, 13, 4, Summer, pp. 527–42.

Rustin, M.J. (1997b) 'What Do We See in the Nursery? Infant Observation as Laboratory Work', *The International Journal of Infant Observation and its Applications*, 1, 1, September, pp. 93–111.

Rustin, M.J. (1999) 'Psychoanalysis: The Last Modernism', in Bell, D. (ed.) *Psychoanalysis and Culture: A Kleinian Perspective*, London: Duckworth, pp. 105–11.

Rylance, R. (1994) *Roland Barthes*, Hemel Hempstead: Harvester.

Salecl, R. (1994) 'Love, Providence or Despair', *New Formations: A Journal of Culture, Theory, Politics*, 23, Summer, pp. 13–24.

Salecl, R. (1998) *Perversions of Love and Hate*, London: Verso.

Sandler, J. and Sandler, A- M. (1994) 'Comments on the Conceptualisation of Clinical Facts in Psychoanalysis', *The International Journal of Psycho-Analysis*, 75, 5/6, pp. 995–1011.

Sandler, Joseph, Person, E. and Fonagy, P. (eds) (1991) *Freud's 'On Narcissism: An Introduction'*, New Haven, CT: Yale University Press.

Sarsby, J. (1983) *Romantic Love and Society*, London: Picador.

Sartre, J. P.[1943] (1989) *Being and Nothingness*, Methuen, London: Routledge.

Sartre, J. P. [1965] (1975) *Nausea*, Harmondsworth: Penguin.

Sarup, M. (1992) *Jacques Lacan*, London: Harvester Wheatsheaf.

Satyamurti, C. (2000) *Love and Variations*, London: Bloodaxe.

Seale, C. (2000) 'Resurrective Practice and Narrative', in Andrews, M., Day Sclater, S., Squire, C. and Treacher, A. (eds) *Lines of Narrative*, London: Routledge, pp. 36–47.

Seidler, V-J (1998) 'Masculinity, Violence and Emotional Life', in Bendelow, G. and Williams, S. J. (ed.) *Emotions in Social Life: Critical Themes and Contemporary Issues*, London: Routledge, pp. 193–210.

Sennett, R. [1977] (1993) *The Fall of Public Man*, Alfred A. Knopf; London: Faber and Faber.

Shibles, W. (1974) *Emotion: The Method of Philosophical Therapy*, Whitewater, WI: The Language Press.

Shuttleworth, J. (1989) 'Psychoanalytic Theory and Infant Development', in Miller, L., Rustin, M.J. and Shuttleworth (eds) *Closely Observed Infants*, London: Duckworth, pp. 22–51.

Shuttleworth, J. (1998) 'Theories of Mental Development', *International Journal of Infant Observation*, 1, 2,

Sodre, I. (1999) 'Death by Daydreaming: Madame Bovary', in Bell, D. (ed.) *Psychoanalysis and Culture: A Kleinian Perspective*, London: Duckworth, pp. 48–63.

Spence, D. (1994) 'The Special Nature of Psychoanalytic Facts', in *International Journal of Psycho-Analysis*, 75, 5/6, pp. 865–71.

Squire, C. (2000a) 'Introduction', in Andrews, M., Day Sclater, S., Squire, C. and Treacher, A. (eds) *Lines of Narrative*, London: Routledge, pp. 13–17.

Squire, C. (2000b) 'Situated Selves, the Coming-out Genre and Equivalent Citizenship in Narratives of HIV', in Chamberlayne, P., Bornat, J. And Wengraf, T. (ed.) *The Turn to Biographical Methods in Social Science: Comparative Issues and Examples*, London: Routledge, pp. 196–213.

Squire, C. (2000c) Seminar on Methodology organised by the Centre for Narrative Research, Tape recording, University of East London, School of Social Sciences, CNR archive.

Steiner, J. (1985) 'Turning a Blind Eye: The Cover Up for Oedipus', *International Review of Psycho-Analysis*, 12, pp. 161–72.

Steiner, J. (1993) *Psychic Retreats: Pathological Organizations in Psychotic, Neurotic and Borderline Patients*, London: Routledge.

Stendhal [1822] (1975) *Love*, London: Penguin.

Stern, D. N. (1985) *The Interpersonal World of the Infant: A View from Psychoanalysis and Development Psychology*, New York: Basic Books.

Stone, L. (1977) *The Family, Sex and Marriage in England 1500–1800*, Weidenfeld and Nicolson.

Storr, A. (1988) *Solitude*, London: Flamingo.

Symington, N. (1986) *The Analytic Experience*, London: Free Association Books.

Symington, N. (1993) *Narcissism: A New Theory*, London: Karnac.

Theweleit, K. (1994) *Object-choice: All You Need is Love*, London: Verso.

Trevarthen, C. (1977) 'Descriptive analyses of infant communicative behaviour', in H.R. Shaffer. (ed.) *Studies in Mother-Infant Interaction*, London: Academic Press, pp. 227–70.

Trowell, J. and Rustin, M. (1991) ' Notes on Infant Observation', *Infant Mental Health Journal*, 12, 3, pp. 233–45.

Tuckett, D. (1994) 'The Conceptualisation and Communication of Clinical Facts in Psycho-analysis', *International Journal of Psycho-Analysis*, 75, 5/6, pp. 865–71.

Tweedie, Jill (1979) *In the Name of Love: An Enquiry into the Past, Present, and Future Possibilities of Love*, London: Cape.

Usher, R. (1997) 'Telling a Story about Research', in McKenzie, G., Powell, J. and Usher, R. (eds) *Understanding Social Research: Perspectives on Methodology and Practice*, London: Falmer Press.

Usher, R. *et al.* (1997) 'Research as Story-Telling: Postmodern Approaches to Social Research', in McKenzie, G., Powell, J. and Usher, R. (eds) *Understanding Social Research: Perspectives on Methods and Practice*, London: Falmer Press.

Waddell, M. (1988) 'Infantile Development: Kleinian and Post-Kleinian Theory, Infant Observational Practice', *The British Journal of Psychotherapy*, 4, pp. 313–29.

Watt, I. [1957] (1987) *The History of the Novel*, Chatto and Windus, London: Hogarth Press.

Welldon, E. (1991) *Mother, Madonna, Whore: The Idealisation and Denigration of Motherhood*, New York: The Guilford Press.

Wengraf, T. (2001) *Qualitative Research Interviewing: Semi-structured, Biographical and Narrative Methods*, London: Sage.

Wetherill, R. (1997) 'Smooth Operators', in Kennard, D. and Small, N. (eds) *Living Together*, London: Quartet Books, pp. 50–60.

Winnicott, D. [1949] (1958) *Collected Papers: Through Paediatrics to Psycho-Analysis*. London: Tavistock.

Winnicott, D. [1958] (1969) *The Maturational Processes and the Faciltating Environment*, London: Hogarth.

Winnicott, D. (1969) *The Maturational Processes and the Faciltating Environment*, London: Hogarth.

Winnicott, D. (1971) *Playing and Reality*, London: Routledge.

Winterson, J. (1994) *Written on the Body*, London: Vintage.

Wittenberg, I. (1983) *The Emotional Experience of Learning and Teaching*, London: Routledge.

Woodward, K. (1997) *Identity and Difference: Culture, Media and Identities*, London: Sage.

Yates, C. (2000) 'Masculinity and Good Enough Jealousy', *Psychoanalytic Studies*, 2, 1, March, pp. 77–89.

Zeldin (1994) *An Intimate History of Humanity*, London: Minerva.

Zizek, S. (1994) *The Metastases of Enjoyment*, London: Verso.

Index